NATURE OF BEND

A Field Guide to Plants and Animals

—— LEEANN KRIEGH ——

T0349429

MOUNTAINEERS
BOOKS

MOUNTAINEERS BOOKS is dedicated to the exploration, preservation, and enjoyment of outdoor and wilderness areas.

1001 SW Klickitat Way, Suite 201, Seattle, WA 98134
800-553-4453, www.mountaineersbooks.org

Printed in China

First printing 2016, third printing 2025

Design and layout for first and second printing: Sarah Craig, sarahcookdesign.com
Updates for third printing: Ellis Failor-Rich
All photographs by the author unless credited otherwise
Maps: Deb Quinlan, Deschutes GeoGraphics, deschutesgeographics.com
Illustrations on pp. 260-261 by Katya Spiecker
Cover photographs, front, clockwise from top left: *Golden Eagle* (Photo by Alan St. John), *Washington lily* (Photo by LeeAnn Kriegh), *black bear* (Photo by Dave Rein), *Shevlin Park* (Photo by Mike Putnam); back, clockwise from top left: *American pika* (Photo by Damian Fagan), *Oregon grape* (Photo by M.A. Willson), *American Kestrel* (Photo by Kim Elton).

Library of Congress record is available at https://lccn.loc.gov/2024045616. Ebook record available at https://lccn.loc.gov/2024045617.

Mountaineers Books titles may be purchased for corporate, educational, or other promotional sales, and our authors are available for a wide range of events. For information on special discounts or booking an author, contact our customer service at 800-553-4453 or mbooks@mountaineersbooks.org.

Printed on FSC-certified materials

ISBN (paperback): 978-1-68051-789-7
ISBN (ebook): 978-1-68051-790-3

An independent nonprofit publisher since 1960

For my mom,
who loved nature as she loved me:
fiercely, joyfully, unconditionally

CONTENTS

ACKNOWLEDGMENTS

Here's the question I asked dozens of complete strangers: "Would you mind sharing your experience and knowledge, plus hours of your time—for free—so I can write a book about local plants and animals?" It's crazy that one person said yes. That nearly everyone did so is humbling and inspiring and shows that Central Oregon is rich in more than just its flora and fauna.

Special thanks to designer extraordinaire Sarah Craig (sarahcookdesign.com), who was the first person to say yes and in doing so made this entire project possible. The photographers and I gave her the raw materials; she turned them into a beautiful and cohesive whole.

Another big thank you to Deb Quinlan, the GIS specialist (deschutesgeographics. com) who created the immensely helpful maps.

And my lasting gratitude to the following incredibly generous naturalists who provided stories and information, and reviewed species, sections, or entire chapters. I could not have done this without you, and of course any remaining mistakes are entirely my own; thank you for reducing their number.

Trees, Shrubs, and Bunchgrasses

- Steve Castillo, district forester, Bureau of Land Management—Prineville District (trees)
- Ron Halvorson, natural resource specialist (botany), U.S. Department of the Interior, Bureau of Land Management, retired (whole chapter)
- James Jaggard, local naturalist (shrubs)
- Ed Keith, Deschutes County forester (noxious weeds)
- Frank Spiecker, local naturalist (sidebars on best-smelling shrubs and trees)
- Brian Tandy, forester, U.S. Forest Service (trees)

Wildflowers

- Ron Halvorson, natural resource specialist (botany), U.S. Department of the Interior, Bureau of Land Management, retired (whole chapter)
- Charmane Powers, botanist, U.S. Forest Service (various)

Birds

- Chuck Gates, creator of the Oregon Birding Site Guide (whole chapter)
- Craig Miller, M.D., local bird expert (various)

Wildlife

- Jim Anderson, local naturalist (various)
- Sue Anderson, lepidopterist (butterflies)
- Damian Fagan (mammals)
- Rich Hatfield, Xerces Society (native bees)
- Jon Nelson, field biologist, High Desert Museum (Sierra Nevada red fox)
- Tom Rodhouse, ecologist, National Park Service (bats)
- Matt Schinderman, senior instructor in natural resources, Oregon State University—Cascades (pikas)
- Alan St. John, herpetologist and author of *Reptiles of the Northwest* and *Oregon's Dry Side: Exploring East of the Cascades Crest* (amphibians and reptiles)

- Amy Stuart, biologist, Oregon Department of Fish and Wildlife, retired (mammals)
- Barbara Webb, wildlife biologist, U.S. Forest Service (mammals)
- Megan Wilkins, park ranger, John Day Fossil Beds (sidebar on ancient species)

But that's not all! Dozens more people answered endless questions, helped me come up with species lists, confirmed which species live where, and provided loads of other helpful insights. I am humbled by their know-how and generosity—especially that of Katya Spiecker, who is a fine artist and the best nature guide I know.

Leslie Bliss-Ketchum

Jeannette Bonomo

Jay Bowerman

Cidney Bowman

Debra Burke

Jim Clark

Dr. Jeff Cooney

Jennifer Curtis

Duayne Ecker

Amanda Egertson

Dr. Stu Garrett

Sarah Garvin

John Goodell

Gena Goodman-Campbell

Corey Heath

Nathan Hovekamp

Marilynne Keiser

Jim Moore

Sarah Mowry

Jon Nelson

Gail Snyder

Katya Spiecker

Dave Stowe

Rebecca Watters

Jen Zalewski

Female Red-winged Blackbird. (Photo by Alice Doggett)

Anise Swallowtail. (Photo by Dave Rein)

*Mule deer fawn.
(Photo by Carolyn Waissman)*

Oregon grape. (Photo by M.A. Willson)

First Street Rapids trail (Photo by Kim Elton)

AUTHOR'S NOTE

While out and about in Central Oregon, have you ever stood in wonder at the sheer beauty of this place—the centuries-old trees with arms stretched wide, the birds strung like kites in the skies above, the fields of wildflowers splayed out before you? And have you ever wished you knew their names? Me too.

And have you also wished you knew more than just the names of the species—their history and habits, their character and quirks? Because you're sure that if only you knew them better, every walk and bike ride, every kayaking and camping trip, would be more fun and fascinating and alive. Again, me too.

Hiking guides tell us where to go and field guides help us identify species, but I've always wanted something more—a book filled with stories about the plants and animals that live right here in Central Oregon. A nature guide that makes you laugh and think and ultimately experience this little patch of the world differently.

That's why *Nature of Bend* exists, with its photos and insights into more than 350 of the most common and interesting plants and animals within an hour's drive of Bend. It's because the views really do get better when we know what's in them. And every adventure becomes so much more rewarding when we feel connected to the living things we walk among.

WHERE ARE WE?

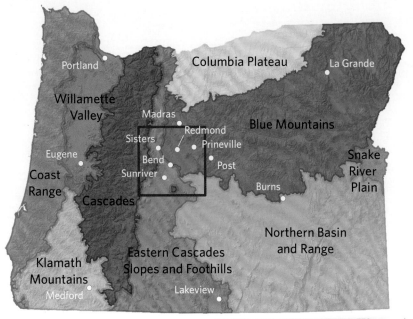

Level III ecoregions of Oregon (source: EPA, epa.gov)

Bend is not the center of the universe, nor even the geographic center of Oregon. The latter honor goes to the little community of Post, which lies a little over an hour east of Bend and is named for the first postmaster of the first post office there. A guy named Post.

But if you look at the map you'll see that Bend, and Central Oregon more broadly, is at the center of things ecologically, surrounded by four very different ecoregions. So what, you say? Well, that map tells you why we can bike through an old-growth ponderosa pine forest on a summer morning and picnic at a subalpine lake in the afternoon. Or wake up early to ski on Mount Bachelor and spend the afternoon hiking through the desert-like landscape of the Badlands Wilderness.

The fact that we're smack-dab in the middle of those diverse ecoregions also means we're surrounded by wonderfully varied plant and animal communities, which are the subject of this book.

As you turn these pages, you'll learn about a shrub that smells like a cigar, a wildflower that flavors soft drinks, a songbird that swims (and walks) underwater, a lizard that freezes solid for months at a time—and so much more.

Frankly, I can't wait to get started.

HOW TO USE THIS BOOK

How to use this book? I always laugh at that. It's a book—read it! Carry it with you! But *Nature of Bend* is not your typical nature guide, so it's worth taking a closer look at what you'll see on the pages to come.

Common and scientific names of over 350 species within about an hour's drive of Bend

Over 600 photos, most by local photographers

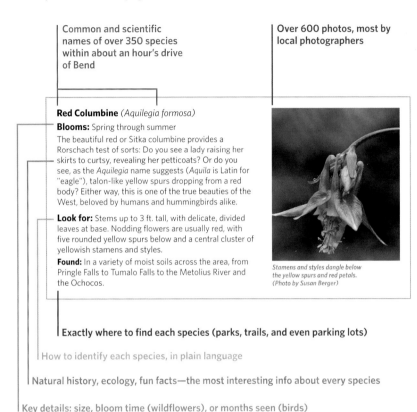

Red Columbine (*Aquilegia formosa*)

Blooms: Spring through summer

The beautiful red or Sitka columbine provides a Rorschach test of sorts: Do you see a lady raising her skirts to curtsy, revealing her petticoats? Or do you see, as the *Aquilegia* name suggests (*Aquila* is Latin for "eagle"), talon-like yellow spurs dropping from a red body? Either way, this is one of the true beauties of the West, beloved by humans and hummingbirds alike.

Look for: Stems up to 3 ft. tall, with delicate, divided leaves at base. Nodding flowers are usually red, with five rounded yellow spurs below and a central cluster of yellowish stamens and styles.

Found: In a variety of moist soils across the area, from Pringle Falls to Tumalo Falls to the Metolius River and the Ochocos.

Stamens and styles dangle below the yellow spurs and red petals. (Photo by Susan Berger)

Exactly where to find each species (parks, trails, and even parking lots)

How to identify each species, in plain language

Natural history, ecology, fun facts—the most interesting info about every species

Key details: size, bloom time (wildflowers), or months seen (birds)

Toward the end of the book, you'll also find treasure hunts for twelve locations where you can find many of the plants and animals described in the main chapters. Because reading about nature is cool. But experiencing and connecting with nature is what *Nature of Bend* is all about.

Black cottonwood. (Photo by Kim Elton)

Western juniper. (Photo by Mike Putnam)

Red columbine. (Photo by Buddy Mays)

TREES, SHRUBS, AND BUNCHGRASSES

I'll let you in on a little secret: This was the most challenging of the four chapters to write. Not because there wasn't a lot of good information out there, but because I had so much to learn.

My hunch is I'm not alone in having largely overlooked our native trees, shrubs, and tough-to-tell-apart bunchgrasses. For many of us, they're just the backdrop that we walk, bike, and run by every day. They're perches for the birds we like to watch, and drab filler that we push past to get to "the good stuff"—cute animals and colorful wildflowers. What an oversight that is!

Douglas-fir.
(Photo by James Jaggard)

Bitterbrush.
(Photo by Ron Halvorson)

Quaking aspen. (Photo by M.A. Willson)

Vine maple. (Photo by James Jaggard)

Purple sage.
(Photo by Ron Halvorson)

As you'll see in these pages, our trees, shrubs, and bunchgrasses are a sensory delight, if you know what you're looking for. Have you smelled a mock-orange bloom or a grand fir needle? Or let the delicate seedheads of Indian ricegrass tickle your palm? Or sat beneath a quaking aspen and listened to the leaves rustle like running water? Or tasted golden currants or wild huckleberries?

If not, let me gently say that you are missing out. And the good news is that you can remedy this oversight immediately—simply by walking outside and taking a closer look at the trees and other plants we see in Central Oregon every single day.

TREES

CONIFERS

Douglas-Fir *(Pseudotsuga menziesii)*

Size: Up to 250 ft., diam. 10 ft.

The Douglas-fir is Oregon's state tree, and for good reason. It grows better and bigger in the Northwest than it does anywhere else, it's native to all but one county in Oregon (Sherman), and the state's economy has long depended on it for everything from timber to Christmas trees.

Animals and plants also depend on Douglas-firs. Woodpeckers and other cavity nesters prefer the tree and its snags, which are also prime breeding habitat for birds, including Brown Creepers, Evening Grosbeaks, and Pine Siskins. Want more? Black bears strip the bark to get at the tasty cambium beneath, deer eat new shoots, and little critters like mice and squirrels gobble up and store seeds from the cones.

One reason Douglas-fir is the most common tree in Oregon is that it prospers in a lot of climates. Coos County has the tallest Douglas-fir in the state (taller than a twenty-eight-story building!), but in Central Oregon, we have fewer and shorter Douglas-firs in our mixed-conifer forests.

Look for: Tall trees with long limbs that sweep upward at the top and have a lot of droopy branchlets. Their giveaway is the cones, which have three-pointed bracts sticking out between the scales like a pitchfork or the hind end of a mouse. Soft, blunt, 1-in. needles surround twigs like a bottlebrush. Brown buds are pointy (not blunt like true firs).

Top: See the mice diving into the holes? (Photo by Ed Jensen)

Bottom: Main branches tend to swoop upward, with branchlets hanging down.

Found: In mixed-conifer forests near Sisters, including along Whychus Creek and near Cold Springs Campground. Also in the Ochocos and Shevlin Park.

FUN FACT

Douglas-firs have that hyphen because they're not true firs. An easy way to tell: While Douglas-fir cones dangle from branches like ornaments, true firs have cones that perch upright like little birds.

Lodgepoles in Yellowstone National Park, rushing to replace a burned stand.

PINES

Lodgepole Pine *(Pinus contorta)*

Size: Up to 100 ft., diam. 2 ft.

Nobody has ever used *majestic* as an adjective to describe lodgepole pines. They don't live long, don't fend off insects very well, don't have gorgeous cones or needles or branches, and don't smell particularly nice. What they do best is reproduce like mad, which is admirable enough in its own way.

Lodgepole seeds are tiny—it takes about 100,000 to make a pound (go ahead, count 'em!). They start producing those seeds at an early age, and the seedlings grow fast once established, making them well suited to move in after wildfires. Alas, lodgepoles typically grow so fast that they become skinny, thin-barked trees susceptible to wind, fire, and insects like the mountain pine beetle.

In burned-over areas, lodgepole seedlings duke it out for early dominance with fellow fast-growers like western larch and quaking aspen. Where lodgepoles succeed, they often develop into deeply crowded "dog-hair" stands; in one such stand, there were 100,000 trees in one acre, with about eight inches between each trunk.

Look for: Our only two-needled pine is skinny and straight (the name comes from their early use as poles for teepees and lodges). The needles are shorter (1–3 in.) and the cones smaller than our other pines. Also note how the branches seem to reach for the sky.

Found: All over, but dominant in much of Sunriver and La Pine because they can withstand cold temperatures and high elevations. Three Creek Lake is a good place to see the damage done by mountain pine beetles.

Top: *Note the bundles of two needles beneath the male pollen cones. (Photo by Jason Hollinger)*

Bottom: *Pinecone-palooza: Sugar pines have the biggest cones, western white cones are banana-shaped, ponderosa cones have prickly bracts, and lodgepole cones are the smallest.*

Ponderosas adding their colors to autumn at Shevlin Park. (Photo by M.A. Willson)

Ponderosa Pine *(Pinus ponderosa)*

Size: Up to 180 ft., diam. 6 ft.

A friend likes to say that Europe's ancient cathedrals are made of stone and Oregon's are made of ponderosa pine. Sit in a park-like forest of old-growth ponderosas some sunny day, and you'll be hard-pressed to disagree.

Ponderosas are the second most common tree in Oregon (behind Douglas-firs), and one of the world's largest ponderosa timberlands stretches from the flanks of the Cascades down through much of Central Oregon, giving way to juniper woodlands to the east. Though fairly common here, old-growth pondo forests are among the most endangered forests in the West, including in Eastern Oregon, where logging has decimated populations in the Wallowas, Blue Mountains, and elsewhere.

Woody cones are female. These are male pollen cones.

Ponderosas and fire

Mature pondos are among the most fire-resistant of all trees, with super-thick bark and lower limbs that fall off to protect the crown. To limit competition from shrubs and other conifers, the trees actively encourage small, frequent fires by sprinkling their long needles all over the forest floor—needles covered in flammable resins. (Yes, you can think of pondos as pyros.)

The problem we hear a lot about these days is that people have been suppressing natural fires since pioneer days. So brush, small trees, and dead fuels build up and up, leading to overly crowded forests and uncharacteristic wildfires that can destroy even older, deeply fire-resistant ponderosas.

Is there anything more beautiful than a pondo? (Photo by Kim Elton)

Life with ponderosas

Ponderosa pine seeds are preferred cuisine for chickadees, doves, finches, grosbeaks, jays, nutcrackers, nuthatches, blackbirds, sparrows, and towhees, as well as beavers, porcupines, chipmunks, squirrels . . . the list goes on.

Even when pondos die, they're extremely valuable as sturdy snags (standing dead trees) that Northern Flickers and other birds drill holes into, forming homes for themselves and later for many other creatures.

Look for: The only Northwest conifer with needles in bundles of three. Needles are exceptionally long (up to 8 in.)—a key differentiator from lodgepole. Cones are 3–5 in. long, with prickly scales.

Found: View (and smell) old-growth stands at Shevlin Park and near Hwy. 20 northwest of Sisters. LaPine State Park is home to many old-growth trees, including 500-year-old "Big Red," the biggest ponderosa of its variety in the country.

FUN FACT

Old-growth pondos (the ones with yellow or orange bark) smell like vanilla. In fact, the wood pulp contains vanillin, which has been used to make imitation vanilla. On a warm day, don't be shy: Go right up to the trunk and inhale deeply. It's one of the most beautiful scents in the forest

Top: The "priest of pines" with arms outstretched.

Bottom: Cones can be twenty inches long. (Photo by Ed Jensen)

Sugar Pine *(Pinus lambertiana)*

Size: Up to 200 ft., diam. 7 ft.

I don't know if it's the grandeur of the foot-long cones or the great size of the trees themselves, but there's something about a sugar pine that takes my breath away. Maybe it's also their rarity, at least in this area, where you have to work hard to find even a handful within an hour's drive of Bend.

It's not just me who loves the sugar pine, the tallest and broadest of all pines. John Muir said, "They are the priests of pine and seem ever to be addressing the surrounding forest." As noble as ponderosas and other trees may be, he wrote, "the sugar pine is easily king and spreads his arms above them in blessing while they nod and wave in signs of recognition."

David Douglas raved that sugar pine was "unquestionably the most splendid specimen of American vegetation." In 1826, he hiked near present-day Roseburg to find the source of the massive pine seeds he'd seen Umpqua peoples eating. When he found a tall sugar pine, he shot down three cones, which attracted the attention of eight none-too-happy Natives. Fearing for his life, Douglas communicated that he'd give them tobacco in exchange for more cones. When the men took the bait and went looking for the cones, Douglas wrote that he "made the quickest possible retreat."

Who knows what the Native Americans thought of someone shooting at a tree. For them, sugar pines were culturally significant and a valuable source of food (the seeds are as big as corn kernels and quite tasty) and of pitch to repair their canoes and fasten arrowheads and feathers to arrow shafts.

Look for: Tall trees with long branches tipped with monster cones. Bluish-green needles are in clusters of five, like western white and whitebark pines, but whitebarks are near timberline and western whites have shorter, banana-shaped cones.

Found: We're at the northern end of their range, but look for small numbers on top of Ann's Butte and on the north side of Davis Mountain and Sugar Pine Butte (and other buttes in that area). They're also on Pringle Butte and near the top of Green Ridge.

FUN FACT

Most of the pine nuts we spend a fortune on at grocery stores come from cultivated pines in Asia and Europe. Most North American pine nuts come from pinyon pine trees, which produce unpredictable crops that are difficult to harvest.

Western White Pine *(Pinus monticola)*

Size: Up to 180 ft., diam. 4 ft.

The first thing to know about western white pine, aka "King Pine," is that it has light, smooth, straight, and strong wood. You know where this is heading, right? Early colonists coveted the eastern white pine, so they were thrilled when they found this larger western species, which became the basis for the timber empires of Weyerhaeuser and other logging companies.

When stock of western whites ran low, companies didn't stop logging. Instead, they turned to foreign nurseries for more stock—and in 1910, a shipment from France brought with it a fungal pathogen that causes white pine blister rust. Thanks to that disease, plus overharvesting, fire suppression, and mountain pine beetles, western whites now cover less than five percent of their historical range.

In the early decades of the 1900s, forestry agencies spent millions trying to stop the spread of blister rust. It didn't work. And when all seemed hopeless, they logged even more western white pines, figuring they could at least make use of the remaining trees before they died. Now we know that rust-resistant strains were developing naturally, and the trees should not have been cut down.

Current conservation efforts focus on identifying, breeding, and planting more rust-resistant western whites. If we successfully restore King Pine to some of its former dominance, it could play a key role in our climate-changed future because it's a particularly hardy, deep-rooted, and fire-resistant tree.

Look for: Five needles, like whitebark and sugar pines, but needles are soft with a whitish tinge. Look for the 6-11 in., banana-shaped cones. Young bark is smooth and white; mature bark is scaled in small squares like an alligator's back.

Found: Uncommon, but here and there in moister areas like Clear Lake, the head of Jack Creek, and in a tiny stand at the Metolius Preserve.

Top: *Banana-shaped cones dangle from branch tips.*
(Photo by Ed Jensen)

Middle: *Smell the sap on the trunks or cones—it's incredible!*

Bottom: *Note the white tinge to the needles (in groups of five).*

DID YOU KNOW?

Pines are the world's most common type of conifer. North America has over thirty pine species, Oregon has eight, and Central Oregon has five.

Whitebark Pine *(Pinus albicaulis)*

Size: Up to 50 ft., diam. 2 ft.

Take a hike up in the Cascades. Keep going. A little higher now. Those last trees you see near timberline, with bark shredded by wind and snow to reveal white trunks polished like bone? Those are whitebark pines, one of our most endangered and starkly beautiful trees.

Whitebarks are a keystone species (a critical species with an outsized affect on its environment) because they regulate runoff, reduce erosion, and produce seeds that nourish birds and mammals. Their most famous relationship is with the Clark's Nutcracker, which buries whitebark pine seeds for retrieval in the lean days of winter. The uneaten seeds are left to germinate—the primary way whitebarks spread.

Sadly, whitebark pines are deeply endangered by blister rust and bark beetle infestations, two human-induced problems exacerbated by climate change. Experts warn that whitebark populations are unlikely to survive blister rust, let alone the beetle infestation. That means one of our most rugged and remote trees may go extinct without further human intervention (of the positive kind), such as the current effort to develop seedlings resistant to blister rust.

Look for: Typically short, wind-battered trees with ragged tops, massive boles (from frost damage), and stiff, yellow-green needles in tight bundles of five. Cones are small and purple but rarely seen on the ground (look for scales).

Found: Near the peaks of high-elevation sites such as Mount Bachelor, Tam McArthur Rim, Tumalo Mountain, Black Butte, and Paulina Peak.

Top: *A whitebark standing up to the weight of winter on Mount Bachelor. (Photo by Bruce Jackson)*

Middle: *One of many whitebarks on Black Butte.*

Bottom: *Yellow-green needles are in bundles of five. (Photo by Ed Jensen)*

FUN FACT

The oldest whitebark pine ever found was about 1,270 years old, in Idaho's Sawtooth Mountains. Height isn't the best indicator of age—a six-foot-tall whitebark pine can be 500 years old!

TRUE FIRS

Grand Fir *(Abies grandis)*

Size: Up to 250 ft., diam. 6 ft.

Grand firs are true firs (none of that confusing Douglas-fir stuff). In fact, they're Oregon's most common true fir, although they prefer moister areas and are far more widespread west of the Cascades than in Central Oregon.

The trees are thin-barked and disease-prone, but if you're in the market for a Christmas tree, it's tough to beat the aptly named grand fir. They grow fast, have a wonderful citrus smell, and their horizontal branches and flat sprays of needles seem specially designed to hold ornaments.

Many, if not most, of our grand firs have hybridized with white firs. It's tough to tell the difference, but you can look for white stomata lines on the tops of needles as a sign that the "grand fir" you're looking at has hybridized with white fir. You can also look at the inner layer of the bark, which is reddish in grand firs and yellowish in white firs.

Look for: Symmetrical trees with whorls of horizontal or slightly downswept branches, often to the ground. Shiny green needles are splayed flat, as if pressed in a book. Needle undersides have two white stomata lines, and tips are blunt and soft. Also look for upright cones in the treetops.

Found: Usually in moister conditions, mixed with Douglas-fir. Common at Black Butte and Shevlin Park, and in and around Sisters.

FACTS ABOUT TRUE FIRS

- The cones of true firs perch on the topmost branches like little birds.

- Needles are "friendly like firs"—meaning the ends are soft, not poky.

- Gently pull the needle of a true fir off its twig, and it'll leave a tiny scar.

- Oregon has more species of true firs than any other state: California red, grand, noble, Pacific silver, subalpine, and white.

Top: *Needles and buds are pointy.* (Photo by Ed Jensen)

Middle: *Branches tend to grow perpendicular to the trunk.* (Photo by M.A. Willson)

Bottom: *It's a true fir, so cones perch upright on branches.* (Photo by Ed Jensen)

Subalpine Fir *(Abies lasiocarpa)*

Size: Up to 100 ft., diam. 2 ft.

If you were a tree that had to make a go of it at upper elevations, how would you adapt? Maybe stiff branches to shed snow? How about an ultra-thin body with a pointy top, also to limit snow accumulation? And maybe a unique way to reproduce that doesn't depend on planting seeds in cold, hard soils? That, in a nutshell, is subalpine fir.

Getting seeds to germinate at high elevations is not easy (just ask the whitebark pine), so many subalpine firs use a clever adaptation called layering. At higher elevations, the trees tend to be shorter and have wide skirts of lower limbs. When those skirts get buried under snow for months at a time, they can take root and create new sprouts—no seeds required.

In cold and windy months, those wide lower branches of subalpine firs also provide a service as shelter for young trees and protection from the elements for birds, rodents, deer, and even mountain goats.

Look for: Most resemble the Eiffel Tower in overall shape, with light-gray bark and stiff, horizontal branches. Short, stiff, blunt, blue-green needles generally point up, with stomata lines on the top and bottom. It's a true fir, so the dark-purple cones, often glistening with resin, perch on branches like little birds.

Found: At higher elevations, including at the Cascade Lakes and along the highway near and beyond Mount Bachelor.

Top: A typical skinny subalpine.

Bottom: Cones point up, and note the tightly coiled branches. (Photos by Ed Jensen)

FUN FACT

For those like me who've had a long time to forget botanical terms, stomata are pores through which trees "breathe," drawing in carbon dioxide and releasing oxygen. To the naked eye, the stomata on the needles of subalpine fir and many other trees look like white strips.

NATIVE TREES

Oregon has at least sixty-seven native tree species, which is far more than Washington. That sounds impressive until you learn that North Carolina has many hundreds of native tree species, and tropical countries like Belize have even more.

OTHER CONIFERS

Engelmann Spruce *(Picea engelmannii)*

Size: Up to 120 ft., diam. 3 ft.

We only have one native spruce in Central Oregon, the lovely Engelmann (named after a physician and botanist from St. Louis). Despite how often you may hear about the blue spruce and see it used in landscaping, the Engelmann is actually the more common tree across the U.S.

Engelmanns grow in cold, shady, wet environments above 3,000 feet in the Cascades and Rockies. If you don't want to climb any mountains, you can spot them in the cold canyon microclimate of Shevlin Park. They're usually in the shade of other trees, and they sometimes grow in tightly packed stands to withstand harsh winds.

Native Americans use spruce as a medicine and a tea, which could be said about perhaps a few hundred other trees and plants. Engelmann spruce is also used to make exceptional violins and other stringed instruments.

Look for: Pyramid shape, with dense foliage often to the ground, and branchlets drooping from main limbs. Gray-green or bluish needles (1 in.) circle the branch and are prickly, four-sided (you can roll them between your fingers, unlike flat fir needles), and perched on woody pegs. Papery, egg-shaped cones dangle from upper branches. Bark is so thin that loose scales flake off.

Found: In moist environments, including along Tumalo Creek in Shevlin Park, near Three Creek Lake, and along the upper Metolius River.

Top: *Note the pyramid shape and bluish tinge. (Photo by Ed Jensen)*

Bottom: *Needles are pointed and prickly.*

FRANK'S NOSE KNOWS

Frank Spiecker is an antique furniture restorer and one heck of a naturalist, with a terrific nose for our native plants. Here's his alphabetical list of our ten most aromatic trees.

- Black cottonwood leaves and buds
- Chokecherry flowers
- Elderberry flowers
- Mountain-mahogany leaf litter and blossoms
- Needles of any conifer
- Old-growth ponderosa pine bark
- Red-osier dogwood flowers
- Water birch leaves
- Western juniper, especially after a rain
- Western white pine sap on cones and trunks

Incense-Cedar *(Calocedrus decurrens)*

Size: Up to 110 ft., diam. 5 ft.

It can be tricky to tell the difference between our many pine and fir trees, but there's really no mistaking the incense-cedar, which has dense, scale-like foliage and truly unusual woody cones. The trees are especially distinctive in winter and early spring, when the branch tips are tinged with golden-yellow pollen cones.

Incense-cedar is the only false cedar in Central Oregon, but across the state there are three others, including the western redcedar, an iconic species on the west side of the Cascades. True cedars only grow on other continents, but the confusion probably began because, like true cedars, Oregon's false cedars have fragrant wood.

Speaking of the fragrance, if you're over the age of forty, you may remember that pencils used to have a strong, "woodsy" smell—that's because they were made from incense-cedar wood. Today's pencils (we still have pencils, don't we?) are often made of tropical woods that lack that distinctive scent.

Look for: Other than junipers, this is our only tree with scale-like leaves that overlap and form flat sprays like a fern. When open, the unique female cones look like a flying goose or a duck's bill with the tongue hanging out.

Found: Common along Forest Service Rd. 11 east of Black Butte and on Green Ridge. Also found in Drake Park and in patches along Rd. 40 between Sunriver and the Cascade Lakes Highway.

Top: *Brown female cones open in fall.*

Bottom: *The dense foliage gives them a unique appearance.*
(Photos by Ed Jensen)

FUN FACT

The hyphen in the common name means that incense-cedar is not a true cedar, just like Douglas-firs are not true firs. That's right, people: punctuation matters!

Scaly leaves on a young tree along the Metolius River.

Mountain hemlocks in winter. (Photo by James Jaggard)

Mountain Hemlock (*Tsuga mertensiana*)

Size: Up to 100 ft., diam. 3 ft.

When John Muir called the mountain hemlock "the very loveliest tree in the forest," he could have been thinking of its colorful nature: blue-green needles, purplish-brown bark, and bluish male cones that release pale-yellow pollen.

But it turns out he was musing on the famous droop of the mountain hemlock, the way the tip of the tree and even the ends of the branches seem to bend under the weight of the world. The tree is "strong not in resistance," Muir wrote, "but compliance, bowing, snow-laden, to the ground, gracefully accepting burial month after month in the darkness beneath the heavy mantle of winter."

A lyrical guy, that Muir. The similar western hemlock is a west-side species that has crept over to this side of the Cascades. But mainly you'll see the mountain hemlock, a survivalist that hangs on in some of our coldest, harshest environments, often intermixed (and competing) with subalpine fir and other high-elevation species.

Look for: Most treetops and branches have that distinctive droop. Cones are up to 3 in. long and purplish-brown; needles are blue-green and very short (under an inch). Branches grow to the ground, so look at the ends to see if needles spiral around in a starlike shape.

Found: Same high-elevation forests as subalpine fir, including at Mount Bachelor and the Cascade Lakes, as well as above Tumalo Falls and in the Three Creek Lake area.

Top: *Droopy tips and droopy branches.*

Bottom: *Look for the short, star-shaped needles. (Photos by Ed Jensen)*

INNOCENT UNTIL PROVEN GUILTY

You may have heard tell of Socrates dying from drinking a potion made from hemlock. That poison did not come from a hemlock tree—it came from a plant called poison hemlock.

Battered junipers in the Badlands Wilderness. (Photo by Kim Elton)

Western Juniper *(Juniperus occidentalis)*

Size: Up to 60 ft., diam. 3 ft.

Everyone loves ponderosa pines, those majestic, straight-trunked, vanilla-scented beauties. It takes a different sort to appreciate battered and craggy old-growth junipers—trees that have been through the worst, stood through the ages, and survived in the midst of our driest, hottest, and least hospitable regions, in something that looks an awful lot like defiance.

Surely there is no better symbol of Central Oregon and the tough characters who live in this area than a gnarled juniper. What's surprising—especially given that North America's largest juniper woodland is north and east of Bend—is that most folks don't know a whole lot about these remarkable trees. So let's fix that.

To survive drought, junipers can cut off water to a branch, resulting in many dead branches on living trees. (Photo by Bruce Jackson)

Are junipers male or female?

That's a bit tricky. They can be male, female, or both, and it appears that some may shift their sex from year to year, possibly in response to environmental conditions. Check to see if the tree has female cones (blue berries) or yellowish-brown male pollen cones, or both.

Are there other kinds of juniper in Oregon?

Yes, there are Rocky Mountain junipers in northeast Oregon and shrub-like common junipers at Sparks Lake and other high-elevation areas.

Are juniper berries edible?

Birds certainly think so! In winter the berries are a critical food source for Cedar Waxwings, Mountain Bluebirds, and many other species. Both robins and solitaires have been known to eat over 220 berries a day, and a Bohemian Waxwing passed 900 berries in five hours!

You can eat the berries too, but they're better dropped into a bottle of water to get rid of the plasticky taste. As for other uses, there's a reason the word *gin* was derived from *ginevre*, the French word for juniper.

A craggy, broken, beautiful old juniper. (Photo by Tyson Fisher)

How can you tell old junipers from young ones?

You can't tell by height or width (which vary based on factors like access to water). Young junipers tend to be pyramid-shaped with pointy tops, while older trees have flattened tops, sparse canopies, twisty trunks, and a lot of dead limbs. Old-growth bark is deeply furrowed and reddish, with lichen on dead branches.

Where are the oldest and biggest junipers?

Oregon's oldest western juniper is about 1,600 years old and is up on Horse Ridge. The state's tallest juniper (sixty-eight feet) is in the Christmas Lake Basin near Fort Rock.

Aren't junipers an invasive species?

No! Many junipers have been here since the Incas ruled Peru, and well before Columbus sailed the ocean blue. Old-growth junipers provide food, shelter, and cavity nesting for birds, coyotes, jackrabbits, porcupines, deer, squirrels, woodrats—and many more native animals.

The "berries" are really female seed cones.

That said, we have too many young junipers, largely because of heavy livestock grazing and fire suppression. Some thinning of young trees is needed, but it needs to be done with care and limited disturbance so the trees are replaced by native plants, not invasives like cheatgrass.

Look for: Distinctive, short trees with scale-like leaves in whorls of three. Old-growth trees are shaggy, with reddish, deeply furrowed bark. Blue "berries" (actually female cones) are a giveaway.

Found: All over, especially in the triangle between Bend, Redmond, and Sisters. The Badlands Wilderness is a convenient place to see contorted old-growth junipers.

Top: *In autumn there's no mistaking these golden beauties. (Photo by M.A. Willson)*

Bottom: *Larch needles in spring, attached to branches in bundled bouquets.*

Western Larch *(Larix occidentalis)*

Size: Up to 180 ft., diam. 4 ft.

After a fire burns through an area, there's a window of opportunity for trees to move in like gold-seeking human settlers, staking their claims to the available nutrients, water, and sunshine. Western larches are often among the first to arrive. They don't like shade so they grow extremely fast, shading other trees that eventually grow up beneath them to create a mixed-conifer forest.

The best-known fact about larches is that they're one of the world's only deciduous conifers, which means they lose all their needles every year. In fall, you can watch as their needles gradually turn yellow and then a deep gold before falling to the ground. Then in spring and early summer, you'll see their bright, grassy-green new needles emerge next to the duller greens of ponderosas, Douglas-firs, and other nearby trees.

Larches' unusual deciduous way of life means that they have to photosynthesize like mad while they have needles, before going nearly dormant during the cold months. One theory holds that by resting much of the year, they extend their lives; we have few old-growth larches left in Central Oregon, but they can surpass 500 years of age.

Look for: Tall, straight trees with short limbs. Needles turn yellow and gold in fall, practically glowing early and late in the day. Spring and summer, look for large clusters of super-soft, bright-green needles.

Found: Hot spots include Shevlin Park and the Metolius River basin, especially at the Metolius Preserve. Also common along Hwy. 26 east of Prineville and in the Ochocos.

LARCH OR TAMARACK?

Western larches are often called "tamaracks," but the tamarack larch is a different species that grows in Canada and the northeastern U.S.

BROADLEAF TREES

Bitter Cherry (*Prunus emarginata*)

Size: Up to 30 ft., diam. 1.5 ft.

Just about every creature you can think of loves to eat the leaves, the twigs, and especially the red berries of bitter cherries: deer, elk, black bears, small mammals, birds, sheep, cattle—which is not to suggest that you should partake. The common name is a tip-off, and the fact that all the plant parts release a little cyanide when eaten should pretty well seal the deal.

Bitter cherries are attractive trees or shrubs that grow in streams and meadows, commonly with ponderosa pines, manzanita, and serviceberry. Like other trees that grow along waterways, they help stabilize banks and provide shelter to wildlife.

Bitter cherry is not a particularly long-lived species because it doesn't tolerate shade well—a problem for a species that often grows in the understory of forests (go figure).

Look for: A small tree or shrub, often with multiple trunks. In spring, small, fragrant, white-to-pink flowers appear in roundish clusters (chokecherry clusters are longer), followed by bright-red berries. Yellowish-green leaves are up to 3 in. long and rounded, with uneven teeth. Reddish-brown bark typically has horizontal lenticels (unlike chokecherry).

Found: Near Sisters at Black Butte, Green Ridge, and Suttle Lake, and along McKenzie Pass. Also at Smith Rock State Park and Shevlin Park.

Top: *A sprawling bitter cherry in spring.*

Bottom: *Flower clusters are rounder and shorter than chokecherry. (Photos by Ben Legler)*

TREES VS. SHRUBS

It's not as easy as you might think to tell a tree from a shrub. Plants like bitter cherries and mountain alders can be either, depending on how big they are (shrubs are generally less than thirteen feet tall) and whether they have one or multiple stems. Tree-ish shrubs and shrubbish trees are all covered in the tree section.

A Western Tanager adds color to a chokecherry. (Photo by Kim Elton)

Chokecherry *(Prunus virginiana)*

Size: Up to 40 ft., diam. 2 ft.

Chokecherries are important sources of food and medicine for many Native American tribes. The cherries, pits and all, can be pounded into a mush and added to dried meat to create pemmican, the early version of Clif Bars. Legend has it that Sacagawea was captured while she collected chokecherry fruits.

Long leaves have pointy tips and are salmon-colored in fall.

It's fun to watch these trees (or shrubs) all year long. In spring you'll see snow-white flowers growing in long, skinny clusters, like upright cones, and you might hear the hum of bees attracted to the strong, sweet fragrance. The flowers eventually flop over, and each develops into a small cherry that ripens from green to red. In fall, the leaves turn a lovely salmon color and the cherries turn purple and then black—at least the ones not eaten by robins, solitaires, Cedar Waxwings, deer, and other wildlife.

Like bitter cherries, chokecherries contain a little cyanide, so you won't want to eat many of the fruits, delicious as they look (they can be made into jam, jelly, butter, and wine, though). Scratch the bark or crush a few young leaves and twigs to smell the bitter, almond-like scent that's a hallmark of cyanide.

Look for: Longer flower and fruit clusters than bitter cherry. Leaves are thick and elliptical, glossy deep-green above and lighter below, with toothed margins (rub your finger backward along the edges to feel the little teeth).

Found: Very common along area waterways, including at Smith Rock State Park and all along the Deschutes River (Drake Park, First Street Rapids, etc.).

Black Cottonwood *(Populus trichocarpa)*

Size: Up to 150 ft., diam. 5 ft.

Black cottonwoods are the largest hardwood trees in the West, and while they're bigger and more common west of the Cascades, Central Oregon has a fair number of them. They're members of the willow family, and like other willows, they're found near water (for pioneers, the sight of a cottonwood was a relief because it meant a water source was near).

Cottonwoods can't tolerate shade, so they move into disturbed areas and grow quickly, racing to beat the competition to the sunlight. Like alders, they do a lot of good along the way, stabilizing riverbanks with their thickly stitched roots and providing food and shelter for wildlife. Large birds like eagles, herons, osprey, and even Canada Geese nest in their sprawling crowns.

Native Americans make dugout canoes, bedding, baskets, and sweat lodges from cottonwoods, and members of the Lewis and Clark Expedition used the trees to make canoes, wheels, and axles. Like other willows, cottonwoods contain salicin, which decomposes into salicylic acid, a precursor to aspirin—so you won't be surprised to hear that the bark has been used raw and in salves to treat everything from headaches to wounds.

Look for: Large trees lining lower-elevation waterways. Mature trees have deeply furrowed gray bark. The branch tips and thick, pointy leaves are sticky and smell sweet when new. Leaves flash silvery-white undersides. Droopy catkins appear in early spring; female catkins later develop fluffy "cotton" seeds that descend like snow.

Found: Fairly common along the shores of the Cascade Lakes and Hwy. 20 between Sisters and Albany. Also at Drake Park, along the Deschutes River, and along Elm St. outside Sisters.

Top: *Cottonwoods give us some of our best fall colors.*
(Photo by M.A. Willson)

Bottom: *Look for big, heart-shaped leaves, like these shown in fall.*

WHY DON'T WE HAVE MORE BROADLEAF TREES?

Ever notice that we have a lot of conifers in Central Oregon but relatively few broadleaf, deciduous trees? It's largely because we don't get much rain or humidity during our long summers, when oaks, maples, and other broadleaves need moisture. That's also why most of our broadleaf trees grow near water.

Curlleaf Mountain-Mahogany
(Cercocarpus ledifolius)

Size: Up to 40 ft., diam. 2 ft.

Curlleaf mountain-mahogany isn't very showy, but it's one of the coolest trees around, if you slow down and take a close look (and sniff) to appreciate what it has to offer.

Let's start with the unique seeds, which are attached to a one-to-three-inch feathery tail (*Cercocarpus* means "tailed fruit"). When the tree drops the seeds, the silky streamer lies on the ground spiraled like a pig's tail. When it rains or gets humid enough, the spiral unwinds, effectively drilling the seed into the ground so it can germinate in the spring.

Mountain-mahogany is a nitrogen fixer like alders, converting nitrogen in the air into a water-soluble form that other plants can use. That's an awfully helpful service, especially in the dry, rocky, and generally inhospitable areas where mountain-mahoganies grow. Deer, elk, and bighorn sheep also feed on the high-protein trees—which helps explain why many of the older trunks are naked and the tops ragged.

Another neat thing about mountain-mahoganies is that their flowers and leaves, especially their leaf litter, have a wonderfully sweet aroma. Be sure to pick up and smell a handful of the inches-deep drifts of white seed piles in August and September.

Look for: Shrubby, contorted trees with rounded crowns. The evergreen leaves curl under (hence the common name). Spring brings tiny whitish-yellow trumpet flowers that develop in late summer into seeds with feathery tails.

Found: On dry, rocky ridges, including on Pine Mountain, at Stein's Pillar, and atop area buttes. In Bend, tiny Laurel Park offers a few specimens of this and other native trees and shrubs.

Top: Silky streamers, ready to carry away seeds. (Photo by Jane Shelby Richardson)

Middle: Trees like this one on Pine Mountain can reach 1,300 years in age.

Bottom: Leaves are dark green and leathery.

MAHOGANY?

The hyphen in the name should tip you off that this isn't a true mahogany. It's actually in the rose family, but the common name refers to its extremely dense, heavy wood, which sinks in water.

Gorgeous clumps of red elderberries. (Photo by M.A. Willson)

Elderberry *(Sambucus* spp.*)*

Size: 3-20 ft.

I'm sorry if you haven't tasted homemade elderberry pie; it's one of life's great pleasures. But even if you don't bake you can at least enjoy the sight of red and blue elderberries on your walks along waterways in Central Oregon.

The west side of the Cascades is known for its red elderberries (*S. racemosa*), but plenty of them grow in our region as well—including on rock outcroppings on Mount Bachelor. We also have a lot of blue elderberry (*S. nigra* ssp. *cerulean*), which better tolerates our hot, dry conditions. Most of the red and blue elderberries in Central Oregon are shrub-sized, but in the right conditions, they can grow up to twenty feet high.

Many birds nest among the long, droopy elderberry leaves, and deer, elk, and birds forage on the berries. You can forage for the berries too, but don't eat them raw—especially if they aren't ripe. Instead, leave them for the birds or use them to make one of those pies.

Look for: In spring, blue elderberry produces yellow-white flowers in flat sprays (not conical like red elderberry), followed by clumps of blue-to-black berries. The leaves are composite in shape, have pointy edges, and can be almost a foot long.

Found: Along irrigation ditches and waterways, including the Deschutes River (look for them at First Street Rapids). Also keep an eye out at higher-elevation locations like Sparks and Hosmer Lakes.

Blue elderberry in Shevlin Park.

Alders tucked along Tumalo Creek. (Photo by Ed Jensen)

Mountain Alder (*Alnus incana*)

Size: Up to 30 ft., diam. 7 in.

Mountain, or thinleaf, alders are extremely common trees, and sometimes shrubs, that don't turn fabulous colors or produce showy berries. But don't overlook them; ecologically speaking, these are among our most beautiful trees.

Alders are nitrogen fixers, which means their roots have small, bead-like nodules filled with bacteria. The tree feeds the bacteria, and in turn the bacteria converts nitrogen from the air into a water-soluble form that's nutritious for the tree. Nearby plants also benefit because alder leaves and roots leach nitrogen-rich compounds. And when the leaves and roots get into the water, they feed phytoplankton, which supports insect and fish life.

The doubly serrated ridges remind me of Broken Top. (Photo by Ed Jensen)

Speaking of life, mountain alders provide forage for deer, elk, muskrats, beavers, cottontails, and more. Pine Siskins, chickadees, and many other birds also feed on the female catkins in winter and early spring, when few other food sources are available.

If all that isn't enough, the root systems also help hold banks together and prevent erosion. That's especially important because alders are among the first trees to move into burned, cut, or otherwise damaged areas, where they stabilize—and then fertilize—the soil.

Look for: Small trees or large shrubs near water. Unlike white alders (found in a few places around Central Oregon), mountain alder leaf edges have double serrations. Long male catkins appear in fall; female catkins emerge in late winter or early spring and look like tiny pinecones.

Found: Sorry, but they don't always grow on mountains and the leaves aren't thin (common names can be misleading). They're all over moist, forested areas, including along area rivers and Tumalo Creek.

Note the thin, flat petioles. (Photo by Ed Jensen)

Quaking Aspen *(Populus tremuloides)*

Size: Up to 80 ft., diam. 2 ft.

A friend's son swears he spent half his childhood removing quaking aspen seedlings from his family's landscaped yard. That's a familiar headache for people living in urban areas, but it's important to separate those frustrations from the very different story of quaking aspen in the wild.

Biological hot spots

Quaking aspen groves play an immensely important role in Central Oregon ecology. While conifer forests can support about 200 pounds of understory growth per acre, an aspen grove can support fifteen times more.

The groves create what naturalist Tom Rodhouse calls "cascading effects through the food chain." A wide variety of insects feed on aspen leaves, which attracts birds and bats. Elk drop their calves in aspen stands, and dozens of bird species nest in the trees. Beavers, cottontails, porcupines, and snowshoe hares eat the bark, rodents depend on the insects and vegetation in the understory, and all of the above activity attracts predators from coyotes to hawks.

Unique reproduction

Unlike most trees, quaking aspens rarely reproduce by seeds; instead, new trees sprout from a parent root system that lies a few inches underground. That's why aspens can grow so fast after fire: Within six weeks after a burn, hundreds or even thousands of new sprouts rise up from the surviving root system, beating conifer seeds to the punch.

When you look at an aspen grove, or clone, consider that the first tree may have sprouted from a seed tens of thousands of years ago. Each tree in the clone is the same sex and roughly the same size, and drops its leaves at about the same time. Pando, a forest of 47,000 aspen clones in Utah, has been growing for at least 80,000 years and is the world's largest organism by mass (a fungal colony in Eastern Oregon covers a larger area).

Declining populations

Many aspen groves are in danger, largely because of fire suppression (which enables larger conifers to "shade out" aspens) and overgrazing by cows, deer, and elk. Since European settlement, quaking aspen occurrence has markedly declined across its western range, and the pace of decline seems to be accelerating.

Measures such as selective fires, removal of encroaching conifers, and reintroduction of wolves and other predators to reduce overgrazing can help restore and protect quaking aspen habitat.

Look for: Thin trees with white bark marked with black. Round or heart-shaped leaves hang on flattened petioles and have pale-green undersides that flash in breezes (listen for the delightful rustling sound). Leaves turn yellow, gold, or red in autumn.

Found: In isolated stands in moist areas, including at Shevlin Park, the Little Deschutes River in Sunriver, and Hwy. 20 near Black Butte Ranch. Also along the Deschutes River above Dillon Falls and near the Aspen trailhead.

Top: *Aspens and ponderosas near Black Butte (Photo by Bruce Jackson)*

Bottom: *Woodpeckers love the soft trunks. (Photo by Ed Jensen)*

FUN FACT

It's said that early trappers believed aspen leaves never stopped trembling because the trees were used to make Jesus's cross. Another explanation is that the petioles are flat, not round, so the leaves flutter in even the gentlest breeze.

Vine Maple *(Acer circinatum)*

Size: 10–40 ft.

If autumn is your favorite season, odds are vine maple is one of your favorite deciduous trees. The little spreaders grow up to twenty feet wide in the understory of our wetter forests, and their brilliant yellow, orange, and scarlet colors are one of the signature signs that fall has arrived.

A vine maple transitioning to fall. (Photo by M.A. Willson)

With enough sunshine, vine maples can grow into decent-sized trees. But deeper in the understory, they tend to twist and contort and sprawl along the forest floor in a slow-motion quest for sunlight. Individual branches can actually grow right into the forest floor, leading to formation of new roots and more chances to creep along in search of the sun.

Along with providing eye candy for hikers, vine maple provides nourishment to wildlife. Deer and elk forage on the leaves and bark, which are especially valuable food sources in winter, and other mammals and songbirds routinely dine on the seeds, buds, and flowers. In spring, the white and wine-red flowers also provide nectar to bees and butterflies.

Look for: One or multiple stems with greenish to red bark and tiered branching. The leaves are lobed like other maples (7–9 lobes with triangular points), turning a soft green to yellow in shade, and bright red to orange in sunny areas or drier soils.

Found: Common in moister soils, including at Fall River and along McKenzie Pass.

Water Birch *(Betula occidentalis)*

Size: Up to 30 ft., diam. 1 ft.

Oregon has two native birch trees: paper and water birch. Water birch is the only one you'll find in Central Oregon, at least natively, but just to make things confusing, we also have the bog birch, which is considered a shrub rather than a tree.

Look for small trunks with copper-colored bark. (Photo by Dcrjsr)

Like other birches, water birches have distinctive horizontal marks called lenticels along their thin bark. (Lenticels are raised pores that provide a gateway through the bark for gases to be exchanged.) Water birches also produce rather unusual fruits—finger-shaped cones that look like furry caterpillars.

Deer and elk browse on water birch, beavers harvest the stems as building materials, and trout appreciate the cool, shaded water they create. The trees also provide important habitat for birds, including warblers and Western Tanagers, and Native peoples have long used the colorful bark (not white like paper birches) as a dye.

Look for: Tall shrub or small tree with multiple stems. Note the horizontal marks on the reddish-brown to coppery bark, and the oval, sometimes sticky leaves with sharp-toothed edges. The 1-in. "caterpillars," or papery cones, are the telltale sign.

Found: Along area waterways. Water birch is more common at lower elevations north and east of Bend, while bog birch (which needs year-round wetlands) occurs at higher elevations along the Deschutes River and areas west and south of Bend.

Colorful willows along the Deschutes River. (Photo by Kim Elton)

Willows *(Salix* spp.)

Size: 3-40 ft.

Walk along just about any waterway in Central Oregon, and you'll come across thicket after thicket of willows. What kind of willow you'll see is harder to say because Oregon has several dozen species that hybridize and are notoriously tough to identify.

The hairs at left carry seeds, leaving the empty capsules at right. (Photo by Al Schneider)

In this region, you're most likely to come across Scouler's willow (*S. scouleriana*), which can grow on slopes away from water, and the typically shorter coyote willow (*S. exigua*), which grows along streams east of Bend and has very long, narrow gray-green leaves.

All willows are hugely important to the environment. They help stabilize and shade streambanks, keeping water cool and clear for fish and other species. Their early blooms also provide one of the first spring food supplies for native bees. And if that's not enough, songbirds nest in their thickets, and beavers, deer, and elk rely on them for food. (When beavers cut them down, willows simply resprout from their trunks.)

Humans are frankly a bit willow obsessed. We describe people as "willowy," write popular books like *The Wind in the Willows*, create characters like Old Man Willow (Tolkien), use willow for everything from medicine to baskets to biomass, and include willow as part of religious ceremonies around the world.

Look for: Leaves are simple, alternate, and shaped like canoes. Male and female flowers (aka catkins or pussy willows) appear early in spring on separate trees. Female catkins develop seeds with white tufts of cottony down that float long distances in the wind or water. Twigs can be colorful through winter (red, orange, yellow, etc.).

Found: Along every river and most streams across Central Oregon.

DID YOU KNOW?

Ancient peoples discovered that chewing willow leaves and bark helped reduce aches and fever. Willow contains salicin, which the body turns into salicylic acid. In the 1890s, German chemist Felix Hoffman developed an altered version called acetylsalicylic acid. His employer, a little company called Bayer, named the new drug aspirin.

Shevlin Park is the perfect place for a treasure hunt! (Photo by Kim Elton)

FOREST TREASURE HUNT

This treasure hunt for the young and young at heart is adapted from *Sharing Nature with Children* by Joseph Cornell. Use it in parks, forests, or other natural areas.

- A feather
- A seed
- Exactly 100 of something
- A pine needle
- A pinecone
- Something round
- Something sharp
- Five pieces of human-made litter

- Something perfectly straight
- Something beautiful
- Something white
- Something that makes a noise
- Something soft
- Something that reminds you of yourself

Autumn blooms on a big sagebrush in Madras. (Photo by Alan St. John)

SHRUBS

Big Sagebrush *(Artemisia tridentata)*

Size: 1-10 ft.

Sagebrush is the iconic symbol of the high desert, the dominant species in ecosystems that once covered about half the American West. Since European settlement, millions of acres of that "sagebrush sea" have been lost, and many more are in danger due to invasive species like cheatgrass, as well as habitat fragmentation, fire suppression (leading to uncharacteristic fires), and energy exploration.

But let's set aside the mega-issues for now and get to know the shrub itself. Big sagebrush is the most common sagebrush species in Central Oregon, and as its name implies, it can be huge—ten feet tall in some areas. The leaves have an unmistakable herbal aroma that's especially wonderful after a spring rain, but this is not the sage used in cooking; it's actually more closely related to tarragon.

Sagebrush at Prineville Reservoir. (Photo by Alan St. John)

Built to survive

How can a little ol' shrub survive drought, heavy winds, hot summers, and extreme cold? Sagebrush is a master of adaptation. It has long taproots to pull water from deep in the ground and shallow roots to absorb ground moisture before it evaporates.

The larger leaves photosynthesize through summer and then drop off to conserve energy, while the smaller leaves keep soaking up the sun through winter. Look closely, and you'll also see that the leaves are covered in tiny hairs that lock in moisture and reflect heat.

All that said, sagebrush is surprisingly fragile and doesn't grow back readily after today's larger and more frequent fires, which are often fueled by cheatgrass.

Other species

There are about 250 species of sagebrush worldwide, many of them tough to tell apart. In Central Oregon, the three most common subspecies are big sagebrush (ssp. *tridentata*); Wyoming big sagebrush (ssp. *wyomingensis*), common on rangelands up to 7,000 feet; and mountain sagebrush (ssp. *vaseyana*), which prefers cooler sites up to 10,000 feet.

In rockier soils, we also have shorter species such as low sagebrush (*A. arbuscula*) and rigid sagebrush (*A. rigida*). In moist areas and dry lakebeds east of Bend, silver sagebrush (*A. cana*) is common.

Who needs it?

Mark Twain said of sagebrush, "Nothing can abide the taste of it but the jackass and his illegitimate child the mule." In fact, more than 350 plant and animal species depend on sagebrush, including elk, mule deer, pronghorn, and Golden Eagles.

Most famously, the imperiled Greater Sage-Grouse relies on sagebrush for every stage of its lifecycle. The sage-grouse is the "umbrella species" for sagebrush habitat, the idea being that if you protect sage-grouse, you will also protect hundreds of lesser-known species that rely on sagebrush.

Small yellow flowers bloom in late summer to early fall. (Photo by Ron Halvorson)

Look for: Gray-green shrubs with small, hairy leaves, usually with three deep notches. Small yellow blossoms appear in late summer and early fall. But really, just smell to see if it's a sagebrush.

Found: All over Central Oregon, from low-elevation, sandy soils north and east of Bend to the open slopes of local buttes and mountains. Within an hour east of Bend is the true sagebrush steppe, where sagebrush is king.

SURVIVAL OF THE FITTEST

See how many of these adaptations you can find on our hardy shrubs:

- Short blooming periods

- Small, rolled, or folded leaves (less surface area to lose water)

- Thick, succulent leaves, stems, or roots to store moisture

- Light colors and a waxy layer on leaves to reflect light

- Hairs on stems and leaves to insulate against heat, cold, and wind

A common pairing of bitterbrush and ponderosas. (Photo by Mike Putnam)

Bitterbrush *(Purshia tridentata)*

Size: 3–8 ft.

Let's start a campaign to rename this shrub because surely bitterbrush is not the best name for one of our most common and important plants, a hardy survivalist that can live a hundred years. 'Tis a crying shame.

One of the sweet smells of spring. (Photo by Ron Halvorson)

In spring and winter, bitterbrush (superbrush? megabrush?) provides crucial nourishment for mule deer, as well as elk and pronghorn. Birds and other small animals cache the seeds for winter food supplies, and a lot of other wildlife (including the occasional sage-grouse) depend on it for cover. Want more? Miraclebrush has also been used for a variety of medicinal purposes and offers up pretty yellow flowers in spring that native bees and other pollinators depend on.

Look for: Three-lobed leaves like sagebrush (but no sagebrush smell). Numerous stiff, brittle branches, many sticking straight up. Yellow flowers appear in spring.

Found: Wherever there's sunshine, so all over Central Oregon. The Deschutes River Trail, LaPine State Park, Shevlin Park, Sunriver, the Badlands Wilderness—you name it.

WHICH BRUSH IS WHICH?				
	Foliage Color	**Leaves**	**Flowers**	**Other**
Big Sagebrush	Gray-green	Thin, gray, typically with three lobes	Yellow (late summer to fall)	Distinctive sagebrush aroma
Bitterbrush	Dull green	Three lobes like sagebrush, but wider and greener	Yellow (spring)	Often tall with erect branches
Gray Rabbitbrush	Silvery-gray	Long, thin, grayish-green or green	Flat-topped or clustered yellow (late summer to fall)	Silvery stems
Green Rabbitbrush	Very green	Greener and stickier than gray rabbitbrush	Rounded yellow clusters (mid-summer to fall)	Greener and often shorter than gray rabbitbrush
Snowbrush (Deerbrush)	Dark green	Thick, like manzanita	Small, white, clustered (late spring)	Flowers and leaves smell like cigar

Black Twinberry *(Lonicera involucrata)*

Size: 1.5–15 ft.

Black twinberry, or bearberry honeysuckle, is the most common and widely distributed honeysuckle in the West. Good thing, too, because it's wonderful at erosion control and restoration of riverbanks.

The shrub is also valuable as a source of nectar for hummingbirds and butterflies and as cover for wildlife. The purple-to-black berries are eaten by numerous small animals and songbirds, but reports are mixed on whether they're edible for humans (stay on the safe side and leave them for the birds). Native tribes use the leaves, berries, and bark to treat everything from dandruff to wounds.

Red bracts with twinned berries in Shevlin Park.

Look for: Opposite leaves are hairy underneath, with pointy tips. Easiest to identify by the yellow tubular or trumpet-shaped flowers in summer, which appear in pairs and are supported by two bracts that turn red to purple.

Found: In moist areas along area streams and lakes, including at the Metolius River, Shevlin Park, and the Cascade Lakes.

Douglas Spiraea *(Spiraea douglasii)*

Size: 2–7 ft.

There are a lot of spiraeas, wild and cultivated. Douglas spiraea, or hardhack, is the most common wild version near Bend, which is on the eastern edge of its habitat.

In early summer, you'll see large stands of the beautiful, erect blooms all over moist areas, but Douglas spiraea doesn't have to get by on its looks alone. It's a particularly fast-growing, deep-rooted shrub that does yeoman's work supporting our streambanks and native pollinators, as well as providing a hiding spot for birds, amphibians, and other small critters.

Look for: Best known for long (4–6 in.), erect, rosy-red flower clusters, like cotton candy on a stick. Spent flower clusters are dark brown and last through winter.

Found: Often in dense stands in moist areas, including along the Metolius River, Deschutes River Trail, and Tumalo Creek (at Shevlin Park).

Top: Long stamens create the fuzzy look. (Photo by Tracy Aue)

Bottom: Spiraea in July at the Old Mill.

Tasty berries at Riverbend Park.

Golden Currant *(Ribes aureum)*

Size: 3-10 ft.

We have a couple very common native currants: wax currants and this golden child, which is prettier, tastes better, and has showier flowers. The golden-yellow flowers have a fragrant, clove-like scent, and Indigenous peoples have long enjoyed the fruits, either fresh or dried and mixed with meat and other ingredients to make pemmican.

Golden currant is also a fantastic shrub to plant in landscapes. The tubular flowers are pretty and preferred by hummingbirds, and fruit-loving birds (and humans) are drawn to them.

Look for: Maple-like leaves with 3–5 lobes (like a catcher's mitt). Tubular yellow flowers in clusters of up to fifteen bloom in spring, later turning orange and violet. Fruits vary from yellow to black.

Found: Fairly common along rivers, streams, ditches, and other moist areas. Hot spots include Smith Rock State Park and elsewhere along the Lower Crooked River. Also at Riverbend Park and at the base of Pilot Butte.

Leaves are narrow and spine-tipped. (Photo by Jim Morefield)

Granite Gilia *('Linanthus pungens)*

Size: 0.5-2 ft.

You're missing out if you visit area trails only in mornings or afternoons. Many animals emerge exclusively at night, when some flowers, such as those of granite gilia (aka prickly phlox), open for business.

From midspring to midsummer, make a point of heading out for a walk in the evening so you can revel in the sweet aroma of the white, yellowish, or pinkish flowers of this otherwise rather prickly and plain-looking shrub. After opening up at night to attract moths, granite gilia's flowers close back up during the day.

Look for: Short or mat-like shrub with small, spiny leaves and spring blooms of trumpet-shaped flowers that are usually white (or yellowish to coppery) and open primarily in the evening.

Found: Sandy, rocky, generally dry areas. Very common in the Cline Buttes area and east of Bend and Redmond at locations such as Chimney Rock.

An unexpected spring beauty, at least in the evening. (Photo by Al Schneider)

Greenleaf Manzanita
(*Arctostaphylos patula*)

Size: 3–10 ft.

The species name *patula* means "wide-spreading," and that's certainly true of this shrub, at least in Central Oregon. Greenleaf manzanita carpets many areas, particularly open, sunny parts of our ponderosa and lodgepole pine forests.

Manzanita ("little apple" in Spanish) stands out because of its gorgeous and twisty reddish-brown stems. It plays a critical role in the ecosystem, providing browse for deer and fruits that are popular with bears, deer, rodents, and birds. Want more? It's also an important plant for pollinators, especially native bumblebees that grab onto the spring flowers and beat their wings like mad to shake the pollen onto their bodies.

Manzanita depends on fire for its survival (small, natural fires, not uncharacteristic ones). Seeds accumulate in the litter at the base of the shrubs, until a fire comes along and cracks open their hard coats, allowing the seeds to germinate. That's why you'll often see manzanita dominating in the early years after a fire sweeps through an area.

Look for: Crooked, reddish-brown stems and thick, leathery, smooth-edged leaves. Look for bell-shaped, pinkish flowers in May and June, followed by fruits that look like dark-brown or black berries.

Found: All over sunny areas in forests and on lava flats and buttes. Hot spots range from Shevlin Park to Pine Mountain to Black Butte and LaPine State Park.

Top: Leaves are shiny and leathery. (Photo by Kim Elton)

Bottom: Scores of pink flowers attract bumblebees in spring.

FRANK'S NOSE KNOWS

Nobody knows the smells of Central Oregon like naturalist Frank Spiecker of Mel's Furniture Restoration. Here, in alphabetical order, is his list of the area's ten best-smelling shrubs.

- Bitterbrush flowers
- Golden currant flowers
- Granite gilia flowers
- Mock-orange flowers
- Oceanspray (whole plant)
- Purple sage leaves and flowers
- Sagebrush leaves
- Snowbrush (deerbrush) leaves and flowers
- Wax currant flowers and leaves (some leaves smell sweet; others like carrion)
- Woods' rose flowers

Huckleberries *(Vaccinium spp.)*

Size: 1.7–5 ft.

"Imagine eating wildness," wrote Asta Bowen in her handbook on the huckleberry. Indeed, if you've never stumbled upon a patch of huckleberries while out on a hike or bike ride, you're missing out on one of the simplest and sweetest of wilderness experiences.

Oregon and Washington have a dozen species of huckleberries. The most sought-after huckleberry for eating is thinleaf or mountain huckleberry (*V. membranaceum*), which is a preferred food for black bears and is also eaten by deer and elk. You can also find the huckleberry species Cascades blueberry (*V. deliciousum*) and grouseberry (*V. scoparium*) at the Cascade Lakes.

Needless to say, post-Columbus immigrants did not discover huckleberries. For thousands of years Native Americans have spent late summer and fall up in the mountains picking, preserving, and eating the berries. Traditionally, they use controlled wildfires to maintain berry patches since the shrubs prefer sunny areas and resprout from their roots after fire.

Huckleberries are tough to tame ("You can take the huckleberry out of the mountains, but you can't take the mountains out of the huckleberry," wrote Bowen), so you'll need to go looking for them in the wild in late August and September.

Top: Mountain huckleberry and its tasty fruits. (Photo by Katja Schulz)

Bottom: They spread by rhizomes, creating large patches. (Photo by Tyson Fisher)

Look for: Mostly oval leaves. Yellowish-pink flowers are shaped like little urns, and berries are black to dark purplish-red.

Found: In forest openings and wet meadows near Odell Lake and many other lakes in our wilderness areas.

HUCKLEBERRY ETIQUETTE

Huckleberries are wild and precious, to us and to wildlife. When you find a patch, don't trample it. Pick some for yourself, savor them for the treat they are, and leave some for wildlife or the next hiker who happens along.

Kinnikinnick *(Arctostaphylos uva-ursi)*

Size: Up to 2 in.

We can thank the Algonquin people for the beautiful but terribly hard to spell word *kinnikinnick,* which they use to describe a smoking mixture made from the leaves of this shrub.

Also called bearberry or pinemat manzanita, kinnikinnick forms a mat in some of our moister areas. It's not tall and showy, but it's a popular source of nourishment for birds, butterflies, bears, foxes, coyotes, and others. The red fruits, which look like tiny apples, are especially valued as a winter food source for native wildlife.

Look for: Low-growing mat of shiny green leaves, with clusters of small white to pink tubular flowers in late spring, followed by red, berry-like fruits. Rounded leaves separate it from the pointy-leaved pinemat (*A. nevadensis*).

Found: Open forest clearings up to timberline, including Black Butte, Sahalie Falls, the Obsidian Trail, and LaPine State Park.

Yellow-green spring leaves darken through summer.

Mahala Mat *(Ceanothus prostratus)*

Size: Mats up to 10 ft. wide

Careful where you step and ride your bike in area forests. That rather nondescript "green stuff" growing off-trail might be a low-growing species like mahala mat, or pinemat, which fixes nitrogen and thus provides valuable nourishment to the bigger, showier plants all around it.

In spring, mahala mat gets its game on with pretty, rounded clusters of flowers. If you happen upon the shrub later in the year, look for the fruits, which are covered in erect little horns.

Look for: A low-growing mat with leathery evergreen leaves about 1 in. long. Leaves have large teeth along the edges. Flowers appear in spring in clusters of blue, lavender, or white.

Found: In dry areas with full sun, often as part of mixed-conifer and ponderosa pine forests. Look for carpets of it along the Cascade Lakes Highway.

Note the sharp teeth on the stiff leaves. (Photo by M.A. Willson)

Top: *They smell as good as they look. (Photo by M.A. Willson)*

Bottom: *A four-petaled beauty at Hollinshead Park in June.*

Mock-Orange (*Philadelphus lewisii*)

Size: 5–10 ft.

Spotting mock-orange is a joy for several reasons. One is that the snow-white flowers smell like orange blossoms (hence the common name). Another is that this shrub grows in numerous habitats but isn't very common or prolific—count yourself fortunate if you spy one or two along any given trail.

Last but not least, it's easy to appreciate mock-orange because it's a do-everything shrub. Deer and elk browse on it, birds and squirrels eat the seeds, and the flowers provide nectar to hummingbirds, butterflies, bees, and other native pollinators. On top of all that, it helps prevent erosion on hillsides and rocky slopes.

Look for: Idaho's state flower blooms from late spring to midsummer. Flowers have four petals and a yellow center, and after petals fall, sepals remain and look like a different kind of small flower. Opposite, oval leaves have three prominent veins and teeth on each side; they turn a soft yellow in fall.

Found: Along the Crooked River at Smith Rock State Park and the Metolius River near the Camp Sherman store. Also at Drake Park and the Old Mill.

Oceanspray (*Holodiscus* spp.)

Size: 3–13 ft.

You can't drive far in summer without seeing this shrub's frothy white sprays of flowers. As with other plants that grow along roadways, oceanspray isn't picky. It grows easily in disturbed areas, so we can enjoy it's blooms on travels across much of Oregon. It's also a hardy garden plant that shelters birds and attracts butterflies and bees.

Oceanspray is also called ironwood because of the Indigenous practice of hardening the already hard wood with fire and polishing it with horsetail to make spears, knitting needles, harpoon shafts, and bows and arrows.

Look for: Leaves up to 3 in. long, with shallow lobes (paler on undersides). In summer, white flower clusters can be 1 ft. long, later turning cream and then brown. Tiny brown fruits hang in clusters through winter.

Found: Bush oceanspray (*H. microphyllus*) grows in the cracks of lava flows and other dry, rocky areas, including along the shores of Hosmer Lake and on area buttes. In moister soils and more forested areas, such as along the Deschutes River Trail and Whychus Creek, there's a taller variety with wider leaves, creambush oceanspray (*H. discolor*).

Top: *Bush oceanspray often grows in the cracks of lava flows. (Photo by Matt Lavin)*

Bottom: *Particularly lush flower spikes. (Photo by Jane Shelby Richardson)*

Oregon Grape (*Berberis* spp.)

Size: Varies

Don't even try to fight me on this: Oregon grape is the best state flower in the country, period. It is found across the state, is pretty and easy to grow, offers countless benefits to wildlife, and has been used as a yellow dye, food source, and treatment for various ailments.

Because it blooms early in spring, Oregon grape is especially valuable to native pollinators. When bees visit the flowers, the anthers literally spring to action and, like a king wielding a scepter, deposit pollen on the bees' heads. (Touch the stamens inside the flowers to see how it works.)

On this side of the Cascades you're most likely to see creeping Oregon grape (*B. repens*), although we also have tall Oregon grape (*B. aquifolium*). Occasionally you might spy dwarf Oregon grape (*B. nervosa*), which is more common west of the Cascades and has narrower leaflets and a longer, narrow inflorescence (flowering part) than creeping Oregon grape.

Look for: Showy yellow flowers in early spring and dark-blue berries in summer to fall (they're not grapes and they're very sour but good as jelly). Compound leaves are dark-green, glossy, deeply jagged, and pointy.

Found: In a variety of habitats, including forest understories and other areas with moist conditions. Look them everywhere you go, including at the Old Mill, Shevlin Park, and LaPine State Park.

Top: *Note the holly-like leaves of this creeping Oregon grape. (Photo by M.A. Willson)*

Bottom: *Tall Oregon grape in bloom. (Photo by Ron Halvorson)*

Pacific Ninebark (*Physocarpus capitatus*)

Size: 5–13 ft.

Ninebark cultivars are extremely popular in area gardens—you can almost see the headline: "Four-season charmer!" Because indeed ninebarks, including this native variety, are pretty all year long.

In spring, maple-like leaves emerge, along with puffy white flower clusters. In summer, reddish-brown fruits surround yellow seeds, and in fall, the leaves turn a pretty rosy-brown. In winter, the bare branches show you where ninebark got its name, as the branches shred layer after layer (not really nine) to reveal pretty, bronze-colored bark.

Look for: Leaves have 3–5 deep, doubly toothed lobes, similar to maples. White flowers bloom in domed clusters in late spring or early summer. Bark is orangish-brown to bronze.

Found: At Suttle Lake and along waterways, especially the Metolius River and Whychus Creek.

Snowball-shaped flower clusters are ready to burst. (Photo by M.A. Willson)

Top: *Gorgeous purple blooms carpet arid ridges in spring.* (Photo by WinterCreek Nursery)

Bottom: *The lovely purple bracts and blue flowers of a purple sage.* (Photo by Ron Halvorson)

Purple Sage *(Salvia dorrii)*

Size: 0.5–2.5 ft.

Many people who know their dry-side shrubs carry a deep fondness for purple sage. It looks like a nondescript round shrub for much of the year, but in May and June beautiful blue flowers shoot up in spikes with purplish bracts. And, oh, the smell! Crush the leaves and you'll quickly realize this is a true sage and not a sagebrush—it's part of the mint family.

By the way, do you remember *Riders of the Purple Sage*, by Zane Grey? Yeah, well, don't go reading that book to learn about purple sage. He was actually referring to sagebrush, but maybe "purple sage" had a better ring to it (evidence that writers cannot be trusted).

Look for: Overall mounded shape. Opposite leaves gray and hairy, with four-angled stems (like all mints). Bluish-purple blooms appear in May and June.

Found: Rocky places in sagebrush communities east of Bend and Redmond, including the Badlands Wilderness, Crooked River Canyon, and Ochoco Viewpoint.

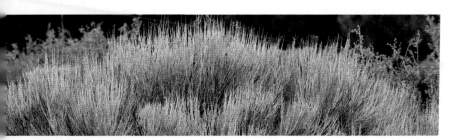

Look for the silvery-gray stems. (Photo by Kim Elton)

Gray Rabbitbrush *(Ericameria nauseosa)*

Size: Typically 0.5–8.5 ft.

Sagebrush gets more attention, but gray and green rabbitbrushes are nearly as common and play a similarly important role in arid regions. Gray rabbitbrush moves quickly into disturbed areas (including after fires), prevents erosion, and provides critical fall and winter cover and desperation forage for birds, deer, pronghorn, black-tailed jackrabbits, and other small mammals.

You'll also hear gray rabbitbrush called rubber rabbitbrush—that's because it can be used to create a high-quality rubber called chrysil. When rubber supplies ran low during World War II, they considered using rabbitbrush, before realizing it would be too expensive and wouldn't meet demand. Scientists also considered using common milkweed, another plant that produces the milky emulsion known as latex.

Look for: Similar to sagebrush, but lacks the sagebrush odor and has narrow, non-lobed leaves. Silvery stems differentiate it from green rabbitbrush. Yellow flowers bloom in showy clusters in late summer, when little else is in bloom.

Found: Extremely common, especially north and east of Bend, from Smith Rock State Park to Pilot Butte, Newberry National Monument, and the Badlands Wilderness.

Green rabbitbrush at left, gray at right.

Green Rabbitbrush *(Chrysothamnus viscidiflorus)*

Size: 1–4 ft.

Like gray rabbitbrush, green rabbitbrush is very common, moves quickly into disturbed areas, and plays an important role in area ecology. Along with providing cover and nesting habitat for sage-grouse and other birds, green rabbitbrush is an essential food source in winter and early spring for animals such as black-tailed jackrabbits.

Traditionally, green rabbitbrush (also called yellow rabbitbrush) is used to treat colds and rheumatism. The leaves can also be mashed into a poultice to treat cavities and stop toothaches.

Look for: Similar to gray rabbitbrush but often shorter and not surprisingly much greener, especially in spring. It's sticky to the touch, with yellow flowers in summer and fall that aren't as showy as those of gray rabbitbrush.

Found: Extremely common in similar areas to gray rabbitbrush. Look for it all over, including on Pilot Butte and in drier, rockier areas of Shevlin Park.

Red-Osier Dogwood *(Cornus sericea)*

Size: 5–20 ft.

Also called western, creek, or redstem dogwood, red-osier dogwood is common across much of North America, except at very high elevations. It's one of the prettiest native shrubs in Central Oregon and is also common in urban landscapes.

The reason for red-osier dogwood's popularity is that it's colorful all year long, with vibrant red stems and large green leaves waving on petioles. In May and June, clusters of pretty white flowers appear, followed by whitish fruits. Just note that the berries aren't tasty and can be toxic in large quantities.

Look for: Lovely red bark is a giveaway. Leaves are oval with pointy tips. Both the flowers and fruits are whitish and appear in clusters.

Found: All along area waterways, often in dense stands with alder and willow. Hot spots include Shevlin Park, Smith Rock State Park, and trails along upper Whychus Creek.

Top: *Red-osier in bloom along Ochoco Creek. (Photo by Ron Halvorson)*

Bottom: *Red-osier in winter along the Deschutes River. (Photo by Mike Putnam)*

Berries persist through fall and winter. (Photo by Kim Elton)

Snowberry *(Symphoricarpos spp.)*

Size: 1.5–10 ft.

Take a walk in the woods on either side of the Cascades and you'll likely come across common snowberry (*S. albus*). On the east side, you'll also find mountain snowberry (*S. oreophilus*) in arid regions and on up through pine and mixed-conifer forests.

It's easy to overlook snowberry in early spring, but from late spring through much of the summer, the shrubs are covered in pretty little pink-and-white flowers. Then comes the big autumn show, when white berries appear all over the many stems. Most of the berries hang on through winter, in part because they're a last-ditch option for wildlife (the berries taste awful to humans, too, and may be toxic).

Look for: Opposite, oval leaves and small, bell-shaped pink-and-white flowers. In fall, white berries grow in small clusters, many remaining through winter.

Found: Common in forests and forest openings, including at Shevlin Park and the Deschutes River Trail. Mountain snowberry is at higher elevations, such as Chimney Rock and Benham Falls.

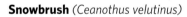

Top: *The beautiful white blooms of a snowbrush. (Photo by WinterCreek Nursery)*

Bottom: *See if you can smell the sweet, cigar-like scent of the blooms. (Photo by M.A. Willson)*

Snowbrush *(Ceanothus velutinus)*

Size: 2–10 ft.

Snowbrush—often called deerbrush or *Ceanothus*—is a quintessential Central Oregon shrub: tough, not overly showy, and a valuable player in the ecosystem. It fixes nitrogen, which helps the plants around it, and it has a deep taproot that helps prevent soil erosion.

Snowbrush is an important shrub for native pollinators. You can also use the blooms to make a soap or use the leaves as a substitute for tobacco (leading to yet another common name, tobacco brush).

Look for: Similar in size and habitat to greenleaf manzanita. Bark is gray-brown. Leaves are opposite, thick, and dark green, with three prominent veins. Small white flowers appear in dense clusters in late spring to early summer (both the flowers and leaves smell like a sweet cigar).

Found: Very common all over the region, from Sunriver to Lava Lands Visitor Center, Tumalo Falls, Shevlin Park, and Camp Sherman.

Spiny Hopsage *(Grayia spinosa)*

Size: 1–5 ft.

The fruits of spiny hopsage look like the commercial hops used in your favorite microbrew, but to me the coolest thing about this shrub is that it's usually dioecious, meaning there are separate male and female plants, each with their own unique features.

Along the base trail around Smith Rock State Park, look for a male spiny hopsage on one side of the trail (with green flowers sticking up in a spike) and a female species on the other side (with flowers enclosed in whitish to red bracts).

Look for: Spine-tipped branches are a giveaway. Smaller stems have alternating gray and tan segments. Leaves are long, thin, and hairy, with brown fruits that look like traditional hops.

Found: In arid regions, including Chimney Rock, Smith Rock State Park, and the rocky hillsides above the Lower Crooked River.

Top: *Oval leaves are fleshy and about an inch long. (Photo by Elizabeth Materna, USFWA)*

Bottom: *Reddish bracts bring color to dry landscapes. (Photo by aspidoscelis)*

Wax Currant *(Ribes cereum)*

Size: 2–5 ft.

Wax currants aren't as showy as golden currants, but the many birds, deer, and other animals that eat the fleshy berries don't seem to mind, and neither do the hummingbirds and other native pollinators that sip nectar from the flowers.

For humans, the reddish berries are generally harmless in small quantities but can cause nausea when eaten in bulk. You can instead turn the berries into a tasty jam or just enjoy the shrub from afar, as the early white blooms are a sign of spring, and the arrival of the colorful berries heralds summer.

Look for: Leaves smaller than golden currant but similarly lobed. Bell-shaped flowers appear in early spring and are white to pinkish. Berries are orange-red to bright red.

Found: Very common across much of Central Oregon. Especially prevalent on the west side of Bend along the Deschutes River and at Shevlin Park.

Top: *Look for small leaves shaped like a catcher's mitt. (Photo by Ron Halvorson)*

Bottom: *Not very tasty but a colorful sign of summer.*

Creamy clusters of clematis blooms.
(Photo by Ron Halvorson)

Western Clematis *(Clematis ligusticifolia)*

Size: 10–67 ft.

A botanist described western clematis to me as "that viney thing climbing over junipers and shrubs." That sums it up pretty well. This is the woody vine that's tangled all over area fences, shrubs, and trees, especially along streambanks (where the mats do a great job of stabilizing the soil).

Also called old man's beard or virgin's bower, western clematis has half-inch white flowers that attract a bevy of bees, butterflies, and other native pollinators.

Look for: Climbing, sprawling vine with opposite leaves divided into 5–7 leaflets. Blooms all summer with cream-to-white flowers in dense clusters.

Found: Along rivers, creeks, and roadsides, including at Smith Rock State Park, Drake Park, and First Street Rapids.

Western Serviceberry *(Amelanchier alnifolia)*

Size: 3–20 ft.

Western serviceberry provides a springtime splash of white in area forests and arid regions where it can access enough water. The shrub goes by many other common names, including western juneberry (referring to when the fruit opens); saskatoon (yep, the Canadian city was named after it); chuckley pear; and my personal favorite, pigeon berry.

The fruits are edible and said to be delicious—bears, chipmunks, birds (presumably including pigeons), and other small mammals certainly think so. Native peoples have used various parts for everything from recovery after childbirth to contraception and prevention of miscarriages.

Look for: *Alnifolia* refers to the alder-like leaves, which are oval and have prominent teeth across the ends. Small, star-shaped flowers are white, have five petals, and smell like apple blossoms. The little red-to-black fruits can be eaten fresh or dried.

Found: In the forest understory at sites like Shevlin Park, LaPine State Park, and Benham Falls.

Top: *Clusters of fragrant flowers along the Lower Crooked River.*
(Photo by Ron Halvorson)

Bottom: *Look closely to see the jagged leaf edges. (Photo by M.A. Willson)*

Woods' Rose (*Rosa woodsii*)

Size: 2–7 ft.

Portland can have its fancy rose gardens (really, they're lovely). If you want to smell that fantastic rosy aroma on the east side of the Cascades, all you have to do is take a walk in late spring through Shevlin Park, along the Deschutes River Trail, or at countless other places across the region.

Woods' rose is the wild rose you're most likely to see in Central Oregon. Along with the wonderful scent of the flowers, the shrubs produce red fruits (rosehips) that provide valuable nourishment all winter for insects, birds, and mammals. Deer and elk forage on the leaves and branches, and people have long used the plant to make everything from tea to jelly and wine.

The light can play tricks, but petals are usually bright pink. (Photo by M.A. Willson)

Look for: Thorns! Also saucer-shaped pink flowers in late spring that have that distinctive rose scent. Fruits, or hips, are deep red and edible, appearing in August to September.

Found: Shrubs form sometimes dense thickets in moist areas. Prevalent all along most area rivers and streams, including at Drake and Shevlin Parks.

Compound leaves have serrated edges. (Photo by Ron Halvorson)

BUNCHGRASSES

Trees are grander and some shrubs are showier, but we wouldn't be here without grasses—the plants that gave us the cereal crops on which civilizations were built. Our native bunchgrasses are the single most important group of plants in the sagebrush steppe, feeding and sheltering wildlife and stabilizing the ground. They're far less common than they were a century ago, when they covered vast swaths of Central and Eastern Oregon, but that just makes it more important to recognize and preserve those that are left.

Top: *With a great view of the Crooked River Canyon.*

Bottom: *Older awns stick out perpendicularly. (Photos by Robert C. Korfhage)*

Bluebunch Wheatgrass
(Pseudoroegneria spicata)

Size: Up to 3 ft.

Different bunchgrasses have different strengths. Bluebunch wheatgrass is a long-lived perennial that provides absolutely critical forage for livestock and native wildlife like elk and pronghorn. But bluebunch has weaknesses too, including that it's sensitive to grazing during its active growing period and doesn't compete well against introduced species like cheatgrass.

An interesting thing to note about bluebunch is that its roots plunge up to six feet into the ground, making this one of the more drought-tolerant of our native bunchgrasses.

Look for: The steely-blue hue of the blades is subtle (often the plants are plain old green). Look for slender spikes that are tightly braided and notched, turning straw-colored with age. The awns (bristles) are straight when young but stick out from the stems like caterpillar legs when mature (put an immature spikelet on your car dash and watch it spread in the heat).

Found: Especially common in open areas, on south-facing slopes, and extremely dry areas such as the Badlands Wilderness.

FUN FACT

?

Bluebunch wheatgrass is the state grass of Iowa, Montana, and Washington. Oregon doesn't have a state grass, although for some reason we do have a state beverage (milk), dance (square dance), and microbe (brewer's yeast).

Bottlebrush Squirreltail (*Elymus elymoides*)

Size: Up to 2 ft.

If you don't like cheatgrass, you have to love bottlebrush squirreltail. After a fire, when cheatgrass and other weeds try to take over, bottlebrush puts up a heck of a fight. Where it succeeds, weeds are less common and other native perennials have a chance to move in and become established.

One secret to bottlebrush's success across many habitats is that it germinates early (late fall and early spring) and at a range of temperatures. It's also self-fertilizing and highly fire-resistant—and if you need yet more reasons to love bottlebrush, it provides forage through winter for a wide array of animals.

Look for: Pale-green base is similar to prairie junegrass but with soft, hairy stems. Spikes are up to 8 in. long, with a bushy seedhead (like a bottlebrush) when mature that eventually breaks apart into segments that roll around on the ground and disperse with the wind.

A sea of bottlebrush seedheads. (Photo by Ron Halvorson)

Found: Common across Central Oregon in a range of habitats. Look for the distinctive, bushy seedheads along just about any area trail.

Great Basin Wild Rye (*Leymus cinereus*)

Size: Up to 6 ft.

Great Basin wild rye is one of those species that make you wish you could travel back in time. Imagine coming upon thick, sprawling stands of this grass waving in the wind above your head or tickling the belly of your horse. Then imagine trying to explain to your fellow travelers that this immense, high-protein forage is not invincible and will not survive decades of overgrazing and cutting and drying like hay.

Alas, that's exactly what happened. And that's the main reason you won't find many large stands of Great Basin wild rye left, just isolated pockets. The giant has been felled. But enjoy it where you see it, and appreciate that in addition to feeding native wildlife and providing bedding, rugs, and matting for Native tribes, it provides exceptional cover and nesting areas for small mammals and birds.

A typical stand of thick-leaved wild rye. (Photo by Robert C. Korfhage)

Look for: By far our tallest native bunchgrass. Bright green, with long, ribbed, very wide leaves. Spikes look like wheat spikes, with large, fat braids.

Found: In moister areas like ravines, meadows, and open woodlands. Look for it along the Crooked River near Smith Rock State Park, in Sunriver, and along Hwy. 26 east of Prineville.

The florets stick out every which way. (Photo by Robert C. Korfhage)

Idaho Fescue *(Festuca idahoensis)*

Size: Up to 3 ft.

Idaho fescue is a widespread perennial—one of the more common bunchgrasses you'll see in Central Oregon, especially in area forests. It may seem odd that it's doing as well as it is, given that it provides popular forage for all sorts of animals, from domestic livestock to deer and elk. But unlike many other bunchgrasses, this one recovers well from limited grazing.

Idaho fescue also has deep and extensive root systems that make it fairly drought-tolerant and helpful for erosion control.

Look for: Little mounds of densely tufted, blue-green bunchgrass. Delicate inflorescences shoot out in all directions like a fireworks display.

Found: All over, especially in open areas and on north-facing slopes, as well as on the north side of trees (especially junipers and ponderosa pines).

Wispy branches end in tiny fruits. (Photo by Robert C. Korfhage)

Indian Ricegrass *(Eriocoma hymenoides)*

Size: Up to 2 ft.

Indian ricegrass is named for its use by numerous Native American tribes, from the Apache and Hopi to the Navajo and Paiute. Traditionally, thousands of the tiny seeds are gathered and ground to make bread, dumplings, and feed for horses.

Even if you buy your bread at the store, you might appreciate Indian ricegrass for its appearance. Nevada's state grass seeds later than most, and the seedheads are delicate and gorgeous—each like a grain of rice, combining to create a fine mist of hair-like branches. Pick a fruit from the end of a branch and look inside to find the tiny black seed; then imagine how many it would take to grind into a useful meal.

Look for: Sparse and rather nondescript before it seeds, with leaves mostly at the base. Open panicles spread like a sparkler, with a single fruit at the end of each hair-like branch.

Found: Prefers full sun. Look for it in dry, open areas with sandy soil, including the Badlands Wilderness and wherever else you see sagebrush and junipers.

Needle-and-Thread Grass *(Hesperostipa comata)*

Size: Up to 3.5 ft.

Needle-and-thread grass is unusual because it grows early in the spring, then goes dormant in the early part of summer before "greening up" again in fall, if there's enough moisture.

The common name comes from another unusual feature of the grass: its long, twisty awns, or bristles, which look like long threads attached to short needles (the seed). When the plant releases its seed, the attached "thread" twists. When moisture comes along, the awn untwists, and when it dries, it twists again, thus drilling the seed into the ground, much like the seeds of curlleaf mountain-mahogany.

Look for: Tall bunchgrass with sparse, tight panicles that loosen when mature. Twisty awns are up to 8 in. long.

Found: Grows well in sandy soils and is often associated with juniper woodlands, so look for it in places like the Badlands Wilderness.

Top: *A tall bunchgrass with long, twisty awns. (Photo by Robert C. Korfhage)*

Bottom: *Long, twisty awns. (Photo by M.A. Willson)*

Prairie Junegrass *(Koeleria macrantha)*

Size: Up to 3 ft.

If you want to get botanists excited, tell them you're going to plant prairie junegrass. "Oh, that's a great choice! I love that one," they'll say. The reason is that it's a beautiful and sometimes underappreciated native grass, an early bloomer with numerous silvery-green seedheads that shimmer delicately in summer breezes.

Prairie junegrass (named for the month it flowers) likes sun and is drought-tolerant. Its roots can reach two feet below the ground, making it good at stabilizing soil, along with simply looking pretty.

Look for: Low, gray-green bunchgrass with soft leaves mostly at base. Panicles are spike-like and spread at maturity into a tree-like form, with short branches clinging to all sides.

Found: Common in the sagebrush steppe and dry, open forests with limited disturbance. Not found in pure stands; often mixed with Idaho fescue.

Top: *Plumes turn tan by midsummer. (Photo by Robert C. Korfhage)*

Bottom: *The spreading panicles are simply gorgeous. (Photo by M.A. Willson)*

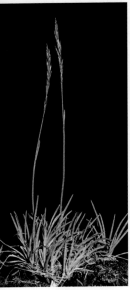

Note the short, thick leaves at the base. (Photo by Robert C. Korfhage)

Sandberg Bluegrass *(Poa secunda)*

Size: Up to 4 ft.

The single most common native bunchgrass in Central Oregon is likely Sandberg bluegrass, which includes several varieties that were once considered separate species. It's a drought-resistant grass that provides important forage in the early spring and in fall because of its unique growth cycle.

Named after a Swedish botanist, Sandberg bluegrass starts growing in March and then hurries right along, like many other native grasses and shrubs. It flowers by May, sets its seed, turns a reddish tint, and goes back to being a dry little tuft of brittle leaves by late June. But it's not quite done. When fall rains come, the plant revives and begins new growth that continues through November.

Look for: Our shortest bunchgrass (although some varieties grow taller than a foot). It's densely tufted with a lot of short, stiff leaves at the base. Like all *Poa* plants, it has two parallel "railroad tracks" (central veins) on its leaves; most grasses have only one. Flowering stalks have a purplish tint and few or no leaves. It's often the first bunchgrass to turn green in spring and again in fall with enough moisture. It takes on a reddish coloration as it ages.

Found: Seriously, it's everywhere, from sagebrush scrub to subalpine habitats, in every type of soil. Most common in the shallow, rocky soils of Eastern Oregon.

Look closely to spot the twice-bent awns. (Photo by Sheri Hagwood, hosted by USDA-NRCS PLANTS Database)

Thurber's Needlegrass *(Eriocoma thurberianum)*

Size: Up to 4 ft.

There are about 150 needlegrass species, all of which have a sharply pointed grain and a long, threadlike awn, or bristle. In Central Oregon, the most common species are Thurber's and western needlegrass (*A. occidentale*).

Thurber's—named after George Thurber, a self-educated botanist and grasses expert in the 1800s—is a common and even dominant grass in many areas across the West. It provides popular forage in spring for livestock and wildlife ranging from black-tailed jackrabbits to juvenile pronghorn. It's also used as cover by sage-grouse.

Look for: Tufted grass with mostly short leaves at the base. Resembles Idaho fescue, but the narrow panicles have flowers with twice-bent awns when mature.

Found: Dry, open sites such as the sagebrush steppe and juniper woodlands.

Keeping lawns green in Central Oregon takes a lot of work, water, and weekends.

The Most Common Grass of All

It wouldn't make sense to talk about grasses without pointing out the most common grass of all: sod, or turf, which is planted all over our urban areas. Sod is grown on specialized farms and is made up of a variety of individual grasses, none of which is native to Central Oregon.

And that's the rub: Sod is not native and thus is not adapted like native bunchgrasses to our hot summers and long winters. To survive, it needs us to help it out with pesticides, fertilizers, and a lot of water. In fact, the typical American lawn sucks up thousands of gallons of added water every year. The sod monoculture also does little for native species and attracts oodles of species like Canada Geese that we then get annoyed with, after rolling out the green carpet for them.

TIPS FOR ENVIRONMENTALLY FRIENDLY LAWN CARE

If you have a lawn, you can take any of several steps to benefit the environment:

- Buy an electric or hand lawnmower (air pollution from an hour of mowing equates to a 45-mile drive in a new car).

- Invest in an automated watering system that detects your precise watering needs.

- Apply organic fertilizer and avoid using pesticides that can harm birds and other wildlife and leech into our water supplies.

- Reduce your total lawn area by interspersing with native plants, gravel, and pavers—get creative!

- Remove your sod and invest in a xeriscaped yard that will use far less water and save money over the long run.

WHAT THE HECK IS THAT?

I've pestered many a hiking partner with my endless pointing and "What the heck is that?" questions (often about the same species we saw a quarter-mile back). This section is designed to reduce your pointing and questioning, and it gives me an opportunity to talk about some really interesting species that don't fit well anywhere else.

Broadleaf Cattail (*Typha latifolia*)

Size: 3-8 ft.

Cattails are perhaps the best-known wetland plants—tall, distinctive perennials that line waterways across the country. What's less appreciated is how vital they are as habitat and food for insects, fish, amphibians, birds, and wetland mammals such as muskrats. Plus, they filter runoff and prevent shoreline erosion.

Humans have also found many uses for cattails. It's said that every part of the plant has been eaten, and the soft down of the seeds can be used as stuffing for pillows, blankets, and mattresses. You can use the fluff to dress wounds, and the long, wide leaves are ideal for weaving mats and baskets. Parts of cattails can also be used to treat burns and other maladies.

Look for: Long, wide, upright leaves on tall stems, with light-brown male flowers at the top of the stems. Thick, dark-brown female flowers form just below the male and combine to look like a big cigar or corn dog. They bloom in late spring or early summer.

Found: Cattails grow in ponds and shallow waters across Central Oregon, including along the Crooked River at Smith Rock State Park and along the Deschutes River Trail at First Street Rapids and the Old Mill.

Top: *A typical stand of cattails.*

Bottom: *Seeds have fluffy parts called pappus that disperse on the wind.*

Common Horsetail (*Equisetum* spp.)

Size: 0.5–3 ft.

Did you know we have living fossils in Central Oregon? Horsetails are the lone survivors from a spore-producing plant family that dominated the understory of Paleozoic forests for over 100 million years. Most spore producers died off long ago when plants started putting out blossoms and seeds, but horsetail hung around.

Horsetail can be used to scour pots and pans and polish everything from canoes to pewter. These and similar uses are why it's also called scouring rush.

Look for: Common horsetail (*Equisetum arvense*) produces two types of stems: fertile (with no bushy branches along the stem) and, later, sterile (which resemble a horse's bushy tail). The stems are green and hollow, with obvious joints.

Found: Needs sun and prefers moist conditions. Look for it at Shevlin Park. Common horsetail also tolerates drier conditions and can be found along roads and in disturbed areas.

Note the notches along the skinny stems.

Galls

Size: Varies

You've probably seen small pouches growing on area plants: soft, round, colorful curiosities that resemble small fruits. Those oddities are galls, which are basically plant tumors—growths created by fungi, bacteria, insects, or other parasites that are using the plant as a host.

Most galls have little impact on the host plant, but some do a lot of damage. For example, Western gall rust (*Endocronartium harknessii*) is common on lodgepoles and ponderosa pines in Central Oregon. It's a fungus that causes galls to form on branches and trunks, limiting the flow of water and sometimes killing saplings.

Look for: Lumps, balls, or other structures on leaves, twigs, or branches. Western gall rust produces bright yellow-orange swellings (round to pear-shaped) on tree branches and stems.

Found: Common on many area trees and shrubs.

Wasp galls look like woody cones on junipers. (Photo by Susan Berger)

A typical juniper littered with mistletoe.

Mistletoe *(Arceuthobium* spp. and *Phoradendron juniperinum)*

Size: Varies

You can take your beloved out to an area forest this holiday season, point to the mistletoe on a tree branch overhead, and enjoy a romantic kiss. But if you do, you'd better hope your loved one doesn't know that our mistletoes are parasitic and suck valuable nutrients and water from the trees to which they're attached. As a metaphor for a relationship, it's not ideal.

We don't have traditional holiday mistletoe here, with its pretty white berries. Instead, we have a lot of dwarf mistletoes *(Arceuthobium* spp.) and juniper mistletoe *(Phoradendron juniperinum)*. Different species of dwarf mistletoes insert their roots into specific conifers, from larches to ponderosa pines. Juniper mistletoe steals water and nutrients solely from junipers *(Phoradendron* comes from the Greek for "thief of the tree"), but at least it produces its own chlorophyll, unlike dwarf mistletoes.

Don't be too hard on our mistletoes, though. Most of the time they don't kill their host trees, and they're immensely valuable to the forest ecosystem; they're even considered keystone species—indicators of a forest's health. Birds, including Spotted Owls, nest in the "witches' brooms" of tangled branches caused by mistletoe, and wildlife ranging from chipmunks to elk eat mistletoe. Juniper mistletoe also produces berries that all sorts of birds rely on, including robins, waxwings, flycatchers, bluebirds, and solitaires.

Look for: Erect, spreading yellow-green branches winding around other trees' branches. Juniper mistletoe is only on junipers and is typically larger than dwarf mistletoe.

Found: Attached to the branches of many area conifers, particularly junipers.

FUN FACT

Some plants spread their seeds by wind or bird. Dwarf mistletoe? Its explosive seed dispersal is more akin to a missile (or is it mistle?) launch.

The fruit rests on a pedicel that bends farther and farther back, eventually blasting the seeds up to fifty feet at nearly sixty miles per hour. The seeds are sticky and attach themselves to conifer needles. When rain comes along, the lubricated seeds slide down the needles to the bark to do their damage.

Where there's one, there are likely to be many.

Mullein *(Verbascum thapsus)*

Size: Up to 6 ft.

I don't mean to be a weed apologist, but as weeds go, common mullein is cool. Yes, it conquers a lot of territory, especially gravelly areas and roadsides, and keeps native plants from thriving, but it's not nearly so noxious as knapweed and its ilk.

As to its more interesting aspects, mullein is a biennial, so the first year you'll see a low-growing rosette of big, velvety leaves up to a foot long. The second year, up sprouts a thick stalk up to six (sometimes even eight) feet tall, topped in summer by a flowering spike of light-yellow flowers. Leaves clasp the long stalk, directing rainwater down the stem to the roots of the plant.

There are many, many uses for mullein, not least of which is that its long, soft leaves provide convenient backcountry toilet paper (be careful; some people have adverse reactions). The leaves have also been used as "Quaker rouge" to redden cheeks, and you can make mullein tea, which is said to soothe respiratory problems. I could go on: These cowboy candlesticks are said to have been used to make everything from lamp wicks to witches' torches.

Another nice thing about mullein? If you don't want it around, all you have to do is pull it out of the ground. Ideally, you should catch it that first year when it's low to the ground, before the 100,000 or so seeds emerge on the tall stalks in year two.

Look for: The first year, look for a low-growing plant with velvety leaves up to 1 ft. long. In year two, there's no mistaking those tall, straight stalks, topped in summer by spikes of yellow flowers.

Found: In just about any disturbed area (roadsides, vacant lots, overgrown yards, gravel bars)—Highway 97 between Bend and Sunriver is but one example.

An owl pellet surrounded by bones and fur. (Photo by Sue Anderson)

Owl Pellet

Size: Varies

Let's say you're an owl that just caught a big, juicy mouse. You fly back to your perch to eat the mouse but find you don't have a knife and a fork. Nor do you have teeth. What should you do? Owls overcome this problem by either swallowing their prey whole or tearing it into big chunks that they swallow without chewing (since they don't have teeth).

Next problem: Owls can't digest bones and other hard stuff, and they lack the crops some birds have to help with the process. So what should they do with the undigestable stuff? Regurgitate it, of course! Owls vomit teeth, claws, skulls, rocks, needles, and other hard material, along with feathers and fur.

Teachers and parents can buy prepackaged, heat-sterilized owl pellets to teach kids about what owls eat—plus it's a great way to study food chains and predator-prey relationships. Scientists are also taking advantage of owl pellets (the fresh variety) to study how species have changed over time.

Look for: Thumb-shaped bundles with hair, bone, feathers, and so forth. Size ranges from a few centimeters (Northern Pygmy-Owl) to a few inches (Great Horned Owl).

Found: Wherever owls hang out. If you see a lot of pellets at the base of a tree, you know that's an "owl tree" where owls roost or nest.

It's in the heath family, so the pink stems have flowers that hang like urns. (Photo by Jacob W. Frank, NPS)

Pinedrop *(Pterospora andromedea)*

Size: 1–3 ft.

When David Douglas heard that pinedrops were growing near Albany, New York, he searched seven hours before he found a specimen. "I have no doubt but it will cultivate," he wrote, which goes to show that great botanists can be bad prognosticators.

To find a pinedrop, you need to go into a forest, not a nursery, where here and there you'll see what appears to be an alien rhubarb stem sticking up near a pine tree or other conifer. Pinedrops live on a fungus that's associated with conifers, and are highly unusual in that they produce very little chlorophyll (so they're sort of purplish-red instead of green) and don't conduct photosynthesis.

Look for: There's nothing quite like a pinedrop. They look like a round, sticky stalk of rhubarb that somebody jabbed into the ground. Midsummer, urn-shaped flowers with yellow, pink, or white petals hang upside-down from the top half of the stem.

Found: Where there are pine trees there are pinedrops, from the ponderosa pine forests in Sisters and Bend to the lodgepole pine forests in Sunriver and La Pine.

Wolf Lichen (*Letharia vulpina*)

Size: Varies

Take a walk in the Badlands Wilderness and many other places around Central Oregon, and you'll see a bright yellow-green lichen covering juniper branches, especially those of old-growth junipers. That's wolf lichen, which also grows on many other conifers.

Wolf lichen's name comes from its barbaric early use as a poison for wolves (mixed with glass and meat), but it also has a more positive use as a favored dye among many Native American tribes.

As a reminder for those of us who haven't taken a biology class in a couple years: A lichen is a composite organism that arises from the symbiotic relationship between a fungus and a photosynthetic partner (usually a green algae). Or to keep it simple, remember: "Freddy Fungus and Alice Algae took a lichen to each other."

Look for: Fluorescent yellow-green or chartreuse lichen (duller colors in drier conditions).

Found: Throughout Central Oregon, especially on older conifers. Look for it on tree bark and branches (often dead), as well as on snags.

A juniper covered in brilliant yellow-green wolf lichen. (Photo by Tyson Fisher)

NOXIOUS WEEDS

Let's not sugarcoat it: Central Oregon has a severe problem with noxious (non-native, invasive, damaging) weeds. They do loads of harm to our native plants and animals, gobble up our precious water, accelerate wildfires, and cause a lot of economic damage. I'm highlighting a handful of the worst offenders so you can identify them and be part of the sustained effort necessary to get rid of them.

Top: *The flowers look so friendly, but this is one tough-to-kill weed.*

Bottom: *Note the fairly dark color, which distinguishes these from native thistle leaves.*
(Photos by Richard Old)

Canada Thistle *(Cirsium arvense)*
Size: 1-4 f

Canada thistle (which is actually native to Eurasia) has a remarkable root system, with horizontal roots spreading twenty feet or more and vertical roots driving down up to fifteen feet. Needless to say, pulling out large numbers of these weeds is a rough way to spend a weekend.

If you spot one or two Canada thistles before they flower in spring, go ahead and pull them, roots and all. Then bag and dispose of them (seeds of these and other weeds can develop even after pulling). For larger infestations, contact Oregon State University Extension or county experts.

Experts can tell you which herbicides to use and how to apply them, although success usually requires a variety of repeated treatments. The trick is to stress the weed so much it uses up the nutrients stored in its expansive root system.

Look for: Long, glossy leaves are clearly pointy and painful to the touch. (Note that we have several native thistles with gray-green leaves; noxious ones like this one have dark-green leaves.) Pink, bristly flowers are packed into a tight little flower head, about a half-inch wide.

Found: Fairly common in moist, disturbed areas across the region, including in wet meadows near ponds and ditches.

HERBICIDES VS. INSECTICIDES

You don't need a sledgehammer to tap a nail into a wall, and you don't need pesticides to kill most weeds.

What you do need is time and energy to pull weeds, repeatedly, until they lose the will to live. Or you can kill most weeds by pouring boiling water or vinegar on them. If you want to get fancy, you can stir up a happy-hour cocktail of vinegar, salt, and liquid dish soap that will do the job.

If you have specific questions about the weeds in your yard and how to deal with them, contact the weed pros:

Crook County weed expert: 541-447-7958
Deschutes County weed expert: 541-322-7117
Jefferson County weed expert: 541-475-4459

They can help you deal with noxious and other weeds while minimizing the harm done to other plants, wildlife, water supplies, pets, and fellow humans.

Don't pull or mow once cheatgrass reaches this stage. You'll only help it spread.

Cheatgrass *(Bromus tectorum)*

Size: Up to 2 ft.

Cheatgrass is the weed that won the West. It's our most prolific weed, infesting over 100 million acres across just about every county west of the Mississippi River. In drier regions of Central Oregon, it occupies more acreage than any other plant.

Cheatgrass was probably shipped to North America in some contaminated grain in the mid-1800s. It "cheats" by germinating early, in fall or early spring, using up precious moisture and nutrients before native perennials get started. Cheatgrass also produces a whole lot of seeds, tolerates grazing, and actually increases after fires (which it helps spread)—all of which spells trouble for wildlife and plant species such as native bunchgrasses and sagebrush, which it routinely displaces.

Sadly, we won't win the war against cheatgrass, but you can still score some small victories. In April, make it a point to pull cheatgrass while it's green. Do not pull or mow the droopy seedheads in summer, when they turn colors—doing so will help them spread, and they definitely do not need our help. Herbicides can work in fall, but contact Oregon State University Extension or local county officials for guidance.

Look for: In early spring, cheatgrass is the first grass to "green up." It's bright green when young, with hairy blades that are wider than most of our native bunchgrasses. Drooping tufts turn from rusty-red or purplish to brown and tan when dried out.

Found: Absolutely everywhere in our dry, open areas, especially disturbed and overgrazed sites.

Technically not a noxious weed, but it's definitely obnoxious.

Dalmatian Toadflax
(Linaria dalmatica)

Size: Up to 3 ft.

Our native wildflowers are generally not three feet high with bright, showy blooms, so when you see a tall, snapdragon-looking flower sticking up in the middle of our dry landscapes, beware. Dalmatian toadflax is only pretty until you get to know it.

Every Dalmatian toadflax plant produces about a half-million seeds. Scary, no? And once the plants are mature (around June), pulling stimulates reproduction from the remaining roots.

The key is to identify the weeds in April or May, when pulling or digging them up is more effective. For help identifying and treating toadflax, contact Oregon State University Extension or local county officials.

Top: For best results, pull toadflax before it gets this big.

Bottom: Proof that you can't always trust pretty things. (Photos by Ed Keith)

Look for: Knee-high stalks with yellow flowers that resemble snapdragons. Leaves are waxy, blue-green, oval to heart-shaped, and clasp the stems.

Found: Thrives in disturbed areas (roadsides, cleared lots, gravel pits, heavily grazed rangeland) and in openings near sagebrush and ponderosa pines. Look for the spikes from La Pine to Sisters, including (at least for now) on Pilot Butte, in Shevlin Park, in the Old Mill, and in a large patch near Horse Butte.

DID YOU KNOW?

Dalmatian toadflax was introduced to this continent in the 1870s as an ornamental flower that soon escaped the bounds of domestication. It's believed that toadflax seeds snuck in as contaminants in wildflower packets handed out for free at gas stations as part of Lady Bird Johnson's well-intended "Let's Beautify America" program in the 1960s.

The moral is not that beautification programs are bad. It's that even very attractive non-native plants can cause big problems—instead, stick to buying and planting our equally pretty native flowers.

Diffuse Knapweed
(*Centaurea diffusa*)

Size: 1–2 ft.

Diffuse knapweed is the equally nasty but slightly less common cousin of spotted knapweed. Like spotted, it chokes out native vegetation and causes other problems for area agriculture and wildlife.

Getting rid of this fast-spreading weed requires a sustained effort that may include pulling, grazing or mowing, chemical, and biological methods. The first and best step is to learn to identify the young plants, and pull them before they develop long roots. Be sure to wear gloves because they can irritate skin.

Once knapweed grows tall and flowers in June, you're too late, but you can still pull the plant or snip off the flower heads to prevent seeding; just be sure to bag and dispose of them. Then make a mental note to pull the weeds the following spring, before they flower.

Look for: Similar to spotted knapweed, but shorter and less bushy, with yellow-brown bracts. Leaves are silvery-green, and numerous flowering heads are white to purple.

Top: Pulling the flowering plant is fine—as long as you bag and dispose of it.

Bottom: Pull it in spring, before the flowers appear. (Photos by Thane Tuason)

Found: In Sisters, Redmond, and the north side of Bend; less prominent in southerly areas like Sunriver.

SO MUCH KNAPWEED

There are many other common knapweed variants, including Russian knapweed (*Acroptilon repens*). You can't kill Russian knapweed by pulling it because it reproduces from a large network of lateral roots—just one more complexity that highlights the need to call weed professionals for guidance.

Spotted Knapweed
(Centaurea stoebe)

Size: 1–4 ft.

Spotted knapweed is a nasty invasive weed shipped here in the late 1800s from Eastern Europe, either in alfalfa seed or in soil used as ship ballast. By 1920 it had a foothold in the San Juan Islands. Sixty years later it was all over the Pacific Northwest. And today it's in all but a few U.S. states.

As with diffuse knapweed, your best bet is to pull spotted knapweed when it's young. If you miss that window, you can pull and bag it after you see it flowering. That won't end the infestation, but it will reduce the spread of seeds and might make you feel better. Contact Oregon State University Extension or local county officials for details on other treatment methods.

Look for: Spotted bracts with black tips under each large, pink to purple flower. Leaves are medium-green with silvery-gray cast. Young leaves are deeply lobed, becoming narrower over time.

Found: It's one of Central Oregon's most adaptable and therefore prolific noxious weeds—found in and around every community.

Top: *Blooms are purplish. (Photo by Oregon Department of Agriculture)*

Bottom: *This is the best time to pull spotted knapweed. (Photo by Ed Keith)*

Photo by Ron Halvorson

AN INNOCENT BYSTANDER

This is not knapweed! But this kindly native aster, called hoary-aster (*Dieteria canascens*), is often mistaken for knapweed because it's a bristly plant of similar size that flowers at the same time, with flowers of about the same color. But note the big difference: The aster has a yellow center. Leave this innocent native in the ground!

Orange Hawkweed
(Hieracium aurantiacum)

Size: Up to 1.5 ft.

Welcome to Central Oregon, orange hawkweed. This bad actor came along in 2008, when a Bend nursery mistakenly sold it as an aster. Stamping out this nasty weed is a statewide priority before it escapes urban areas and enters our forests and other wild areas, as it has in other states.

Deschutes and Crook Counties offer free herbicide treatments to get rid of orange hawkweed. If you catch it before it flowers, you can pull it. Otherwise, pulling can stimulate growth, so call county officials to come out and treat it for you free of charge.

Look for: Hairy, lance-like leaves are up to 5 in. long and exclusively at the base of the plant (stems have no leaves). Blooms are a distinctive bright orange, with clusters on each stem.

Found: Most common on the west side of Bend (Awbrey Butte, Old Mill District), but also in La Pine, Redmond, and Sisters.

Top: *The hairy leaves are doing their job here, holding on to moisture. (Photo by Ed Keith)*

Bottom: *Once these pretty flowers bloom, call officials for help. (Photo by Richard Old)*

WHAT CAN YOU DO?

Here are some simple tips to prevent the spread of noxious weeds:

- Learn to identify young weeds, so you can pull them before they're established.
- Plant native vegetation to keep weeds at bay (don't leave empty lots or medians for long periods).
- Be persistent with treatments—it often takes repeated efforts, but don't give up!
- Stay on marked trails. Weeds like disturbed areas, so don't create more of them.
- Check your dogs: Cheatgrass awns have barbs that can get stuck in dog paws, ears, and nether regions, causing serious infections.

Puncturevine (*Tribulus terrestris*)

Size: Mats up to 5 ft. diam.

This weed goes by a lot of names (goathead, bullhead, devil's thorn, tackweed, etc.), but in bike-loving Central Oregon, most folks call it puncturevine, often preceded by a curse. While tumbleweed rolls and many other weed seeds blow in the wind, puncturevine sticks its hard, thorny seeds in anything that rambles by (foot, hoof, bike tire, car tire), spreading itself by the most obnoxious means possible.

Barbed and ready for you and your tires. (Photo by Richard Old)

Puncturevine was introduced from southern Europe in the early 1900s and has since spread across the U.S., including into every county east of the Cascades. It's especially prolific in the Hermiston area, where melon growers appreciate the plant's ability to stabilize topsoil. Others are less appreciative, as the spiny seeds can do great harm to wildlife and livestock.

If you identify this weed before it matures and develops seed, you can simply use a shovel to break the taproot and kill the plant (it's an annual so it won't regrow). If the seeds are already there, contact Oregon State University Extension or county experts for details on what to do.

Look for: Grows in mats with pinnately compound leaves, like fern fronds, with hairs on each leaflet. Flowers are yellow with five petals, developing into circular, spiny fruits that break into sections when ripe.

Found: Any heavily disturbed site will do, including barren lots and along paved or gravel roads, sidewalks, and bike paths.

Look for dense mats with half-inch yellow flowers. (Photo by Vengolis)

Top: *Pull in spring when you see fleshy leaves with spines at the tip.*

Bottom: *In Southern California, tumbleweed is so prolific some people make "snowmen" out of them in winter, stacking them up and spray-painting them white. (Photo by Ed Keith)*

Russian Thistle (Tumbleweed)

(Salsola tragus)

Size: 1–3 ft.

It's odd, isn't it, that this invasive plant from Russia is an iconic symbol of the American West? Tumbleweed stowed away in a shipment of flax seed from the Ukraine in the late 1870s and subsequently became engrained in our landscapes and Old West mythology.

Tumbleweed is remarkable in that it does all its growing in late summer, just as most other plants are packing it in for the winter. In late fall or early winter, many thousands of tumbleweeds across Central Oregon magically turn themselves into wheels, breaking off near the base and rolling along in the wind, dropping up to a quarter-million seeds per plant as they travel for miles before settling against my fence.

Tumbleweed soaks up precious moisture, displaces our native plants, shelters harmful insects, increases fire danger . . . and the list goes on. It's hardly deserving of its iconic stature. When plants are young and green, you can hand-pull, dig up, or mow (repeatedly) small infestations. Contact Oregon State University Extension or local county officials for help with larger problems.

Look for: Young tumblers resemble pine tree seedlings, with long, stiff, sharp leaves. As they mature, they branch out, becoming rounder and woody, with spines on the many branches.

Found: Common north and east of Bend. Tumbleweed loves abandoned fields and is one of the first weeds to occupy disturbed sites. In hot spots such as Alfalfa, thousands can occur in a single acre.

ANOTHER TUMBLER

Tumble mustard (*Sisymbrium altissimum*) is another noxious weed that spreads its seed by tumbling around. It's an annual that lacks deep roots, so you can pull it even after its yellow flowers appear— just make sure to safely dispose of the plant.

Scotch Thistle
(Onopordum acanthium)

Size: Up to 12 ft.!

Plants in the genus *Onopordum* are said to be so named because of their ability to cause flatulence in donkeys (*onus* is Greek for "ass" and *porde* is Greek for "flatulence"). That doesn't have much to do with anything, but it's the only funny thing to say about Scotch thistle.

Introduced as an ornamental, Scotch thistle causes real problems for ranchers, native plants, and wild animals because it forms dense stands that exclude animals and other vegetation. The roots are not deep, so it's an easy weed to dig up—until it spreads so fast it gets out of hand. Where it has spread, a combination of control methods is best, and as always, Oregon State University Extension and local county officials are the best sources of information.

Look for: Usually 6 ft. or under, with broadly winged stem. Spiny leaves are up to 2 ft. long and 1 ft. wide, covered with dense hair, giving it a grayish appearance (unlike most invasive thistles). Flowers are violet to reddish.

Found: Common on the east side of Bend and near Redmond and Terrebonne, especially in pastures and other disturbed sites, such as along fences and roadways.

Top: *If you dig up a flowering weed, get all the roots and bag and dispose of the whole thing so it doesn't go to seed and defeat your hard work.*
(Photo by Ed Keith)

Bottom: *Dig these thistles up when you see them!*
(Photo by Richard Old)

THE PRIDE OF SCOTLAND

One region's noxious weed is another's national emblem. Legend (not backed or bothered by historical evidence) has it that some sleeping Scottish warriors were saved from ambush by an invading Norse army when one of the attackers stepped on a thistle with his bare feet. His yelps raised the alarm, and the sleeping Scots woke to defeat the invaders, *Braveheart* style.

Beargrass with a view of Mount Jefferson. (Photo by Mike Putnam)

Paintbrush, lupine, and bog orchids. (Photo by Susan Berger)

Washington lily. (Photo by John Nelson)

WILDFLOWERS

Let's be honest: Central Oregon is never going to be mistaken for Hawaii or any other tropical isle overflowing with large, lush, brazenly colored vegetation. Most of our wildflowers play it safe, growing low to the ground and building up their energy all year long for one brief burst of color.

Is that disappointing? Nah. I'd say it only deepens the pleasure. When the snow finally melts and the wildflowers begin to bloom, it's a spectacle unlike anything you might experience in lusher environments. As E. R. Jackman wrote in *The Oregon Desert*, "Their vivid colors flash as suddenly into view as a startled antelope."

Columbia lily. (Photo by Kermit Williams)

Western trillium.
(Photo by Bruce Jackson)

Wildflowers at Broken Top. (Photo by Bruce Jackson)

Get to know our native wildflowers, and you'll be astounded not only by their beauty but also by the adaptations that enable them to survive here, at elevation, in sandy and volcanic soils, and in a climate that is variously too dry, too hot, too cold, too snowy, and too unpredictable for so many others.

On your next hike, look closely at the wildflowers you pass. Feel the hairy leaves that trap moisture. Admire the hair-trigger stamens coated with pollen. Note the showy colors, and smell the often grand (and sometimes foul) odors that attract pollinators.

In other words, enjoy the show, knowing it won't last long.

A field of beargrass blooms on Coffin Mountain. (Photo by M.A. Willson)

WHITE OR WHITISH FLOWERS
3 OR 6 PETALS

Beargrass (*Xerophylllum tenax*)

Blooms: Late spring to midsummer

Beargrass is one of the biggest and most distinctive wildflowers around, a stately perennial that stands up to five feet tall. Yes, bears do eat beargrass leaves. The strong, grass-like leaves can also be woven into baskets and hats—including the rain hats made by Clatsop women that were worn by members of the Lewis and Clark Expedition.

Beagrass blooms only once every few years or so (more often in ideal conditions, like after a fire). That's because the flowers, stalks, and leaves all die after each blooming period, and it takes a long time for the underground rhizomes to build up the nutrients necessary to do it all over again.

Look for: It's tough to miss plants several feet high, topped with cream-colored flower heads up to 20 in. long. The rough-edged leaves stretch up to 3 ft.

Found: En masse on open slopes and open areas of forests, often in volcanic or disturbed soils. Look for pockets along roads and trails throughout the Sisters area (including at the Obsidian Trail and Canyon Creek Meadows) and beside highways as you cross the Cascades.

Bog Orchid (*Platanthera dilatata*)

Blooms: Summer

This lovely orchid is also called a bog candle because of its tall, sturdy shape. It pays to get up close to the flowers, first because they smell so wonderful you can even wash with them, and second because when you get close, you can see that at the back of each flower is a nectar-filled pouch, or spur, that only moths and other insects with very long proboscises can reach.

Look for: 12–45 in. tall. Leaves all along the stem, shorter at top. Small white to pale-green flowers in clusters along the candlestick, with spur at back of each flower.

Found: In bogs, swamps, marshes, and other very moist areas, including Todd Lake, Walton Lake, and Shevlin Park.

Note the spurs at the back of each flower. (Photo by Susan Berger)

Look for little white, or greenish white, flowers. (Photo by Ron Halvorson)

California Corn Lily *(Veratrum californicum)*

Blooms: Summer

This tall and distinctive plant is sometimes called false hellebore, but it's not a hellebore. It's sometimes called skunk cabbage, but it's not related to the real skunk cabbage. And even though it looks like corn and is called corn lily, alas, it's not actually related to corn.

It is a lily, and it's found in our moister areas, especially high meadows and open woods, where it grows in dense colonies, spreading by its root system. Corn lily is poisonous to livestock and people and considered invasive.

Look for: Corn-like stalks 4–6 ft. tall, with thickly veined leaves 8–15 in. long clasping the stems. Spikes of green-white blossoms. Easy to mistake for green corn lily (*V. viride*), which has more greenish flowers.

Found: In wet woods and meadows all over the region, including at Todd Lake and in the Ochocos at spots like Walton Lake and Lookout Mountain.

Washington Lily *(Lilium washingtonianum)*

Blooms: Early summer

Washington lilies are few and far apart—celebrate when you see these tall beauties, which are named in honor of Martha, not our neighbors to the north nor our capital to the east.

The lilies stand several feet high and the smell of the blooms will knock your socks off. Just don't pick them; they'll provide an emotional lift to other hikers if you leave them be.

Look for: One of our tallest wildflowers, with stems 2–5 ft. high. Leaves of up to 5 in. are in whorls around the stem. The trumpet-shaped flowers are 2–5 in. long, white or pinkish at first, fading to pink or purple.

Found: Keep an eye out at Tumalo Falls, Shevlin Park, Suttle Lake, the road to Camp Sherman, and other areas west of Sisters.

One of our biggest and best-smelling wildflowers.

81

The grass-like leaves at the base can be almost two feet long. (Photo by M.A. Willson)

Death Camas
(Toxicoscordion paniculatum)

Blooms: Early spring

As the common name suggests ever so delicately, death camas is a toxic plant that can kill livestock as well as any humans who mistake the bulb for that of an edible camas (*Camassia quamash*). So don't do that. But do stop to appreciate this pretty early bloomer that survives in some of our driest areas.

Look for: We have foothill (*T. paniculatum*) and meadow death camas (*T. venenosum*). Both are like a miniature beargrass, with pale-yellow flower spikes atop stems that rise up to 20 in. Iris-like leaves curl outward from the base.

Found: In dry, open woodlands (ponderosa and lodgepole) and sagebrush flats. Look for them at the Badlands Wilderness, Chimney Rock, Steelhead Falls, and Whychus Canyon Preserve.

Each panicle (loose cluster) has at least twenty little flowers. (Photo by M.A. Willson)

False Solomon's Seal
(Maianthemum racemosum)

Blooms: Midspring to early summer

False Solomon's seal is a large and distinctive plant that's interesting to watch from spring through fall. In spring, the arching stems with leaves up to ten inches long will catch your eye. Then smell the plumes of tiny snow-white flowers in late spring or early summer, which are followed by green berries. In fall, the leaves fade in color and bright-red berries steal the show.

Look for: Arching stem with egg-shaped opposite leaves (3–10 in.). Soft-looking plume of white flowers, followed by berries that go from green to red by fall. Star Solomon's seal (*M. stellatum*) is similar but with a smaller spray of flowers and darker berries.

Found: In every state but Hawaii. Common here in moist areas along streams and rivers—Benham Falls, Shevlin Park, and Suttle Lake are good places to look.

TRUE OR FALSE?

There is a "true" Solomon's seal (*Polygonatum biflorum*), but it doesn't grow in Oregon and only superficially resembles false Solomon's seal. The name is said to come from scars on the rhizome (root) that look like the Seal of Solomon (the Star of David in Jewish tradition).

Mountain Lady's Slipper
(Cypripedium montanum)

Blooms: Early summer

This beautiful, long-lived, and fragrant orchid is a reminder of the care we need to take when harvesting timber and building roads and trails. If we're not careful, we could easily destroy the remaining habitat for this disturbance-intolerant flower, which would be a shame.

Once found in most counties of the state, mountain lady's slipper is now a truly rare find, and populations are steadily declining. If you're fortunate enough to spot one, appreciate it from afar, but don't dig up this or any other native wildflower.

Look for: 10–30 in. high. One to three flowers on each stem, each with maroon-brown or purple petals and sepals surrounding a distinctive white pouch or slipper. Also note the yellow column at the throat of the slipper.

Found: A rare but beautiful find in mixed-conifer forests. Watch for it along roads and trails in the Ochocos (one sighting was reported near the Ochoco Forest Campground).

The purplish brown parts are sepals that protected the budding flower.
(Photo by M.A. Willson)

Queen's Cup *(Clintonia uniflora)*

Blooms: Early summer

As you've walked through shaded forests, have you ever wondered why there are so many plants with white flowers? Not purple, red, or blue, but white? One reason is that white stands out against the backdrop of all that dense greenery, attracting the attention of native bees and other pollinators.

Queen's cup, or bride's bonnet, produces one of those white flowers and is also easy to spot because of its big green leaves and blue berries in late summer.

Look for: White lily about 4 in. tall with six petals (actually tepals, which are basically a mix of sepals and petals). Each plant has two or three big, pointy, glossy-green leaves 4–6 in. long.

Found: In moist forests up to timberline, including at Tumalo Falls and Suttle Lake and along the Cascade Lakes Highway.

Count the six stamens, matching the six tepals.
(Photo by M.A. Willson)

Sand Lily *(Leucocrinum montanum)*

Blooms: Early to midspring

Portlanders have fun trying to spot the first trilliums of spring in Forest Park. In Central Oregon, sand lilies provide the equivalent spark of bright-white flowers that lets you know spring has arrived.

It really is just a spark: By late May or June, the blooms are gone and the aboveground parts of sand lilies wither away. The fruit pods are buried and later spread by insects that dig up the seeds.

Look for: No stems, just narrow, grass-like leaves close to the ground, up to 8 in. long. Fragrant white flowers (1–2 in.) sit on stalks a few inches high. Note the six yellow anthers in the middle.

Top: *Look for grass-like leaves and six-petal blooms. (Photo by M.A. Willson)*

Bottom: *It's a simple truth: When you see these, spring is here. (Photo by Ron Halvorson)*

Found: All over sandy and rocky soils—which means all over Central Oregon, from the Badlands Wilderness to Pilot Butte, Smith Rock State Park, and open lots near you.

Subalpine Mariposa Lily *(Calochortus subalpinus)*

Blooms: Summer

It pays to memorize the look of this lily's grass-like leaves so you can spot them when they first peek through the soil in spring. Then come back in summer to admire the beautiful blossoms and feel the soft, hairy fringe of the petals, which gives the plant its other common name, cat's ear lily.

Nurseries have long tried to cultivate lilies like these, nearly loving many of them to death. It's better simply to enjoy them where they grow in the wild.

Note the hairy inner face and the ragged edges of the petals. *(Photo by Susan Berger)*

Look for: Flat, grass-like leaves at base. Stems rise up to 15 in., with up to five yellowish-white flowers, 1.5–2 in. wide with yellow centers and often a purple arc near the base.

Found: In dry meadows, gravelly subalpine slopes, and volcanic soils along the Cascades, especially west of Sisters. Search for them near Camp Sherman, the Cascade Lakes Highway, and Elk Lake.

Western Trillium (*Trillium ovatum*)

Blooms: Early spring

My brothers used to warn me not to pick the pretty trilliums that grew near our house because they said the flowers only bloom once every seven years. That's not quite true, but it's close.

Most of the western trilliums you see in the wild sprout regularly from underground rhizomes. But if you were to plant a trillium seed, it could take seven years or longer to bloom. That's largely because the plants prefer deep shade so they don't get a lot of sunlight to support photosynthesis.

An early sign of spring in wet forest understories. (Photo by Tracy Aue)

Look for: The big, long leaves (2–8 in.) are technically bracts that lie under the three-petaled white flowers (1–2.5 in.). Petals fade to pink, purple, or red over time.

Found: Mainly a west-side species, but you may get lucky and spot some along the Cascade Lakes Highway or west of Sisters in moist and boggy areas.

4 PETALS

Bunchberry (*Cornus unalaschkensis*)

Blooms: Late spring to midsummer

Bunchberry, or dwarf dogwood, is the ground-cover version of the dogwood tree you may be more familiar with. The four whitish "petals" are actually bracts, or modified leaves.

The flowers are in the center, and they contain a surprise: When pollinators bump into the tiny antennae that stick up from the unopened buds, the flowers open suddenly and release a small explosion of pollen to cover the insects.

Look for: Low-growing, with four to six oval leaves (1–4 in.) on short stalks. Leaves are white on the undersides, with obvious parallel veins. Flowers can be greenish-white to yellowish or purplish. Bunches of red berries by September are edible but tasteless.

Found: Along the Cascade Lakes Highway, at Clear Lake, and in other shady, forested areas.

The bracts are white; the petals in the middle are only about a millimeter long. (Photo by M.A. Willson)

The flowers tumble down beside the stem, which can rise up to three feet. (Photo by Paul Slichter)

Holboell's Rockcress (*Arabis holboellii*)

Blooms: All summer

We have numerous species and subspecies of rockcress, which typically do not have showy flowers but do have interesting seedpods. As the name suggests, rockcresses (including this one) tend to prefer rocky or gravelly soils, as well as dry and disturbed areas—any place that struggles to support other life will do.

Look for: Erect plant (6–36 in.) with hairy leaves at base about 0.5–2 in. long. Flower petals are white to purplish pink, and the seed stalks curve abruptly downward along the main stem.

Found: In dry, rocky, and sandy soils, disturbed areas, and areas with juniper and sagebrush, including at Pilot Butte, the Badlands Wilderness, and Scout Camp.

The exquisite white blooms fade to pink. (Photo by Susan Berger)

Tufted Evening Primrose (*Oenothera cespitosa*)

Blooms: Late spring to early summer

All evening primroses are a delight, if you head out late in the day to catch them in action. They bloom in the evening to attract sphinx moths and other night-flying insects; then they wilt the next morning.

Look closely at the backs of evening primroses and you'll see that they have a long, thin floral tube to make sure only highly qualified, long-tongued pollinators can reach the nectar within. But don't just look—be sure to smell these fragrant beauties too.

Look for: Large (2–4 in.) flowers (usually white or yellow) growing low to the ground with long, narrow, fuzzy, gray-green leaves up to 8 in. long. Petals are heart-shaped, with eight yellow anthers.

Found: Sunny, dry hills; rocky slopes; and meadows in the Ochocos, as well as farther afield near Christmas Valley.

SWEET-SMELLING WILDFLOWERS

Trust me: These common native wildflowers are worth a whiff.

- Arrowleaf balsamroot (like chocolate!)
- Bog orchid
- False Solomon's seal
- Milkweed
- Oregon grape
- Tufted evening primrose
- Wallflower
- Washington lily

The outer flowers of the clusters are often bigger than the inner ones. (Photo by M.A. Willson)

5 PETALS

Cow Parsnip *(Heracleum maximum)*

Blooms: Late spring to early summer

You wouldn't expect a plant named after Hercules to be small, and indeed *Heracleum maximum* is anything but, rising up to ten feet tall, with leaves over a foot long. The tender stems and Frisbee-size flowers are popular among deer, elk, black bears, bighorn sheep, and well over one hundred insect species, but don't be tempted yourself: It's too easy to mistake this plant for poison hemlock and other decidedly inedible species.

Look for: Tall, strongly scented plant (3–10 ft.) with huge, maple-like leaves (4–16 in.). Umbrella-like clusters of white flowers are tough to miss.

Found: In moist or forested sites, including along streams and roads. You'll see cow parsnip along Sparks Lake, Whychus Creek, and the Deschutes and Metolius Rivers.

Large-fruited Desert Parsley

(Lomatium macrocarpum)

Blooms: Early spring

When you see an umbrella-shaped cluster of white flowers on a low-growing plant, point and declare, "It's a *Lomatium*!" You'll impress your friends and avoid having to figure out which of the seventy or so North American species of *Lomatium* it is.

Or, if you're up for a challenge, look closely and try to distinguish among the common varieties. This one, for instance, has stamens that stick out of the flowers a long way, making it memorable as the *Lomatium* having a bad hair day.

Look for: Hairy, compound leaves with purple undersides. Flower clusters can be white or yellow, sometimes tinged with purple. Fruits are long and narrow.

Found: Widespread in dry, rocky areas, including at Scout Camp and Whychus Canyon Preserve.

A Lomatium with messy "hair."
(Photo by Ron Halvorson)

The fused leaves form platters on which the flowers are served. (Photo by Susan Berger)

Miner's Lettuce *(Claytonia perfoliata)*

Blooms: Late spring

What do Gold Rush miners and the famous foodie Alice Waters have in common? Little, I suspect, except an appreciation for miner's lettuce. Crunchy and with a pleasant, mild taste, miner's lettuce staved off scurvy among early miners and has satisfied the sensitive palates of many a refined diner at Waters' Chez Panisse.

Miner's lettuce is common in Central Oregon, but make sure it's miner's lettuce before you add it to your lunch on the trail.

Look for: Low-growing plant (2–12 in.) with oval leaves at the base. The stem leaves are fused together to form disks beneath the flowers, which range from white to pale pink.

Found: Common in a lot of open, shady, and slightly moist areas, including Whychus Canyon Preserve, Scout Camp, Smith Rock State Park, and elsewhere near Redmond and in the Ochocos.

Egg-shaped leaves are up to two inches long. (Photo by Jacob W. Frank, NPS)

One-sided Wintergreen *(Orthilia secunda)*

Blooms: All summer

One-sided wintergreen, or pyrola, is an unassuming little perennial with vibrant green leaves that typically grows in large colonies. The common name comes from the fact that the stem arches over to support up to eight small flowers on a single side.

One-sided wintergreen is used in folk medicine to treat everything from fibroids to cancer.

Look for: Just 2–10 in. tall, with egg-shaped, toothed leaves at the base. True to its name, the cream to pale-green flowers dangle from one side of the leafless, arching stem.

Found: In shady conifer forests along the Cascades, especially west of Sisters at Black Butte and at the Cascade Lakes.

Pussypaws *(Calyptridium umbellatum)*

Blooms: Late spring into summer

Pussypaws are funny little plants. The first thing that gives them away is their succulent, teaspoon-shaped leaves. Then look for those kitty paws—the fuzzy white to rosy-pink balls of flowers that resemble the bottom of a cat's foot (it's a bit of a stretch).

The stems and flowers usually lie on the ground, like my cat, but during the day all those paws sometimes rise up, possibly to shade the leaves from the hot sun or to attract more pollinators.

Look for: Low-growing (2–10 in.) with reddish flowering stalks radiating out from the succulent leaves in the middle. Round and fuzzy flower clusters are white to pink.

Found: Mostly in forested areas with sandy and pumice-filled soils, including at Newberry Crater, Three Creek Lake, and Todd Lake.

The "paws" rise up during the day, then lie back down at night. (Photo by M.A. Willson)

Wild Strawberry *(Fragaria virginiana)*

Blooms: Late spring to early summer

My first job was picking strawberries for $2.50 a flat—but thankfully those were cultivated varieties and not the much sparser wild strawberries you'll find growing in area forests.

This is our most common wild strawberry plant, more specifically called Virginia or mountain strawberry. The berries aren't as sweet as Hoods and other cultivars (few things are), but they're a welcome treat along the trail.

Look for: Low-growing mat with blue-green leaves, divided into three leaflets on little stalks, toothed from middle to tip. Pretty, rounded white petals surround a golden middle.

Found: In meadows and open woodlands and along streambanks, including at Shevlin Park, LaPine State Park, Paulina and East Lakes, and Suttle Lake.

The virginiana *variety is an especially sweet wild strawberry. (Photo by Ron Halvorson)*

Look for mounds with tiny leaves and open-faced blooms. (Photo by Ron Halvorson)

5 PETALS FORMING TUBE

Hood's Phlox *(Phlox hoodii)*

Blooms: Late spring to early summer

The fact that *phlox* means "flame" should give you some idea as to the subtlety of the vibrant, open-faced blooms.

Hood's phlox is one of the more common varieties in Central Oregon. In fact, it's found almost entirely east of the Cascades, where the open, colorful petals and golden centers brighten our dry forests and areas dominated by sagebrush and juniper.

Look for: A ground-hugging mound with spiny, pointed, quarter-inch leaves. Half-inch white, pink, or blue petals seem to rest on top of the leaves.

Found: Common across dry regions, including at Whychus Canyon Preserve and Scout Camp.

The usual penstemon shape, in an unusual color. (Photo by Ron Halvorson)

Hot Rock Penstemon *(Penstemon deustus)*

Blooms: Early summer

Your eyes are not deceiving you: Most of the hundreds of varieties of penstemon are blue or purple, but this rugged individualist has creamy-white blooms instead.

You'll notice hot rock penstemon here and there on rocky ledges and roadsides, where most other plants fear to tread. Get up close and you'll see the red-to-purple lines in the flower throats, guiding bees to the nectar within.

Look for: Erect plants with stiff stems rising up to 18 in. Leaves are opposite (like most penstemons) and there are a lot of them (unlike most penstemons). The small, creamy-white flowers are in dense clusters, with distinctive lips and tubular shape.

Found: In dry, rocky places and volcanic soils, including in the Ochocos and near Lava Lands Visitor Center.

Silverleaf Phacelia *(Phacelia hastata)*

Blooms: Late spring to early summer

I can't help it: I start singing Simon and Garfunkel's "Cecilia" to myself every time I see a phacelia, which in the case of silverleaf phacelia is quite often.

A lot of silver hairs cover the broad leaves of silverleaf phacelia. It and the rather similar varied-leaf phacelia (*P. heterophylla*) grow in some tough neighborhoods, including shrublands and rocky and barren slopes.

Look for: Height varies from 6 in. to 3 ft. The long, narrow leaves at the base extend up to 5 in. White or lavender flowers emerge in dense, coiled clusters (like scorpion tails), with long stamens sticking out.

Found: Abundant all over the region, including along the Deschutes River Trail and at Pilot Butte, Horse Ridge, and Cove Palisades State Park.

Long stamens create a fuzzy appearance. (Photo by Ron Halvorson)

COMPOSITES

Common Yarrow *(Achillea millefolium)*

Blooms: All summer

Yarrow is one of the most common and easiest-to-spot wildflowers in Central Oregon. If you don't see it in the wild, you'll surely see the cultivars in area gardens, with their yellow, pink, red, and other supernatural colors (and names like "Saucy Seduction").

By the way, the genus *Achillea* is named after Achilles, the Greek mythological hero who was taught by his centaur friend to treat soldiers' wounds with yarrow extract. The connection makes sense, since yarrow contains salicylic acid.

Look for: Hairy, fern-like leaves are distinctive. Grows from 0.5 to 3 ft. tall, with flat or rounded clumps of fragrant white flowers (crushed leaves also have a strong odor).

Found: Extremely common in open places all across Central Oregon, including urban areas.

Look for fields full of yarrow. (Photo by Ron Halvorson)

A mat of low pussytoes.
(Photo by Ron Halvorson)

Low Pussytoes (*Antennaria dimorpha*)

Blooms: Midspring

It's a stretch to suggest that the flowers on low pussytoes resemble the toe pads of a cat, but at least the name is memorable (just don't confuse it with pussypaws).

Low, or dwarf, pussytoes are only a couple inches tall, with male and larger female flowers on separate plants. Rosy pussytoes are similar, but they're taller and the bracts are pinkish, not brown.

Look for: A many-branched mat about 1–3 in. high, with single flower heads on each stem, almost hidden among the leaves. Flowers are a dull white inside a large cup of brown bracts.

Found: In dry places, including at Chimney Rock and the Crooked River Canyon.

Top: *A bee feeding on the yellow flowers.*

Bottom: *The leaves are very narrow and hairy (feel 'em!). (Photos by Susan Berger)*

Pearly Everlasting (*Anaphalis margaritacea*)

Blooms: Early to late summer

Pearly everlasting is a beautiful name, isn't it? The white "pearls" of the plant look like petals, but they're actually modified leaves, or bracts, that surround the yellow flowers in the middle.

It doesn't make much difference what you call the pearls, I suppose, except it helps explain why these plants are "everlasting" in dried flower arrangements—unlike petals, the hardy bracts keep their fresh appearance for a long time.

Look for: Bunches of woolly-stemmed plants 1–4 ft. tall. Leaves are narrow, whitish above and green below. Dense blooms have yellow disk flowers in the middle; the white bracts have a dark spot at the base. Pussytoes look similar but lack yellow flowers.

Found: Common (even weedy) in open areas, especially roadsides. Look for them near Hand Lake and all along the Cascade Lakes Highway.

Rough Eyelash (*Blepharipappus scaber*)

Blooms: Spring and early summer

Rough eyelash, or rough eyelashweed, is a little looker with slender stems topped by a daisy-like flower head. I thought the "eyelash" moniker referred to the delicately lobed ray flowers, but in fact the name comes from the fruit, which has a few stiff bristles that resemble human eyelashes (*pappus* is Greek for "eyelash").

Look for: Stems 4–12 in. tall with numerous narrow leaves, topped by white flower heads. Look closely at the white, three-forked ray flowers that have purple on the undersides.

Found: In dry, open flats with sagebrush and juniper. Hot spots include Cove Palisades State Park, Prineville Reservoir State Park, and Cline Buttes Recreation Area.

Purple anthers add color to the middle of the blooms.
(Photo by M.A. Willson)

Showy Townsendia (*Townsendia florifer*)

Blooms: Late spring to early summer

Townsendia is a genus of asters, and showy townsendia is just that—a showy aster with up to thirty white to lavender ray flowers surrounding a bunch of yellow disk flowers.

To tell this composite flower from others, look for tufts of hair sticking out of the disk flowers, as well as spatula-shaped leaves that are broad at the ends and narrower at the base.

Look for: Small daisy (2–8 in.) with a lot of spatula-shaped, ash-gray leaves on the stems. Flower heads have 18–30 white or pinkish ray flowers, with yellow disk flowers in the middle.

Found: In sandy, gravelly areas of arid regions, including at the Badlands Wilderness, Chimney Rock, and Tumalo State Park.

Note the messy "hair" of the central disk flowers. (Photo by Ron Halvorson)

The petal-like sepals surround numerous yellow stamens and greenish pistils. (Photo by M.A. Willson)

White Marsh-Marigold (*Caltha leptosepala*)

Blooms: Early spring

If you tromp through a snowy forest in early spring and get up near the tree line, you might get lucky and spot a spread of white marsh-marigolds. The alpine variety in Central Oregon prefers the wet soils found at higher elevations, where the flowers often start blooming even before the snow melts.

Look for: You can't see stems on this low-growing plant—just leaves sticking straight up from the ground, up to 6 in. long and heart-shaped, with a rounded tip. Flowers are white with a thick yellow center.

Found: In wet soils at the edges of snowmelt, including at Tumalo Creek and the Cascade Lakes.

Top: *White mule's ears cover wet meadows in spring.*

Bottom: *The ray flowers are whitish, not yellow like northern mule's ears.*
(Photos by Ron Halvorson)

White Mule's Ears (*Wyethia helianthoides*)

Blooms: Late spring to early summer

The species name *helianthoides* gives you a hint that this radiant plant is in the sunflower family, and the common name tells you to look for long leaves that resemble a mule's ears.

A lot of pollinators are fond of this beauty, from butterflies and native bees to flies and moths. You'll like it too, if you get lucky and see a profusion of the large blooms sprinkled across area foothills.

Look for: Clumps of upward-pointing leaves 10–16 in. long. Each stem bears one 1–2 in. flower head with 13–21 rays around a yellow center.

Found: Moist places and open areas, including along Crystal Creek and near Indian Creek in the Ochocos.

> "At some point in life the world's beauty becomes enough. You don't need to photograph, paint, or even remember it. It is enough. No record of it needs to be kept and you don't need someone to share it with or tell it to."
> —Toni Morrison, *Tar Baby*

YELLOW FLOWERS
3 OR 6 PETALS

Glacier Lily *(Erythronium grandiflorum)*

Blooms: Early spring

This big beauty gets a head start by photosynthesizing under the snow at higher elevations, even pushing its leaves and buds right up through the snow. Like other lilies, it has six petals (actually tepals) that in this case curve upward, revealing the colorful anthers within.

If you're lucky, you'll see the drooping heads en masse on an alpine meadow in the Cascades, although the common name is a bit of a misnomer—glacier lily is actually found in a variety of habitats.

Look for: Tall (4–12 in.), with long, thin leaves (4–8 in.) and erect stems with one or two golden-yellow flowers. Anthers can be cream-colored, yellow, or even dark red.

Found: Moist alpine and subalpine areas, as well as drier forests and even areas dominated by sagebrush. Look for them at lakes across the Cascades.

Bumblebees rely on these lilies in early spring. (Photo by Jacob W. Frank, NPS)

Parsley Desert Buckwheat

(Eriogonum heracleoides)

Blooms: Spring and early summer

We have a number of buckwheats like this widespread one, each topped by distinctive balls of flowers. To tell parsley desert buckwheat from other varieties, look for the big whorl of bracts about halfway up the stem.

Though rather unassuming in appearance, buckwheats are one of the most important plant species in the shrub-steppe, ranking just behind grasses and sagebrush. Among their many ecological benefits, the plants provide a critical nectar source for native bees, especially after most other flowers have gone dormant. The seeds are also a significant food source for birds and rodents.

Look for: Loose mats up to 16 in. across, with most leaves at the base and lower stem, and a large whorl of bracts mid-stem. Long stalks end in clusters of cream-colored (not bright-yellow) flowers that turn red with age.

Found: On sandy and gravelly slopes in dry areas east of the Cascades, including at the Badlands Wilderness, Steelhead Falls, and Lava Lands Visitor Center.

Look for the cream-colored clusters of buckwheat blooms. (Photo by Ron Halvorson)

Sulphur-Flower Buckwheat
(Eriogonum umbellatum)

Blooms: Summer

Buckwheats are popular plants in drought-tolerant landscapes across Central Oregon, in part because they're pretty at every stage, from foliage to flower to seed.

I think the flower heads of sulphur-flower buckwheat are especially attractive, with the bright-yellow or cream-colored blooms aging gracefully to a glorious reddish-yellow.

Look for: A mat of leaves with flower stems up to 2 ft. tall and little balls of bright-yellow or cream flowers. Compared to parsley desert buckwheat, the leaves are more elliptic and there's no whorl of leaf-like bracts halfway up the stems.

Found: Widespread in the same sandy and gravelly soils as other buckwheats. Look for them all over, including at the Badlands Wilderness, Scout Camp, Steelhead Falls, and Lava and Pilot Buttes.

Top: *Stems are generally leaf-free.*

Bottom: *Blooms get even more beautiful as they age. (Photos by M.A. Willson)*

Yellow bells don't last long, and petals turn red as they age. (Photo by M.A. Willson)

Yellow Bell *(Fritillaria pudica)*

Blooms: Early spring

Like sand lilies, yellow bells are a harbinger of spring in Central Oregon—one of the first blooms to brighten our open and lightly wooded areas.

Yellow bells are dainty little flowers, and once you know that the species name *pudica* is Latin for "ashamed" or "bashful," you'll smile at the way they hide their faces from view. After they bloom, watch for the contrasting seedpods, which stand tall and proud, with "heads" like little aliens.

Look for: 3–12 in. tall, with a handful of strap-like leaves and one or two nodding, bell-shaped flowers at the top of the erect stems. Blooms turn from yellow to orange to dull red as they age.

Found: All over, from juniper woodlands to open forests and meadows. Look for them at Whychus Canyon Preserve and Chimney Rock.

4 PETALS

Golden Bee Plant

(Peritoma platycarpa)

Blooms: Late spring to early summer

The golden bee plant, or golden spiderflower, is a striking sight, with bright, tight clusters of golden-yellow flowers bursting atop stems up to three feet tall.

The plant is found near Bend but is perhaps best known as a common flower at the Painted Hills in the John Day area, where it adds a golden tint to the hills after spring rains.

Look for: 0.5–3 ft. tall, with leaves up to 2 in., divided into three leaflets. Long, hairy stems have a purple tint, with bright-yellow flower clusters at the ends.

Found: In ashy, clay soils, including at Bear Creek and Prineville Reservoir State Park.

Six stamens stick out beyond the petals of each flower. (Photo by Ron Halvorson)

Tansy-leaved Evening Primrose

(Taraxia tanacetifolia)

Blooms: Summer

This is one of several gorgeous evening primroses that you can appreciate in summer. Tansy-leaved evening primrose is also called tansyleaf suncup, which is appropriate given the bright-yellow cups of low-growing flowers.

One of my favorite things about this wildflower is that—unlike so many others—it has almost no practical use to humankind. It is nothing but beautiful.

Look for: Low-growing rosettes or mats covered in hairs. Deeply lobed leaves can be quite long (2–12 in.). Each plant has a lot of flowers, each forming a little cup that turns from deep yellow to red.

Found: In open locations that are moist in spring, including along the Cascade Lakes Highway and in alkaline areas that dry by summer.

Top: Blooms turn purplish to red with age.

Bottom: The leaves are almost fern-like, like tansies. (Photo by Ron Halvorson)

Look for large clusters of four-petaled flowers. (Photo by Ron Halvorson)

Western Wallflower (Erysimum capitatum)

Blooms: Summer

I could never figure out why such a tall, showy flower (aka prairie rocket) was called a wallflower. Well, here's the story: There's a similar European species that was named a wallflower because it literally grew on walls. The name has stuck for relatives like this one, even though they grow in dry, sandy, and decidedly wall-free areas.

Look for: Tall (2–4 ft.) with hairy, pointy-tipped leaves (up to 10 in.). Strong, erect stems are topped by clusters of fragrant yellow to orange flowers with four petals.

Found: In drier habitats, including the Badlands Wilderness, Smith Rock State Park, Steelhead Falls, and Whychus Canyon Preserve.

5 PETALS

Blazing Star (Mentzelia laevicaulis)

Blooms: Summer

Blazing star is appropriately named, as it stands up to several feet tall and bursts forth in summer with large golden blooms.

The plant is also called nature's Velcro because the leaves easily fasten themselves to fur or fabric, thanks to hairs ringed by barbs or bristles. Blazing star flowers close during the midday heat but open for a second showing by early evening.

Look for: The plant is rough to the touch and has whitish, widely branching stems 9–40 in. tall. Check for long leaves at the base (7–10 in.) and along the stem (1–4 in.). Five pointy yellow petals form a star shape with fifty-plus stamens shooting out.

Found: In sandy, gravelly, or rocky slopes and roadsides, including at the Badlands Wilderness and Prineville Reservoir. Head up Pilot Butte after the Fourth of July fireworks to see these beauties lighting up the hillsides.

Top: Note the sawtooth-edged leaves.

Bottom: One of our showier summer blooms. (Photos by Ron Halvorson)

Goosefoot Violet (*Viola purpurea*)

Blooms: Late spring

In Central Oregon we have a number of plants in the *Viola*, or violet, genus. Most, like goosefoot violet, produce small, five-petaled flowers that sit atop short and sometimes unnoticeable stems.

Like many other wildflowers, the center of goosefoot violets features colored lines (in this case brownish-purple or maroon) that help guide pollinators to the sweet spot within.

Look for: Up to 4 in. tall, with fleshy, shallowly lobed, rather triangular leaves up to 1 in. long. Flowers are bright yellow with maroon veins on the lower three petals.

Found: In dry, open areas, including roadsides and among sagebrush and ponderosa pines east of Bend and Sisters.

Look for purple veins on the lower three petals. (Photo by Gerald Corsi)

Gray's Desert Parsley (*Lomatium grayi*)

Blooms: Spring

This is another of our many umbrella-shaped lomatiums, or desert parsleys. This one is especially attractive, with dark-green leaves and bright-yellow flowers atop leafless stems. Just beware that the strong, parsley-like odor isn't for everyone.

Look for: 6–14 in. tall, with leaves divided into hundreds of crowded, narrow segments in different planes, making the base look thick. Tightly clustered yellow flowers top the leafless stems.

Found: In dry, rocky slopes and foothills, including at Whychus Canyon Preserve, Chimney Rock, and lower elevations of the Ochocos.

Look for the dense understory of leaves and check for the parsley scent. (Photo by Ron Halvorson)

The egg-shaped leaves are different from most lomatiums. (Photo by Ron Halvorson)

Indian Celery *(Lomatium nudicaule)*

Blooms: Spring

A First Food for some tribes, this plant has also been used to address medical ailments, ranging from headaches to tuberculosis. While it has been used for food, it looks enough like poison hemlock that it's safer to settle for giving the blooms a sniff—they have an interesting, spicy smell.

Look for: Erect stems (10–30 in.) with leaves mostly at the base. Flower stalks branch every which way, with clusters of creamy-yellow blooms at tips.

Found: Not common close to Bend, but it's found in open areas with rocky or sandy soils, including at Big Summit Prairie and the Ochocos.

Look for reddish stems and red on the petals. (Photo by M.A. Willson)

Lanceleaf Stonecrop *(Sedum lanceolatum)*

Blooms: All summer

Like the name suggests, these intriguing little plants grow in rocky (stony) areas, where they survive the wind exposure and lack of soil by conserving water in their succulent stems and leaves.

There are a lot of stonecrops across Oregon, but lanceleaf and wormleaf stonecrop (*S. stenopetalum*) are the two most common in arid regions.

Look for: Fat, succulent leaves at the base. Flowering stems 1–8 in. long, with upward-pointing leaves. Yellow, star-like flower heads are up to 2 in. across with obvious stamens. The stems of wormleaf stonecrop are thinner and twistier (wormier).

Found: In rocky soils at high elevations, including the Ochocos, Chimney Rock, and Whychus Canyon Preserve.

Nineleaf Desert Parsley
(Lomatium triternatum)

Blooms: Mid-to late spring

The *Lomatium* family (aka biscuitroot or desert parsley) includes carrots, parsnips, celery, fennel, and dill—as well as poison hemlock (not all parsleys are edible). The family also includes this plant, which does ID-inhibited folks like me the favor of bearing leaves divided into three segments that are further divided into threes—hence, "nineleaf" desert parsley.

Look for: Stems 6–30 in. tall with 3–8 in. leaves at base. Flower stalks are topped with compact bundles of yellow flowers in loose, flat umbels (meaning "umbrella-shaped").

Found: Widespread across foothills, sagebrush, and ponderosa pine forests, including at the Badlands Wilderness, Shevlin Park, Chimney Rock, and Cove Palisades State Park.

Look for long, thin, and divided leaves at the base. (Photo by M.A. Willson)

Roundleaf Alumroot
(Heuchera cylindrica)

Blooms: Late spring to early summer

There are nearly forty species of alumroot and a lot of hybrids too; this one (including several subspecies) is among the more common in our region.

The most distinctive feature is the long, leaf-free stem, which is topped with a bottlebrush-shaped flower spike. The flowers of alumroot, or coral bell, resemble strings of popcorn.

Look for: 5–22 in. tall, with mound of lobed, toothed, round leaves at base. Leafless stems end in narrow flower spikes with bell-shaped flowers.

Found: Along steep cliffs and rocky slopes, including at Benham Falls, Shevlin Park, and Paulina Lake.

The cream-colored blooms grow in poor, rocky soils. (Photo by M.A. Willson)

Look for fleshy leaves and a lot of stamens and pistils. (Photo by Ron Halvorson)

Sagebrush Buttercup (*Ranunculus glaberrimus*)

Blooms: Spring

Sagebrush buttercups are another of those early spring jewels that bring beauty to the shrub-steppe and juniper woodlands.

Buttercups are rather obviously named for the buttery color of the blooms. What's less known is that buttercups as a group are poisonous, and the sap can blister your skin—whatever you do, don't let kids put parts of the plant, including the blossom, in their mouths. Let bees and other pollinators do the touching. For us, buttercups are a pleasure best enjoyed from a distance.

Look for: Low-growing (2–6 in.) with fleshy leaves at the base and bright-yellow flowers 1 in. wide with four to seven petals. Petals often fade to white with age.

Found: Fairly widespread across moister sites in juniper woodlands and other arid regions, including at Smith Rock State Park and Big Summit Prairie.

5 PETALS FORMING TUBE

Columbia Puccoon (*Lithospermum ruderale*)

Blooms: Late spring to early summer

Also known as western gromwells, Columbia puccoons are unusual-looking plants that grow in tall, crowded clumps and have long leaves at the top that seem to be doing their best to hide the pretty little flowers within. The various puccoons are named for the red dyes made from their roots ("puccoon" comes from the Powhatan word *poughkone*).

Look for: Clusters of hairy stems 8–30 in. tall. A lot of long, narrow leaves (1–3 in.) near the top, with small pale-yellow to greenish-yellow flowers (petals flare open). The seeds are like little white stones.

Found: Scattered along dry hillsides, open forests, and other areas, including at First Street Rapids, Cove Palisades State Park, Chimney Rock, and Tumalo State Park.

In bloom near McKay Saddle in the Ochocos. (Photo by Ron Halvorson)

Seep Monkeyflower (*Erythranthe guttata*)

Blooms: All summer

Walk along Fall River on a summer afternoon, and you might come across some of these golden beauties blooming on a log in the middle of the river.

Seep monkeyflower grows in and alongside all sorts of waterways across the West, including in every county in Oregon. The plant causes tissues to contract, so traditionally some Native tribes rely on it as a poultice for wounds and cuts.

Look for: From tiny to 3 ft. tall with pointy leaves (upper leaves clasp the stem). Each stem has five or more yellow, snapdragon-like flowers, each with one or many red dots in the throat.

Found: In and along most streams, irrigation ditches, seeps, stock tank overflows, and other waterways in Central Oregon. The Deschutes, Metolius, and Fall Rivers are all good bets.

A typical spread of beautiful seep monkeyflowers. (Photo by M.A. Willson)

Towering Lousewort (*Pedicularis bracteosa*)

Blooms: Summer

Talk about an unfortunate name. Louseworts are not warty, and they don't carry lice. They got their lousy moniker from an old and mistaken belief that livestock that grazed on a European species of *Pedicularis* became plagued with lice. As teenagers might say: So. Not. Fair.

This lice-free lousewort (also called bracted lousewort or wood betony) is wonderfully unusual, with hairy spikes and colorful, hooded flowers.

Look for: Erect stems (1–4 ft.) with fern-like leaves 1–6 in. long. Dense flower spikes are 2–7 in. long, with flowers ranging from yellowish to brownish-red or purple. The upper lip forms a hood and often has little beaks poking out.

Found: In damp forests and meadows, including at Todd Lake and elsewhere near Broken Top.

Look for hooded flowers, usually greenish yellow. (Photo by M.A. Willson)

Look for large leaves clumped at the base. (Photo by Ron Halvorson)

COMPOSITES

Arrowleaf Balsamroot *(Balsamorhiza sagittata)*

Blooms: Late spring to early summer

Just when you've begun to appreciate and even revel in the small charms of our arid regions, like little yellow bells and gold stars, along come these big, bold beauties that blanket entire fields. They're not just good-looking, either; deer and elk browse arrowleaf balsamroot, and Native Americans value just about every part as food.

Given its golden, wide-open blooms, it's not surprising that arrowleaf balsamroot (and its look-alike, *B. careyana*) is in the sunflower family. To figure out if you're looking at a balsamroot or a true sunflower, look at the leaves: Balsamroots have clumped leaves at the base and no leaves along the flowering stalks, while true sunflowers are just the opposite.

Look for: Clumps of very long, arrow-shaped leaves. Erect stems rise 1–3 ft., with bright-yellow flower heads about 2–4 in. wide.

Found: Common in large patches at sites like Lake Billy Chinook, Scout Camp, Prineville Reservoir State Park, and Smith Rock State Park.

Top: Look for narrow, grayish leaves.

Bottom: They have up to forty-five ray flowers. (Photos by Ron Halvorson)

Desert Yellow Daisy *(Erigeron linearis)*

Blooms: Summer

Like many other daisies, desert yellow daisy is also called fleabane (lineleaf fleabane, to be precise). Fleabanes got their common name from an old belief that dried clusters could be used to prevent or end flea infestations.

Just to complicate things further, fleabanes like the desert yellow daisy look a lot like asters. One key difference is that fleabanes usually flower earlier and are "busier" than asters, with more, larger, and narrower ray flowers (the long petals surrounding the flower head).

Look for: One of the first fleabanes to flower. Small clumps are 2–12 in. tall, with very narrow leaves (*linearis* refers to the long, thin leaves). The bottom of stems is hard and shiny. Small flower heads have twenty or more yellow ray flowers surrounding a yellowish-orange disk.

Found: Common all over rocky soils in areas, including Chimney Rock and Steelhead Falls.

False Dandelion *(Agoseris glauca)*

Blooms: Late summer

Many sources call this plant pale or prairie agoseris, but I prefer the more descriptive name of false dandelion, which is also applied to several other wild plants. It's an appropriate moniker because it's easy to confuse this plant with the dandelions in your yard— or is it just my yard?

If you tear the leaf tissue of real or false dandelion, a milky juice will dribble out that solidifies into a rubber-like substance that can be chewed like gum (very bitter gum, apparently).

Look for: Long, narrow leaves at base. Leafless stems 8–20 in. tall, with a single bright-yellow flower head.

Found: Most common in higher and moister areas with sagebrush and ponderosa pine, including Horse Ridge and Big Summit Prairie.

Top: *The blooms aren't as dense as on dandelions.*

Bottom: *Note the narrow leaves.*
(Photos by M.A. Willson)

Gold Stars *(Crocidium multicaule)*

Blooms: Early spring

If we conducted a survey of people's favorite Central Oregon wildflowers, I have a feeling gold stars would be near the top of the list. These are the tiny gold flowers—also called spring gold or gold fields—that emerge before just about anything else, creating spectacular displays across entire slopes.

As suggested on a Deschutes Land Trust hike, a fun way to think of gold stars is as the literal gold sprinkled by a gold miner with holes in his pockets.

Look for: Little annuals (3–6 in.) with alternate leaves that are thick like a succulent. There's one flower head per stem, less than a half-inch across. Look closely to spot woolly hairs between leaves and stem.

Found: As early as late April in dry, open fields and sandy areas near Sisters. Watch for brief blooms at Whychus Canyon Preserve, Scout Camp, and the Tam-a-láu Trail.

Top: *Count the petal-like ray flowers—there should be five to thirteen.*

Bottom: *A sprinkling of gold stars.*
(Photos by M.A. Willson)

Heartleaf Arnica (*Arnica cordifolia*)

Blooms: All summer

We have about a dozen species of arnica in the Northwest, which is a good thing to know if you sprain your ankle while out hiking. The dried leaves have been used for centuries to treat muscle strains and bruises.

This particular arnica stands out because of its lovely, heart-shaped leaves, which is said to have led some Native tribes to use it in love potions.

Look for: One or a few erect and hairy stems, 6–24 in. tall. Heart-shaped leaves at the base are in opposite pairs, with finely toothed edges. Single yellow flower heads top each stem, about 2–3 in. across.

Found: Carpets lightly shaded regions of area forests, including in the Ochocos and at Black Butte and other areas along the eastern slope of the Cascades.

Top: *Look for broad, heart-shaped leaves.*

Bottom: *Blooms are two to three inches wide. (Photos by Ron Halvorson)*

Longleaf Hawksbeard (*Crepis acuminata*)

Blooms: Midspring

There are about 200 hawksbeard species, most of which at least somewhat resemble dandelions and, like dandelions, produce a milky sap that can be chewed like gum.

Longleaf, or tapertip, hawksbeard is one of the more common varieties in our area, and it lives up to both common names with leaves over a foot long that end in sharp points.

Look for: Tall (8–28 in.), with long leaves at the base (up to 16 in.) that have a lot of deep, narrow lobes. From 20 to 100 showy yellow flower heads sit atop branched stems.

Found: In sandy, gravelly soils, often with sagebrush, at the Badlands Wilderness, Powell Butte, Horse Ridge, and Cline Buttes Recreation Area.

Note the long, dandelion-like leaves at the base. (Photo by Paul Slichter)

Northern Mule's Ears (*Wyethia amplexicaulis*)

Blooms: Late spring to early summer

The common name for this plant refers quite obviously to the foot-long leaves that look like the ears of a mule.

The genus refers to Nathaniel Wyeth, aka the Cambridge Iceman, an interesting fellow who led two expeditions to Oregon in the 1830s. Wyeth wasn't a botanist, but he collected plants during his four years in Oregon and spent several months exploring the Deschutes River.

Look for: Stems 1–2 ft. tall, with pointy, lance-shaped leaves at the base 12–15 in. long; stem leaves smaller. Deep-yellow flowers are 2–3 in. wide. Similar to arrowleaf balsamroot, but leaves are on the stem (not solely at the base).

Found: In open, dry meadows, including Big Summit Prairie and other sites in the Ochocos.

Leaves grow at the base and along the stem. (Photo by Ron Halvorson)

Oregon Sunshine (*Eriophyllum lanatum*)

Blooms: Late spring through summer

If you're going to lend our state name to a plant, this one's an awfully good choice (even if it's most common in California).

Like many Oregonians, Oregon sunshine is as hardy as it is pretty, blooming in dry, sandy, and rocky conditions. Also like many Oregonians, Oregon sunshine wears a lot of wool; woolly hairs cover its stems, leaves, and the leaf-like bracts that surround the flower heads.

Look for: Clumps of green, deeply lobed leaves (0.5–3 in.) covered with fine white hairs, creating a soft, grayish appearance. Plants grow 4–24 in. and have single flower heads (1–2 in.) on long stalks, with 7–15 yellow ray flowers surrounding darker-yellow disks.

Found: All over sunny areas, especially in sandy soils. Common sites include Pilot Butte, Tumalo State Park, Gray Butte, and the Badlands Wilderness.

Top: *Gray-green leaves are deeply lobed.*

Bottom: *The sunny blooms last several months. (Photo by M.A. Willson)*

Goldenrod beginning to bloom in mid-July at Shevlin Park.

Goldenrods (*Euthamia* and *Solidago* spp.)

Blooms: Late summer

We don't have many wildflowers that bloom in late summer. Those that do, including several varieties of goldenrods, are hot commodities for hungry native pollinators. You might see bees, butterflies, beetles, moths, and flies buzzing about the goldenrods in your yard and our wild places.

If you have late-season allergies, you can still plant goldenrods. They happen to bloom when our heads get stuffy, but their heavy pollen is carried by insects, not the wind.

Look for: Usually 1-4 ft. tall with long, thin leaves. Stems are topped with fluffy clusters of golden flowers. It's tricky to tell all the different species apart, so use a detailed field guide for help.

Found: Along streams and in other damp places such as Shevlin Park and Cline Falls State Park.

Western Groundsel (*Senecio integerrimus*)

Blooms: Late spring to early summer

Western, or lambstongue, groundsel is yet another of what botanists lovingly refer to as "damn yellow composites," or DYCs. It's said that even the flower-loving Lady Bird Johnson used the term, so don't feel too bad if you do as well.

To distinguish western groundsel from other DYCs, look for flower heads that are clustered on short, hairy stalks, and black tips on the bracts beneath the petals.

Look for: Stout, erect stems 8–30 in. tall. A lot of lance-shaped to nearly round leaves at base, with matted hair when young (smoother with age). Ray flowers can be yellow to nearly white; disks in middle are prominent and yellow.

Found: In a variety of habitats, including forests, alpine ridges, and the shrub-steppe. Look for them at the Badlands Wilderness, Horse Ridge, and many locations near Sisters.

The short, hairy stalks and prominent yellow disks are giveaways. (Photo by Ron Halvorson)

MANY OR NO OBVIOUS PETALS

Skunk Cabbage (*Lysichiton americanus*)

Blooms: Early spring

Skunk cabbage is so named because it's pretty like the lush coat of a skunk. Or, okay, that's a lie. As with most things called "skunk," this plant smells bad. Really bad. The foul odor attracts flies, beetles, and other pollinators and has the added benefit (to the plant) of driving away people.

Along with native pollinators, other animals also appreciate skunk cabbage, including deer that forage on the leaves and bears just out of hibernation that dig up the roots for much-needed nourishment. You probably don't want to forage for it yourself since it has oxalate crystals that will irritate your mouth.

A beautiful—and stinky—plant. (Photo by M.A. Willson)

Look for: Grows to 1–3 ft., with huge, deep-green, elliptical leaves up to 2 ft. long. A bright-yellow hood partially surrounds the greenish-yellow flowering stalk (called a spadix), which bears a lot of tiny yellow-green flowers.

Found: Primarily a west-side species, but look for it in wetland areas at Suttle Lake and along the Metolius River.

Yellow Pond-Lily (*Nuphar polysepala*)

Blooms: Midsummer to late summer

It's easy to paddle right by these water-loving plants on your stand-up paddleboard or in your kayak or canoe. Slow down, though, and there's a lot to appreciate. Beneath the large, waterproof leaves and bright-yellow blooms, see if you can spot the roots—which can be fifteen feet long. Also, look inside individual flowers to spy the red-tinged stamens.

Think too about the many uses of this perennial (aka spatterdock or cow-lily). It's been used to treat just about every disease you can think of, and the seeds are said to pop like popcorn.

Look for: Large, often heart-shaped leaves (4–18 in.) float or rise above water. Bright-yellow, cup-shaped flowers are about 4 in. across, sometimes with a green or red tint.

Found: In shallow ponds, slow streams, and standing water, including at Hosmer and Sparks Lakes and along the Metolius River.

Look for leaves over a foot long floating on the water. (Photo by Paul Slichter)

*Like many true lilies, this one's leaves are arranged in whorls.
(Photo by M.A. Willson)*

Columbia Lily *(Lilium columbianum)*

Blooms: Early summer

Orange is an uncommon color for wildflowers in our region—they stand out when you see them. And none stands out more than this stunner, which is also called Cascade, Oregon, or tiger lily.

Standing as tall as four feet on this side of the Cascades and topped with golden-orange flowers covered in distinctive brown spots, Columbia lilies will stop you in your tracks. At which point you should take a whiff of the beautiful blooms (they have a light, peppery scent).

Look for: 1–4 ft. tall, with leaves (2–4 in.) in whorls. A lot of flowers top the bent stalks. Blooms are 1–2.5 in. across, light to dark orange with brown spots, and bell-shaped. Stamens droop below the petals.

Found: Meadows, forests, and roadsides on the western edge of Deschutes County, including along the Metolius River.

5 PETALS

Orange Globe Mallow *(Sphaeralcea munroana)*

Blooms: May through summer

Did you know that marshmallows were originally made from the root of the common marshmallow (*Althaea officinalis*)? The whole mallow family is interesting and diverse, with well-known members like cacao, cotton, and okra.

Orange globe mallow is the apricot to red-orange mallow you'll see occasionally in these parts, especially in more arid regions where pronghorn, deer, elk, and a lot of smaller animals eat it.

Look for: Usually less than 1 ft. tall, with grayish appearance due to hairs on the lobed leaves. Upper stems have clusters of distinctive orange flowers that form bowls with a lot of yellow stamens inside.

Found: In landscaped yards and arid regions, including Prineville Reservoir State Park and the Ochocos.

*Look for hairy, heart-shaped leaves.
(Photo by Ron Halvorson)*

Fiddlenecks (*Amsinckia* spp.)

Blooms: Spring

Fiddlenecks are truly unusual-looking plants, with orange-yellow flowers that curl over at the top of the stem, forming what looks for all the world like the head of a fiddle. Though interesting to look at, fiddlenecks are not popular among ranchers because they're notoriously poisonous to livestock.

In Central Oregon we have at least a couple common varieties of fiddlenecks: Bugloss (*A. lycopsoides*) and Menzies' (*A. menziesii*). The differences are subtle enough that we'll settle for recognizing a fiddleneck when we see one.

Look for: 4–30 in. tall, with stiff hairs. Flowers coil like the head of a fiddle (or a scorpion tail, if you prefer).

Found: Here and there at Todd Lake, Scout Camp, Pilot Butte, and Chimney Rock, and in disturbed areas.

Look for red dots in the center of most blooms. (Photo by Thayne Tuason)

Large-flowered Collomia (*Collomia grandiflora*)

Blooms: Early and midsummer

Large-flowered collomia is one of the most common wildflowers in the dry areas of Central Oregon, including on Pilot Butte. Don't let the name fool you, though: The flowers are actually quite small; the name refers to the fact that they're larger than those of other collomias.

That intrepid botanist David Douglas spotted large-flowered collomia along the Columbia River in 1828. But the genus name *Collomia* is not derived from "Columbia"—it's from the Greek word *kolla*, which means "glue" and refers to the sticky seeds.

Look for: Erect stems up to 3 ft. tall with flowers bunched at the tip. Flowers have long tubes and are usually salmon in color (or white or yellow).

Found: Very common in dry soils at Pilot Butte, Chimney Rock, Cove Palisades State Park, the Badlands Wilderness, and many other locations.

Take a gander at the middle of each bloom to spot the deep-blue pollen. (Photo by M.A. Willson)

Stigma and stamens dangle from each trumpet. (Photo by M.A. Willson)

5 PETALS FORMING BELL

Orange Honeysuckle *(Lonicera ciliosa)*

Blooms: Late spring to early summer

There are about 180 varieties of honeysuckles clambering up trees and fences worldwide. This native one (more common on the west side of the Cascades) is known as a hummingbird magnet, although it's also popular with birds that eat the orange-red berries and with butterfly larvae that munch on the leaves.

Look for: Climbing vine (6–18 ft.) with orange, trumpet-shaped flower clusters that hang just beyond two fused leaves. Fruits are red.

Found: In forests and thickets in wetter regions on the west side of Deschutes County, including at Suttle Lake and the Metolius River.

COMPOSITES

Orange Agoseris *(Agoseris aurantiaca)*

Blooms: Summer

If you spy what appears to be a burnt-orange dandelion in the wild, you're probably looking at orange agoseris.

This member of the sunflower family, which is native to our mountainous regions, has the misfortune of looking similar to the dreaded orange hawkweed (see Noxious Weeds). There should be no confusion, though, because thus far orange hawkweed has not become common in our wild areas.

Look for: Naked flower stalks 4–24 in. tall, typically topped with dense orange flower heads. Leaves at base are hairless and egg-shaped.

Found: Widespread across both wet and dry regions, including at Paulina and East Lakes and along the Tam McArthur Rim Trail.

Top: Aurantiaca means "orange-red," but the petals can also be pink or purplish.

Bottom: The blooms sit atop long, leafless stems. (Photos by M.A. Willson)

Green-banded Mariposa Lily

(Calochortus macrocarpus)

Blooms: Late spring to midsummer

There's something hopeful and poignant about seemingly delicate plants like the green-banded mariposa lily that persist in some of our harshest environments.

This little-flower-that-could sprouts from underground bulbs that are so tough they can survive wildfires, although grazing can destroy them. In late spring, the blooms draw cheers—beauty has defied the odds again.

Look for: Erect stems (8–23 in.) with a single grass-like leaf. Flowers are lavender, purple, or white, with three long, thin sepals and three broad petals.

Found: In full sun in ponderosa pine forests and arid regions, including at the Badlands Wilderness, Pilot Butte, Scout Camp, and Whychus Canyon Preserve.

Note the dark-purple band at the base of the petals. (Photo by Ron Halvorson)

Tolmie's Onion *(Allium tolmiei)*

Blooms: Early summer

When a friend introduced me to the wonders of wild onions on a hike at Lookout Mountain—sprinkling a few pieces on our sandwiches—I was smitten. However, there are a lot of onion species and plenty of other plants that you might confuse with them, including the aptly named death camas, so be careful, and note that wild onions smell like onions.

If you decide to spice up a trailside meal, please don't dig up the lovely Tolmie's onion—a few petals will do the trick.

Look for: Low-growing, with two wide, thick, sickle-shaped leaves about twice as long as the stem, or scape (leafless stalk growing directly from ground). Blooms are umbels (umbrella-shaped), with 10–40 flowers with pink or white petals.

Found: Dry, often rocky areas with clay soils north and east of Bend, including many areas in the Ochocos.

Long scapes trail below the blooms. (Photo by M.A. Willson)

Hummingbirds love the drooping hearts. (Photo by M.A. Willson)

4 PETALS

Bleeding Heart (*Dicentra formosa*)

Blooms: All spring

Bleeding hearts are one of those wildflowers that elicit yelps of joy. Who can resist a drooping pink flower shaped like a Valentine's heart?

Just to rub it in, the species name *formosa* means "beautiful"—and its beauty is a large part of the reason bleeding hearts have been cultivated in the U.S. since the early 1800s.

Look for: Upright perennials with fern-like leaves at the base and stout stems (8–20 in.). Pink (sometimes white) flowers hang above the leaves in drooping clusters.

Found: In moist sites near area lakes and streams, including along Elk, Todd, and Sparks Lakes.

Note the long leaves and reddish stems. (Photo by Ron Halvorson)

Dagger Pod (*Phoenicaulis cheiranthoides*)

Blooms: Midspring to early summer

Dagger pods did not get their common name from their long, lance-shaped leaves. The "daggers" are actually the distinctive seedpods.

The colors may also grab your attention: The gray of the leaves offsets the beautiful pink to purple flowers, which provide a burst of spring color in some of our driest areas. The stems are also colorful—*Phoenicaulis* combines *phoni* ("reddish purple") and *caulis* ("stem"), in reference to the reddish stems.

Look for: Gray, hairy leaves at base, 4–10 in. long. Flowering stalks up to 8 in. long with reddish-purple, pink, or white flowers in dense clusters.

Found: In moist habitats within our more arid regions, including at Big Summit Prairie.

Fireweed (*Chamerion angustifolium*)

Blooms: Summer

Fireweed often gets overlooked, perhaps because it's common and stuck with that "weed" name. But make no mistake: This is a native plant that also happens to be beautiful and ecologically valuable.

In burned-out European cities and on Mount St. Helens after it blew, fireweed was one of the first on the scene. And unlike typical weeds, fireweed soon yields to other plants—moving on to stabilize the next burned or damaged area.

Look for: Very tall (2-9 ft.), with often unbranched stems topped by a long, dense spike of pink to magenta flowers.

Found: In burned, clearcut, and otherwise disturbed areas, including in urban areas and along the Deschutes River Trail and Cascade Lakes Highway.

This "weed" is tall, pretty, and ecologically important. (Photo by Susan Berger)

Ragged Robin (*Clarkia pulchella*)

Blooms: Late spring to early summer

Meriwether Lewis got it right in 1806 when he described ragged robin as a "singular plant." Two of its other common names—elkhorn and deer horn—refer to the unusual, deeply divided petals, which resemble antlers.

Many people enjoy the unique appearance of the blooms (also called pink fairies), and butterflies and bumblebees make the most of the nectar they produce.

Look for: Erect, hairy stems (6-18 in.) with pointy leaves 1-3 in. long. Lavender to rose-purple petals generally have three lobes, with a wider central lobe.

Found: In rocky, sandy, and loamy habitats north and east of Bend. Look for blooms at Powell Butte and the Ochocos.

Top: One of our most distinctive wildflowers.

Bottom: That's a big white stigma in the center of the flower. (Photos by Ron Halvorson)

The two inner petals fuse to form the muzzle of the steer. (Photo by Susan Berger)

Steer's Head *(Dicentra uniflora)*

Blooms: Early spring to early summer

Pretty, showy, distinctive—several adjectives apply to the many wildflowers of Central Oregon. But steer's head is one of the few that deserves another descriptor: bizarre.

As the common name suggests, the blooms of this toxic member of the bleeding heart family look a whole lot like tiny skulls, complete with horns and a long snout.

Look for: Tiny plants (2–4 in.) with lobed leaves 2–3.5 in. long (look for waxy powder on the undersides). Single flowers are white to pinkish, with two outer petals curved back like horns.

Found: On open ground in foothills and subalpine slopes. It's rare and tiny, but look for it at sites like Todd Lake.

Top: You probably won't see leaves or a stem—only blooms. (Photo by M.A. Willson)

Bottom: A rare beauty in rocky areas. (Photo by Ron Halvorson)

5 PETALS

Bitterroot *(Lewisia rediviva)*

Blooms: Spring

Bitterroot is a magical plant with blooms that seem to drop down from the stars each May to brighten some of our harshest terrain. Salish Indians especially prize and honor bitterroot and are said to have traded one basket of the tasty roots for a horse. It's also Montana's state flower and the source of the name for the Bitterroot River, as well as the valley and mountains.

The genus is named after Meriwether Lewis, who dug up some bitterroot plants in Montana, dried them whole, and sent them to the Academy of Natural Sciences in Philadelphia. When those dried roots were planted years later, they sprouted to life, leading to the species name of *rediviva*.

Look for: Very low-growing plant, often tucked under a rock or two. Fleshy leaves frequently wither before the flower matures, so you'll see little more than the white to rose-colored blooms (1–3 in. wide), with a dozen or more petals.

Found: In rocky soils at Chimney Rock, Scout Camp, Powell Butte, and Whychus Creek Preserve.

Brown's Peony *(Paeonia brownii)*

Blooms: Late spring to midsummer

Aren't peonies Asian or Eurasian species? Well, yes. Mostly. There are two *Paeonia* species—this one and *P. californica*—that are native to western North America.

Brown's peonies, with their multicolored flowers, are certainly an unusual sight in the midst of fields of bitterbrush and bunchgrasses. Up in the foothills in early spring, they provide a critical source of nectar for native pollinators, when their energy supplies are at their lowest.

Look for: 8–24 in., with fleshy leaves. Blossoms are 3–4 in. wide and sometimes so heavy they weigh stems to the ground. Leathery sepals, greenish to purple, surround the petals, which are deep red to brownish and have yellow to greenish edges. Seeds are housed in the leathery green fruits at the center of each bloom.

Found: In arid regions and open pine forests, including along the Deschutes River Trail, at Lookout Mountain, and near Sisters at Indian Ford Campground and Black Butte.

Top: *Blooms are green, red, and yellow. (Photo by Ron Halvorson)*

Bottom: *Stems are thick and leaves are fleshy.*

Giant-Head Clover *(Trifolium macrocephalum)*

Blooms: Spring

A lot of people know about cultivated clover species used in agriculture, but I think it's safe to say far fewer know about our many species of native clovers. This one is especially noticeable, with big, round flower heads of dramatic colors.

Giant-head clover is said to be edible (and nutritious) when cooked, although native bees, flies, and other pollinators like it just fine as it is.

Look for: Low-growing (3–8 in.), with rare exceptions. Compound leaves have up to nine egg-shaped leaves (sorry, no four-leaf clovers here). Up to sixty white, cream, pink, or purple flowers bloom in large clusters.

Found: Abundant in dry, rocky sites in ponderosa pine forests and arid regions, including at Scout Camp and Powell Butte.

The one-inch flowers are usually a mix of cream and purple. (Photo by Ron Halvorson)

Stem is reddish and long styles dangle beyond the petals. (Photo by Susan Berger)

Heart-leaved Pyrola *(Pyrola asarifolia)*

Blooms: All summer

Pyrolas are also called wintergreens because the leaves maintain their green color through winter. You'll understand why heart-leaved pyrola is also known as pink wintergreen when you see the pink undersides of some of the leaves.

Over the years, people have used various wintergreens to treat everything from rheumatism to gonorrhea. That's because the leaves are high in methyl salicylate, a substance that serves as a natural painkiller.

Look for: 2–14 in. tall, with glossy-green leaves at base and pink, cup-shaped flowers along the reddish stem. A flower style sticks out beyond the petals, like the clapper in a bell.

Found: Moist sites in forests west of Bend, including Odell Lake, Black Butte, and Suttle Lake.

Top: Note the fern-like leaves at the base.

Bottom: Hairs cover the stem, leaves, and red sepals. (Photos by Ron Halvorson)

Old Man's Whiskers *(Geum triflorum)*

Blooms: Late spring to midsummer

Old man's whiskers are a sight to see when the seeds develop. Each seed attaches to more than two inches of feathery tails that together create a purplish haze (hence the whisker's name, as well as the other common name, prairie smoke).

The multicolored flowers are pretty too; they're droopy at first, but the stems straighten out over time, often rising well over a foot high.

Look for: Clumps of fern-like leaves at base. Erect stems are 8–20 in. long, with one leaf pair near the middle. Usually three flowers weigh down each stem, with five red sepals curved outward and pink to yellow petals tucked inside.

Found: Fairly common in a variety of habitats, including along Hwy. 26 east of Prineville and throughout the Ochocos.

Oregon Checker Mallow (*Sidalcea oregana*)

Blooms: Late spring through summer

Along with orange globe mallow, we have the lovely Oregon checker mallow, one of the more sun-loving members of the mallow family.

The checker mallow, or Oregon checkerbloom, is also one of the more common meadow plants in the Ochocos, with tall stems and beautiful, hollyhock-like pink blossoms.

Look for: Upright plant 2–4 ft. tall, with rounded, gently lobed leaves at base (leaves get sharply toothed farther up). Pink to deep-rose flowers bloom in loose, spike-like clusters.

Found: In a variety of habitats, including the Great Meadow in Sunriver, Walton Lake, Discovery Park, streams in the Ochocos, and drier areas with sagebrush and juniper.

Top: *Look for lobed leaves at the base.*

Bottom: *Petals are usually notched.*
(Photos by Ron Halvorson)

Pink Mountain Heather

(*Phyllodoce empetriformis*)

Blooms: All summer

You'd be excused for mistaking pink mountain heather for a young or dwarf pine tree, given the way the evergreen leaves roll up into a needle-like shape. But once summer hits and the blooms open, there's no mistaking the bell-shaped pink flowers. They might remind you of the heather (or "heath") that covers the wild hills of Scotland or the moody Yorkshire moors of *Wuthering Heights*.

Look for: Matted shrub with stems 4–15 in. tall. There are a lot of needlelike leaves and small clusters of bell-shaped pink to red flowers, with styles hanging down.

Found: In moist meadows and open forests of subalpine to alpine locations, including at Todd Lake and Broken Top, and across the Three Sisters area.

Note the evergreen-like leaves and the pistil sticking out of each flower. (Photo by M.A. Willson)

The petals bend back, exposing ten stamens. (Photo by Susan Berger)

Pipsissewa (Chimaphila umbellata)

Blooms: All summer

Pipsissewa is a semishrub that grows in heavy shade—a difficult feat for photosynthesis-craving wildflowers, and one pipsissewa accomplishes by living in part off underground fungi (mycorrhizae). Pipsissewa is the Cree name for the plant; it's also called western prince's pine.

Look for: There's a lower-growing little pipsissewa (*C. menziesii*), but this one is 6–14 in. tall, with opposite pairs or whorls of long, sharp-toothed leaves. Small, whitish-pink to rose-colored flowers hang in small clusters from the stem tips.

Found: In leaf mold of moist forests, including at Cultus, Paulina, Elk, and Suttle Lakes.

The purplish stem is sticky and hairy, with few leaves. (Photo by Ron Halvorson)

Prairie Star (Lithophragma parviflorum)

Blooms: Early spring

Prairie stars are yet another of our harbingers of spring, appearing in open areas as early as March. The reddish to purplish stems are distinctive, as are the pretty petals, which are divided into three pencil-like lobes. There are several species and varieties of prairie stars—you'll know you're looking at the variety *parviflorum* if the flowers are fragrant.

Look for: Sticky, hairy stems 4–12. in. tall, with sharp-toothed leaves at base. Blooms have five pink or white petals, each divided into three lobes.

Found: All over dry, open areas of sagebrush and juniper. Look for it at Whychus Canyon Preserve and Chimney Rock, and along the Crooked River.

FUN FACT

Pipsissewa has long been used as a medicine to treat rheumatism and other issues. You've probably had some yourself—but not for that reason. It's also used to flavor root beer and is said to be (or has been) one of the secret ingredients in Coca-Cola and Pepsi.

Red Columbine *(Aquilegia formosa)*

Blooms: Spring through summer

The beautiful red or Sitka columbine provides a Rorschach test of sorts: Do you see a lady raising her skirts to curtsy, revealing her petticoats? Or do you see, as the *Aquilegia* name suggests (*Aquila* is Latin for "eagle"), talon-like yellow spurs dropping from a red body? Either way, this is one of the true beauties of the West, beloved by humans and hummingbirds alike.

Look for: Stems up to 3 ft. tall, with delicate, divided leaves at base. Nodding flowers are usually red, with five rounded yellow spurs below and a central cluster of yellowish stamens and styles.

Found: In a variety of moist soils across the area, including at Pringle Falls, Tumalo Falls, the Metolius River, and the Ochocos.

Stamens and styles dangle below the yellow spurs and red petals. (Photo by Susan Berger)

5 PETALS FORMING TUBE

Cusick's Monkeyflower *(Diplacus deschutesensis)*

Blooms: Late spring through summer

Especially in early summer, Cusick's monkeyflowers put on a show you don't want to miss—and in places you might not expect. Keep an eye out for their colorful, monkey-like faces in arid regions.

This one (technically called Deschutes monkeyflower, but better known as Cusick's) is one of several monkeyflowers in our area and is especially similar to *D. cusickioides*, although that one is more common north and east of Central Oregon.

Look for: Hairy, upright plants 1–10 in. high. The plant is taller than dwarf monkeyflower and the leaves are rounder with pointy tips. Flowers are pink to deep magenta, with yellow bands in the throat.

Found: In sandy soil and cinder grit of juniper woodlands and other arid regions, including at the Badlands Wilderness, Scout Camp, and Pilot Butte.

A field of Cusick's monkeyflowers in the Badlands Wilderness. (Photo by M.A. Willson)

Dwarf Monkeyflower (*Diplacus nanus*)

Blooms: All summer

Dwarf monkeyflowers are another of our many species of monkeyflowers—all with open, pretty faces beloved by humans and pollinators alike.

Some monkeyflowers grow up to four feet in height, but this one (and the similar *D. cascadensis*) sticks close to the ground, which is a sensible adaptation since it grows in rugged, arid regions.

Look for: Very low-growing (0.5–6 in.) plant. Leaves are fairly narrow with rounded tips and a purplish tint underneath. Blooms pink to purplish, with darker colors and two yellow folds within.

Found: In sandy and disturbed soils throughout the Bend and Redmond areas, including at the Badlands Wilderness, Tumalo State Park, and Steelhead Falls.

Top: *The two large upper lobes and three lower lobes are a hallmark of monkeyflowers.*

Bottom: *In some years, they carpet arid regions (Photos by Dr. Stu Garrett)*

Lewis's Monkeyflower (*Erythranthe lewisii*)

Blooms: All summer

And you thought the monkey face at Smith Rock State Park was the only one in Central Oregon. Lewis's monkeyflower is a perennial (not an annual like Cusick's and dwarf monkeyflowers). It also stands apart because it prefers moist habitats.

Whichever monkeyflower you come across, lean in for a closer look at the ingenious design of the monkey's face: When bees and others enter the flowers, the three lower lobes press against the two larger upper lobes to thoroughly cover the insects with pollen.

Look for: A tall monkeyflower (1–4 ft.) with long, pointy, and hairy leaves (1–3 in.) clasping the upright stems. Flowers about 1 in. wide and pink (note the yellow spots or nectar guides in the throats).

Found: In seeps and other moist locations, including at Three Creek Lake and near the creek on the east side of Broken Top.

Look for this tall monkeyflower in moist locations. *(Photo by M.A. Willson)*

Elephant's Head Lousewort *(Pedicularis groenlandica)*

Blooms: Summer

Sometimes it seems like nature has a sense of humor. Case in point is the flower of this plant, which looks for all the world like the forehead, trunk, and big ears of a pink elephant. Elephant's head lousewort is actually a member of the broomrape family, so quite unlike real elephants, this one is parasitic, piercing the roots of other plants and drawing nutrients from them.

Look for: Fern-like leaves and reddish-purple stems 8–32 in. tall, with dense flower clusters at the ends. Flowers are light pink to dark purple, with upper petal tapering to form the "trunk" and the three lower petals resembling the ears and lower mouth.

Found: In wet meadows and along streambanks. Fairly common in the Cascade Lakes area, including at Todd, Sparks, Green, and Three Creek Lakes, and at Trout Creek Swamp.

The colorful stems can be nearly three feet tall. (Photo by M.A. Willson)

Paintbrush *(Castilleja* spp.*)*

Blooms: Late spring to midsummer

Paintbrush is one of our best-known and most easily recognized wildflowers, with dozens of varieties in colors ranging from yellow to green to red (the most common). What's less well known is that these beauties are hemiparasitic, meaning they often draw some of their nourishment from sagebrush and other host plants while also photosynthesizing on their own.

Look for: Generally 1–3 ft. tall. The bright colors (red, pink, yellow, green) come from the bracts, which surround inner petals.

Found: All over Central Oregon. Hot spots range from Shevlin Park to Steelhead Falls and Pine Mountain, but really they're everywhere.

One of our most common, and showy, wildflowers. (Photo by Sue Dougherty)

> "Remember you're this universe and this universe is you, that you have a place, and so do the plants, and so do the animals."
> —Joy Harjo

Look for long, pointy leaves and leafless stems. (Photo by M.A. Willson)

Jeffrey's Shooting Star *(Dodecatheon jeffreyi)*

Blooms: Early to midsummer

We have a few varieties of beautiful shooting stars, including this one (aka tall mountain shooting star) and the usually paler-pink Bonneville shooting star (*D. conjugens*). All the shooting stars are among the eight percent or so of all wildflowers that are buzz pollinated, meaning the stamens that hang down below the petals spew pollen in response to the furious vibrations of bumblebees and other pollinators.

Look for: 6-24 in. tall, with long leaves (up to 20 in.). Flowers are up to 1 in. long with 4-5 pink to purple petals that are white, cream, or yellow at the base. Stamens hang down and sepals are swept back, creating the unique look of a shooting star.

Found: The flowers carpet moist meadows, marshes, and seepy areas up to higher elevations, including at Three Creek, Todd, Green, and other Cascade Lakes.

Milkweed *(Asclepias* spp.*)*

Blooms: All summer

Milkweed is the only plant eaten by Monarch caterpillars, so when the iconic butterflies pass through Central Oregon in spring and fall, you can bet they're looking for our two common and native milkweeds: showy (*A. speciosa*) and narrow-leaved (*A. fascicularis*). Unfortunately, both of these plants are far less common today than in the past.

To help deeply at-risk Monarch populations, plant your own native milkweed (it's easy, and the blooms are big and fragrant). Contact Deschutes Land Trust or WinterCreek Nursery to learn how.

Look for: Both native milkweeds grow to about 4 ft., with rounded clusters of beautiful, purplish-pink flowers.

Found: Uncommon, but occasionally found along streams and roadsides that haven't been sprayed. Many of Bend's community gardens now feature waystations of milkweed and other native plants helpful to pollinators.

Top: Showy milkweed is a gorgeous, and ecologically important, plant.

Bottom: Do pollinators a favor and plant this beauty! (Photos by Ron Halvorson)

Naked Broomrape (*Orobanche uniflora*)

Blooms: Spring

And the winner of the award for worst common name for a wildflower is . . . naked broomrape. That unfortunate appellation apparently has an innocent origin: a combination of the English word *broom* (an old word for legumes) and the Latin *rapum*, for "tuber." It's also called one-flowered cancer root, which is not a whole lot better.

Making matters worse, the genus name is from *orobos* ("clinging plant") and *ancho* ("to strangle")—because, like all broomrapes, naked broomrape is a parasitic plant that sucks water and nutrients from the roots of other plants.

You might see another broomrape—clustered broomrape (*O. fasciculata*)—in drier areas, where it feeds off sagebrush and buckwheats and blooms into early summer.

Look for: Up to 3 in. tall, with purple to yellow blooms horizontal to the ground. They lack chlorophyll, so look for yellowish stems.

Found: In mostly wooded habitats, including Big Summit Prairie and Lookout Mountain. Clustered broomrape is found at Horse Ridge and the Prineville Reservoir.

Top: *Blooms vary in color. (Photo by M.A. Willson)*

Bottom: *Yellowish stems lack obvious leaves. (Photo by Ron Halvorson)*

Scarlet Gilia (*Ipomopsis aggregata*)

Blooms: All summer

The striking blooms of scarlet gilia, or skyrocket, were designed for hummingbirds. How can you tell? The long, tubular flowers are one giveaway, but also the bright-red color: Most insects can't see red, but hummingbirds can.

Interestingly, in places where hummingbirds migrate south by August, the blooms of scarlet gilia sometimes switch from red to white in late July and August—because moths don't see red flowers well, but on their nighttime forays they do visit white flowers.

Look for: Bright-green, comb-like leaves and stems 1–3 ft. tall, topped with loose clusters of red flowers (sometimes white or yellowish with hints of pink or red). Flower tubes flare open to form a five-pointed star with stamens extending outward.

Found: Common in dry meadows and gravelly roadside areas. Good spots to look include Virginia Meissner Sno-Park, the Ochoco Ranger Station road east of Prineville, and Canyon Creek Meadows.

The trumpets flare open to reveal five stamens. (Photo by Ron Halvorson)

Give the delicate-looking flowers a sniff (they're fragrant). (Photo by Ron Halvorson)

5 PETALS FORMING BELL

Twinflower *(Linnaea borealis)*

Blooms: All summer

Carl Linnaeus, the father of modern taxonomy and self-described "Prince of Botanists," liked to hold sprigs of twinflowers in his portraits, and though he never named a single plant after himself, he asked a colleague to name this one after him. Not generally known as a humble man, Linnaeus was nonetheless just that when he wrote that twinberry is "lowly, insignificant, flowering but for a brief space, after Linnaeus who resembles it."

Look for: A creeping evergreen vine, 2–6 in. tall, inconspicuous until blooming. Flowers in pairs (twins) are pale pink and shaped like trumpets or bells.

Found: In moist, shady forests west of Bend, including at Black Butte and Suttle Lake, and along McKenzie Pass.

COMPOSITES

Cushion Fleabane *(Erigeron poliospermus)*

Blooms: Spring

This low-lying daisy of our drier areas offers us a chance to talk about ray and disk flowers in composite flowers. At a glance, you might think those are whitish petals surrounding the golden middle of cushion fleabane. But they're actually more than a dozen ray flowers surrounding a whole bunch of tiny yellow disk flowers.

The ray and disk flowers each contain flower parts too small for us to see at a glance, but they're there. And that's why botanists cringe when we say of composites like this, "What a pretty flower!"—it's a little more complicated than that.

Look for: Diminutive daisy (3–6 in.) with narrow, hairy leaves only at the base. Flower stalks have single blooms, about 1 in. wide, with white, pink, or lavender ray flowers around yellow disk flowers.

Found: In dry, rocky sites where sagebrush grows. Chimney Rock, Horse Ridge, and Cove Palisades State Park are good places to look.

The ray flowers are usually pink to dark purple—here, more whitish. (Photo by Ron Halvorson)

Rosy Pussytoes *(Antennaria rosea)*

Blooms: All summer

Botanists appear to have a thing for cats, as the common names for some of our area wildflowers include cat's ears, pussypaws, and pussytoes. The clustered blooms of rosy pussytoes feature white to pinkish bracts surrounding white disk flowers (which resemble the pads on the underside of a cat's foot).

Most rosy pussytoes reproduce asexually, with the ovules maturing into seeds without being fertilized by pollen. The blooms you see are likely female clones that have spread by runners, or stolons.

Look for: Mats with multiple upright stems 3–16 in. tall and long, hairy, spatula-shaped leaves at the base. Flower heads have clusters of white disk flowers surrounded by pink bracts.

Found: Common and fairly widespread in a variety of habitats. You can find them at Horse Ridge, LaPine State Park, Shevlin Park, Tumalo State Park, and the Badlands Wilderness.

They're pretty, grow easily, and blooms last for months.

VIOLET TO BLUE OR BLUE-PURPLE FLOWERS
3 OR 6 PETALS

Blue-Flag Iris *(Iris missouriensis)*

Blooms: Late spring to midsummer

This is one of my favorite wildflowers because it's a quirky combination of showy, unusual, and lethal. Irises are, of course, gorgeous. And blue-flag irises (aka Rocky Mountain irises) spread by rootstalks, or rhizomes, so you'll typically see a number of them beautifying one small area. Look at the middle of the grouping, because as the population spreads, the central, older individuals die, leaving only the outer ring of plants.

As for the lethal part, the rootstalks contain a toxic material called irisin traditionally used by Plains Indians to poison arrowheads.

Look for: Small, dense populations, with upright, strap-like leaves. Stems 1–2 ft. tall, with two or four pale-blue to bluish-purple flowers on top, 1–3 in. wide. Deep-blue lines often radiate from the center of the petals.

Found: In meadows and seasonally moist areas across the region. Good places to look include the Deschutes River Trail and Sunriver's Great Meadow.

Look, smile, admire, but don't imbibe. (Photo by Susan Berger)

A long-stemmed Howell's triteleia.
(Photo by Ron Halvorson)

Triteleias *(Triteleia* spp.*)*

Blooms: Spring through summer

In Central Oregon you can easily find a couple *Triteleia* species: Howell's triteleia (*T. grandiflora*) and hyacinth tritileia (*T. hyacinthina*).

The story goes that hyacinths are named after a Greek youth who was accidentally killed by the god Apollo. The flowers are said to sprout from the blood of the boy, although technically they grow from corms, or bulbs.

Look for: Howell's triteleia has pale to deep-blue flowers on long stems, with a cup-like base. Hyacinth triteleia is found in wetter areas and has white or blue-tinted flowers that form a shallow bowl.

Found: In a variety of habitats across Central Oregon, including dry slopes in the Ochocos.

5 PETALS

Larkspurs *(Delphinium* spp.*)*

Blooms: Typically early summer

Larkspurs are among our most common and beautiful wildflowers. The giveaway for all larkspurs, including common varieties like upland larkspur (*D. nuttallianum*) and the meadow larkspur pictured (*D. distichum*), is the long tube, or spur, at the back of each bloom, which led to the common name.

Delphinium is Greek for "dolphin." To understand the reference, look at the top two flower buds in the photo at left. They really do resemble graceful dolphins.

Look for: Up to about 2 ft. tall, with many showy blue to purple blooms along erect stems. Tube-shaped spurs stick out the back of the blooms.

Found: All over Central Oregon, from streambanks to meadows and drier areas. You'll find them at Riley Ranch, Whychus Canyon Preserve, and the Metolius Preserve.

Long, thin spurs behind the flowers are the hallmark of larkspurs.
(Photo by Ron Halvorson)

Lupines *(Lupinus spp.)*

Blooms: Spring to summer

Lupines are so common across Central Oregon that trying *not* to see them would be an interesting challenge. They're notoriously difficult to differentiate, but a few of the most common species to look for are silvery lupine (*L. argenteus*), broadleaf lupine (*L. latifolius*), and dwarf lupine (*L. lepidus*).

The common name means "wolflike" or "ravenous," which refers to a mistaken belief that lupines steal nutrients from the soil. In reality, it's just the opposite: Our lovely lupines are valuable contributors to the soil, depositing nitrogen that provides nourishment for nearby vegetation.

Look for: Height varies, but the palmately divided leaves are distinctive (resembling the outstretched fingers of a hand). Flower spikes tend to taper at the top, with many blue to purplish blooms.

Found: All over the region, from high elevations to forests and urban environments. Look for them growing beside just about every area trail and all along Hwy. 97.

Flower spikes taper to a point, making it easy to identify them from a distance. (Photo by Ron Halvorson)

Western Blue Flax *(Linum lewisii)*

Blooms: Midspring to summer

Western blue flax is another of our more common wildflowers; in both urban and wild areas, you can't miss its pretty blue blooms sitting atop long stems.

This isn't the flax used to make flax oil, but it is the type many Native peoples use to make cordage for nets, snowshoes, baskets, and more. The cultivated common flax (*L. usitatissimum*) is the one used for flax oil and, since ancient times, to make linen cloth.

Look for: Tight clumps of slender stems (0.5–3 ft.) topped by blooms with five blue (occasionally white) petals streaked with purple. Look for yellow at the base of flowers.

Found: All over! Keep an eye out for the beautiful blue blooms in urban areas and along the Pilot Butte base trail and Deschutes River Trail.

The simple, exquisite beauty of blue flax. (Photo by Ron Halvorson)

Woolly-Pod Milkvetch (*Astragalus purshii*)

Blooms: All spring

You could easily walk right by this little wildflower without seeing it, even when its pretty pink-purple flowers are in bloom. But toward the end of spring, when those blooms turn into seedpods that look for all the world like inch-high cotton balls, they'll almost certainly catch your eye.

Milkvetches like this one are in the pea family. Their odd name comes from an ancient belief that goats feeding on the plants would produce more milk.

Look for: Low-growing perennial (2–6 in.). Stems and compound leaves are covered with a lot of silver or gray hair. Pea-shaped flowers are white, yellow, or purplish, with long tubes.

Found: In dry areas with juniper or sagebrush north and east of Bend, including the Badlands Wilderness and Chimney Rock.

Top: *Note the short, hairy leaves.*

Bottom: *A bounty of woolly pods.*
(Photos by Ron Halvorson)

5 PETALS FORMING TUBE

Bluebells (*Mertensia* spp.)

Blooms: Early spring to summer

Bluebells are one of the better-known and easily recognizable wildflowers, although there are many varieties that can be difficult to tell apart. All are beautiful, with nodding clusters of colorful flowers dangling from the ends of the stems.

Our common varieties include leafy bluebells or trumpet lungwort (*M. longiflora*), and sagebrush bluebells or prairie mertensia (*M. oblongifolia*).

Look for: Erect stems up to 1 ft. tall, topped by tight, nodding clusters of tubular flowers less than 1 in. long.

Found: Mainly in arid regions and ponderosa pine forests, although you might spot them in moister locations such as Todd Lake. Farther afield, look for them at Lookout Mountain, Big Summit Prairie, and Coffin Mountain.

Drooping clusters can have well over a dozen flowers. (Photo by Ron Halvorson)

Small-flowered Blue-eyed Mary
(Collinsia parviflora)

Blooms: Spring

The blue-eyed Mary is a beauty in miniature, with the blooms stretching to reach a quarter-inch wide.

You'll see the diminutive flowers each year around Easter, which suggests that the common name may refer to the Virgin Mary; whether that's the case or not, it's a handy way to remember this little wonder. Look closely to appreciate the gorgeous deep blue of the lower lobes.

Look for: 3–15 in. tall, with leaves that can be maroon or purplish on undersides. Tiny flowers have two white to pale-lavender upper lobes and three dark-blue lower lobes.

Found: All over open areas in the foothills, along the Deschutes River Trail, at the Badlands Wilderness, and at Indian Ford Campground.

Note the maroon tinge under the leaves. (Photo by Ron Halvorson)

Dirty Socks *(Eriogonum pyrolifolium)*

Blooms: All summer

This little plant goes by some other names, like alpine buckwheat and pyrola-leafed buckwheat. But the name you're not likely to forget is dirty socks—an appropriate moniker given the foul odor of sweaty, unwashed socks that emanates from the flowers. You can't blame the plant, though: The smell is a great way to attract flies and other pollinators.

Look for: Low-lying (2–5 in.) buckwheat with oval leaves at the base. Small, crowded flower clusters have white to greenish-white petals that fade to pink or red.

Found: On rocky slopes and sandy or pumice-covered areas—hike the South Sister or Tam McArthur Rim Trails in summer, and you'll smell those socks.

To confirm a buckwheat is dirty socks, give it a whiff. (Photo by brewbooks)

A gentian in late August near Three Creek Lake. (Photo by Charmane Powers)

Newberry's Gentian *(Gentiana newberryi)*

Blooms: Late Aug. to Sept.

The meadow on the north end of Todd Lake is a precious place filled with delicate species. Depending on the time of year, you'll find western toads and Pacific treefrogs hopping through, as well as loads of wildflowers, from buttercups to shooting stars. Late in the year, you'll also see Newberry's, or alpine, gentian, a sensitive species that should be treated as delicately as the meadow.

The hundreds of gentian species worldwide are used medicinally to treat urinary infections and stimulate digestion. Traditionally, gentians have also been used to treat headaches and defend against witchcraft, although a writer with the Forest Service notes, "More study is needed to determine if [gentian] has efficacy in warding off witches."

Look for: A low-lying plant with trumpet-shaped flowers. Between the five lobes, look for a pointy sinus appendage.

Found: In meadows and other moist areas at high elevation, including the meadow at Todd Lake and near Three Creek Lake. Stay on marked trails!

Yellow styles dangle from the bowl-shaped blooms. (Photo by Susan Berger)

Jacob's Ladder *(Polemonium spp.)*

Blooms: Summer

We have several varieties of very pretty and very blue Jacob's ladder, which grow in a variety of habitats. The "ladder" of the name refers to the leaflets, which have an orderly, ladder-like arrangement. In the Old Testament, Jacob's ladder is a ladder to heaven that Jacob sees in a dream.

Look for: Up to 3 ft. tall, with leaves divided pinnately into a lot of leaflets. They're in the phlox family and look similar, with blue petals surrounding a yellowish-white throat.

Found: In a variety of wetlands, forests, and rocky areas. *P. micranthum* is common all over Central Oregon in areas with sagebrush and junipers. Other varieties grow in moist, higher-elevation areas, including Todd Lake.

Meadow Forget-Me-Not (*I lackelia micrantha*)

Blooms: All summer

The common name of this much-loved plant is said to stem from one of several German legends. The general idea in each is that God names all the plants except one beautiful, lonely outlier that cries out, "Forget me not!"

Over the years, forget-me-nots like this one (we have several) have been used as a symbol of everything from marital fidelity to remembrance of those killed in war.

Look for: 1–3.5 ft. tall clumps with saucer-shaped blue flowers on widely spreading branches of the upper stem. Flowers have a white or yellowish eye and little raised folds in the center of the petals.

Found: In moist areas, often with quaking aspen. You can spot them along the Deschutes River Trail, including at First Street Rapids.

They're also called blue or Jessica stickseed after their prickly nutlets. (Photo by Susan Berger)

Davidson's Penstemon (*Penstemon davidsonii*)

Blooms: Midsummer

Ever feel like you've seen a lot of penstemons around? You probably have. Penstemons are the largest genus of flowering plants native solely to North America, and Oregon has the fifth-most native species of any state, with forty-six.

Davidson's is a mat-forming penstemon that often grows along rocky slopes where it provides a valuable service in stabilizing the soil.

Look for: Dense mat, 2–5 in. high, with leathery leaves and tube-like flowers that range in color from blue to purple.

Found: In rocky areas at high elevations, including along the Cascade Lakes Highway and at Lava Butte, Sparks Lake, Paulina Peak, and Tam McArthur Rim.

Top: The "tongue," or infertile stamen, is hairy.

Bottom: You'll often see Davidson's clinging to rocky slopes. (Photos by Dr. Stu Garrett)

Note the opposite leaves and blooms along the long stems. (Photo by Paul Slichter)

Lowly Penstemon (*Penstemon humilis*)

Blooms: Midsummer

This is one of our more common penstemons, and it shows off some of the typical penstemon characteristics. The leaves are opposite (that is, the leaf pairs are attached at a single node, not alternating up the stem). And although penstemon flowers come in all sorts of colors, this one's bright-blue to purple blooms are what many people envision when they think of penstemons.

Look for: Erect stems 4–10 in. tall, with spoon-shaped opposite leaves up to 3 in. long. Blooms appear along the stem and have very narrow tubes with nectar guides inside.

Found: All over the region, including in juniper woodlands and urban areas. Look for this and showy penstemon at Shevlin Park.

Showy Penstemon (*Penstemon speciosus*)

Blooms: Early summer

The showy, or royal, penstemon is a beautiful plant that stands tall and seemingly proud, displaying its gorgeous blue flowers for all to see.

Take a good look at the blooms and you'll see a common characteristic of penstemons: the long, straight, infertile stamen (staminode), often covered with hairs. The staminode's purpose might be to force pollinators to climb around it, spreading pollen. In any case, it's why penstemons are also called beardtongues.

Look for: Sturdy stems 6–30 in. tall, with leathery, blue-green leaves, including long-stalked leaves at the base. Flowers are a vivid blue with a white throat.

Found: All over dry, rocky sites, including at Black Butte, urban areas, and arid regions north and east of Bend.

Top: Look inside the blooms to spot the long staminode.

Bottom: Showy penstemons grow taller than lowly penstemons. (Photos by Ron Halvorson)

LOWLY OR SHOWY?

Showy penstemon is generally taller and, well, showier than the mat-forming lowly. Showy also has fewer leaves at the base and a lot of them along the stem (lowly only has a few leaf pairs on the stem).

Threadleaf Phacelia (*Phacelia linearis*)

Blooms: Spring to early summer

In wetter years, this plant will stand tall and show off an abundance of lavender to dark-blue blooms. In dry years, the plants are much smaller and unbranched, producing only a few pale and, let us say, sad little flowers. Either way, watch for these plants in spring, when the pretty blue or lavender flower buds appear.

Look for: Often in dense colonies with stems 3–20 in. tall and long, narrow leaves. Wide, bowl-shaped flowers are pale lavender to dark blue, with a paler center.

Found: In dry and frequently sandy sites, including the Badlands Wilderness, Chimney Rock, Pilot Butte, and Tumalo State Park.

Look for the narrow leaves and pale-centered flowers. (Photo by Ron Halvorson)

COMPOSITES

Asters (Various)

Blooms: Summer to early fall

There are so many types of asters I get a headache just thinking about it. The hundreds of species formerly in the *Aster* genus have now been divided into no fewer than eight genera.

The general features to look for in the many varieties of asters in Central Oregon are a star-like shape (*aster* means "star") and numerous ray flowers surrounding a prominent (often yellow) central disk.

Look for: Asters are similar in appearance to fleabanes, but asters tend to bloom later and have many bracts layered like shingles (fleabanes have fewer bracts).

Found: All over, especially in meadows and open woods.

Top: A typical aster with ray flowers around a central yellow disk. (Photo by Susan Berger)

Bottom: Look at the layered bracts behind the blooms to confirm it's an aster. (Photo by Paul Slichter)

Threadleaf Fleabane (*Erigeron filifolius*)

Blooms: Late spring to early summer

Threadleaf fleabane, or threadleaf daisy, is a pretty member of the enormous aster family, which also includes sunflowers. "Threadleaf" recognizes the extremely narrow leaves.

The variety *filifolius* has several flower heads per stem, while the variety *robustior* that's common east of the Cascades has only one flower head per stem. Note that "He loves me, he loves me not" will take a while with either, since each flower has up to seventy-five rays.

Look for: Clumps of daisies 8–40 in. tall, with erect, hairy stems. Ray flowers are blue, pink, or white, surrounding a yellow center.

Found: Very common in dry places, often in association with sagebrush, including at Tumalo State Park, the Badlands Wilderness, and Cove Palisades State Park.

BROWN OR GREEN FLOWERS
3 OR 6 PETALS

Checker Lily (*Fritillaria atropurpurea*)

Blooms: Midspring

If you're fortunate enough to spot a checker lily (aka spotted mission bells, chocolate lilies, purple fritillaria, and more), savor the sight of this increasingly uncommon plant and its unusual appearance.

The nodding blooms seem to be attempting camouflage with their distinctive brown, red, or purple mottling. If you're not sure you're looking at a checker lily, give the flower a good sniff—it has an odor only a fly could appreciate.

Look for: 1–3 ft. tall with narrow, alternate leaves. Nodding flowers have brown, red, or purple checkering on petals.

Found: Uncommon in cool, moist areas among shrubs and trees. Populations are dwindling, but you can search for them along the Metolius River and Deschutes River Trail.

Blue-eyed Mary. (Photo by Tracy Aue)

Beargrass and red columbine.
(Photo by M.A. Willson)

Golden bee plant. (Photo by M.A. Willson)

False Solomon's seal. (Photo by Evelyn Sherr)

WHY GARDEN WITH NATIVE WILDFLOWERS?

Look, I love tulips and daffodils and crocuses and dozens of other gorgeous, non-native plants and understand their appeal. But this chapter shows that there are plenty of native wildflowers that are just as colorful and generally far more beneficial to the environment. As the Forest Service points out, the benefits of adding native plants to your landscape include that they:

- Provide nectar, pollen, and seeds to feed native animals.
- Don't require as much (or any) fertilizer and pesticides.
- Need less water than lawns and help prevent erosion.
- Help reduce air pollution (no mowing needed).
- Provide shelter for wildlife.

California Quail. (Photo by Chuck Gates)

Female Red-winged Blackbird. (Photo by Sue Dougherty)

Cliff Swallow. (Photo by Chuck Gates)

Great Horned Owl. (Photo by Sue Dougherty)

BIRDS

Once you get to know the birds of Central Oregon, you'll never hike, bike, or kayak alone again. Now of course you were never alone to begin with, but it's only when you know what to look for and how to listen that birds can become an integral part of your outdoor experience.

The great thing about birds is that you can experience them in a way most other animals won't allow. Think about it: From beavers to bears, most wild animals want nothing to do with us; they hide, they growl, they slink into the shadows. But birds? They sing! They flash their colorful bodies! They court and hunt and build nests right in front of our eyes—even in our own backyards.

Bald Eagle with fish. (Photo by Rick Derevan)

House Finch. (Photo by Kim Elton)

Common Merganser. (Photo by Dave Rein)

By inviting our voyeurism, birds allow us to connect with them in unique ways. And since Oregon ranks high in bird diversity, with over 350 species living in or passing through Central Oregon, you can spend a lifetime building those connections.

So go ahead, listen for that first Red-winged Blackbird of spring. Feel your heart skip a beat when you spy a Great Horned Owl asleep on a branch. Marvel at the acrobatics of a swallow in summer.

Get to know the birds of Central Oregon, and I guarantee you'll spend more time looking up and smiling, even laughing, and you'll feel more connected and more joyful every time you go outside.

We may hear nothing but honk, but they have about thirteen calls. (Photo by John Williams)

WATERFOWL

Canada Goose *(Branta canadensis)*

Seen: Year-round

Canada Geese are the least popular Canadian export since Nickelback, but it wasn't always that way. When they neared extinction in the U.S. in the 1960s, an aggressive effort was launched to save what was then a beloved species. It worked, and today there are over 3.5 million Canada Geese across the U.S.—but it's not a straightforward success story.

The problem is that we've replaced much of our native lands with sod, which has led many lawn-loving Canada Geese to turn in their passports and stay in the U.S. year-round. Their droppings are considered such a nuisance that over a hundred of the geese were gassed to death in Bend in 2012. Thankfully the public spoke up and helped end that control method, but today we still spend thousands of dollars each year to haze, relocate, and otherwise reduce their populations.

Look for: Big birds with long black necks and white cheeks with a chinstrap. Similar Cackling Geese have shorter necks and smaller bills.

Found: In parks and on golf courses and sports fields. Hot spots: First Street Rapids, Sawyer Park, Drake Park, and Farewell Bend Park.

BIRDS OF A FEATHER

Some birds flock together and others—well, these are some of the funny and unusual names for their groupings:

- Cinnamon Teals: a seasoning
- Cormorants: a gulp
- Ducks: a raft (on water)
- Eagles: a convocation
- Hawks: a kettle (in flight)
- Jays: a scold
- Larks: an exaltation
- Owls: a parliament
- Ravens: an unkindness
- Sapsuckers: a slurp
- Starlings: a murmuration
- Woodpeckers: a descent

Wood Duck (*Aix sponsa*)

Seen: Year-round

There's nothing subtle about the most colorful ducks in North America. During the breeding season, male Wood Ducks look like they're wearing aerodynamic and iridescent helmets from the Tour de France.

As their name suggests, Wood Ducks are associated with timbered wetlands. In fact, they're one of the few ducks to perch and nest in trees, which creates an interesting challenge for their young. Less than two days after hatching, the tiny fluff balls have to make a giant leap for duckling kind, jumping (or falling) from their tree cavity or nest box to the ground, where Mom awaits to take them to food.

Look for: Males have red eyes and a crested head with multicolored plumage, including a white flare down the neck. Females are mostly dark gray with a whitish throat and white patches around the eyes.

Found: In park settings with large trees near the water. Hot spots: First Street Rapids, Sawyer Park, Drake Park, and Farewell Bend Park.

Top: *You could excuse males for reveling in their handsome reflections.*

Bottom: *Breeding females have yellow rings around their eyes. (Photos by John Williams)*

American Wigeon (*Anas americana*)

Seen: Year-round

Like Mallards, Cinnamon Teals, and many other ducks, American Wigeons are dabblers—sticking their bill in the water and their rear in the air to feed on underwater vegetation.

There is one big difference between wigeons and other dabblers: They have a shorter, sturdier bill that allows them to pluck vegetation right out of the ground. That's why you'll see wigeons in pastures and golf courses, grazing in a most un-duck-like way.

Look for: Medium-sized, short-billed ducks. Breeding males have a white forehead, iridescent-green face patch, and white shoulder patch on each wing. Females are mostly gray and brown.

Found: In and near golf courses and shallow ponds. Hot spots: Hatfield Lake, Tumalo Reservoir, and Drake Park.

Top: *Males have a green patch on their faces. (Photo by Kim Elton)*

Bottom: *Females have rustier-brown bodies. (Photo by John Williams)*

A handsome male, or drake. (Photo by Buddy Mays)

Mallard *(Anas platyrhynchos)*

Seen: Year-round

Mallards are the most abundant and widespread of all waterfowl. Head to Drake Park (named after a developer, not a male Mallard) or just about any other area waterway, and you'll see a combination of wild, domestic, and in-between Mallards.

The males are famously bad fathers, at least by human standards. They often mate with multiple females, sometimes drown females while trying to mate with them, and generally leave as soon as the eggs hatch. It's worth noting, however, that the gaudy plumage of the males could attract predators, so it may be better that they take off.

Look for: Males have a glossy green head with white ring around the neck, a yellow bill, and a pale body. Females are mostly speckled brown in color. Both sexes have white in the tail.

Found: In and along ponds and other areas with shallow water. Hot spots: Hatfield Lake, Drake Park, and Redmond Fireman's Pond.

FUN FACT

Female Mallards lay one egg a day for up to two weeks, but all dozen or so eggs hatch within hours. How is that possible? Researchers think that the mother and her young communicate with each other while the young are still in their eggs.

Males have glowing red eyes. Females have a dull-blue shoulder patch. (Photo by John Williams)

Cinnamon Teal *(Anas cyanoptera)*

Seen: Late March to late Sept.

Cinnamon Teals have been living in Oregon since at least the last Ice Age. They're graceful swimmers and low, swift flyers (reaching at least sixty miles per hour). They're also beautiful birds, with cinnamon-red bodies and light-blue wing patches that they show off in flight.

Look along the edges of area ponds in late spring and try to spot a group of the birds—also known as a seasoning of Cinnamon Teals. They're tough to identify from August on, so late March to the end of July is your best bet.

Look for: Small ducks. Males have a cinnamon head and body, red eyes, and a light-blue patch with a white border on the upper wings. Females are gray-brown with a white area at the base of the mostly black bill.

Found: In and near ponds with grassy sides. Hot spots: Hatfield Lake, Bend city parks near the Deschutes River, and Redmond Fireman's Pond.

Bufflehead *(Bucephala albeolu)*

Seen: Early Oct. to May (some year-round)

Buffleheads got their fabulous name from the archaic word *buffle*, meaning "buffalo." It's in reference to their big black-and-white head, which an imaginative or perhaps nearsighted person thought looked like the head of a buffalo.

Buffleheads are small enough to nest in old woodpecker holes—they especially like those made by flickers. They're also unusual among ducks in that they're mostly monogamous, returning to the same mate for at least several years.

Look for: Very small ducks with big, rounded heads. Males have a white body, black back, and big white patch around the back of the head. Females are gray-brown with a white cheek patch.

Found: In and near ponds and other slow-moving, shallow waters. Hot spots: First Street Rapids, Sawyer Park, Drake Park, and Farewell Bend Park.

Top: *The right light shows off a male's gorgeous purple-green head.*

Bottom: *In flight, look for white patches on the upperwings.* (Photos by John Williams)

Barrow's Goldeneye *(Bucephala islandica)*

Seen: Early Oct. to mid-April (some nest in summer at high elevations)

We're fortunate to have the uncommon Barrow's Goldeneye (named for the statesman Sir John Barrow), as well as Common Goldeneyes, although the latter are found here only during the colder half of the year.

As you'd expect, the "goldeneye" name refers to their boldly colored eyes. But the interesting thing is that those eyes change colors through the year, from gray-brown at hatching to purple-blue, blue, green-blue, and finally bright yellow in males and pale yellow in females.

Look for: Medium-sized ducks. Males have a purplish-black head with a white patch on the side; the rest of their body is black and white. Females have a chocolate-brown head and white flanks, belly, and breast.

Found: In and near rivers and ponds in winter (First Street Rapids, Sawyer Park, Drake Park) and at high mountain lakes in summer (Suttle and Scout Lakes, Wickiup and Crane Prairie Reservoirs).

Top: *Females are generally brownish and males black and white.*

Bottom: *The white cheek mark has a wheelbarrow shape.* (Photos by John Williams)

Hooded Merganser *(Lophodytes cucullatus)*

Seen: Early Oct. to May

As you might expect, these mergansers are not so common as Common Mergansers. But the birds are similar in that they are both "fish ducks" that dive underwater to catch fish in their serrated beaks.

When underwater, a transparent extra eyelid called a nictitating membrane protects their eyes, like a pair of goggles. On land, Hooded Mergansers are not nearly so comfortable. They have an awkward, chicken-like walk because their legs are set far back on their bodies.

Look for: Small ducks with thin bills and crested, oversized heads. Males are black above with a white breast, chestnut flanks, and large white patch on the head. Females are gray and brown with tawny-cinnamon tones on the head. Males have golden eyes; females dark eyes.

Top: A male shows off his black, white, chestnut, and gold colors.

Bottom: Females have fluffy brown crests. (Photos by John Williams)

Found: Along shorelines of rivers and ponds that have fish. Hot spots: First Street Rapids, Sawyer Park, Drake Park, and Farewell Bend Park.

FUN FACT

Hooded Mergansers often lay their eggs in nests belonging to other mergansers. A female will only lay about a dozen eggs but may find herself incubating more than forty.

Common Merganser *(Mergus merganser)*

Seen: Year-round

Most ducks eat plants and small invertebrates, but mergansers have slender bills with saw-like edges that enable them to grip and consume small fish. To pursue those fish, Common Mergansers can actually dive up to fifteen feet underwater (*merganser* means "plunging goose").

When you're near area rivers, keep an eye out for their underwater activities: A friend watched in amazement as a group of Common Mergansers swam like a school of fish under the bridge at First Street Rapids.

Look for: Large ducks with red bills. During breeding season, males have a creamy-white body with greenish-black head, and wings that are mostly white on the inner half and black on the outer half. As with most waterfowl, from July to October the sexes look alike—in this case, mostly gray with reddish-brown heads and white chins.

Top: A male in breeding season (note the red bill). (Photo by Tom Lawler)

Bottom: Females have shaggy hairdos. (Photo by Sue Dougherty)

Found: In and near most area rivers (where the fish are). Hot spots: First Street Rapids, Sawyer Park, Drake Park, and Farewell Bend Park.

QUAIL AND GROUSE

California Quail *(Callipepla californica)*

Seen: Year-round

California's state bird probably didn't arrive in Oregon until after 1900, when hundreds were brought in for hunters. Since their arrival, these adorable pot-bellied birds have made themselves at home in neighborhoods and rural areas that provide shrubs for cover. With their floppy topknot, Alfred Hitchcock profile, and oddly regal demeanor, quail are a favorite subject for area sculptors, painters, and photographers.

In spring and summer, you may find yourself waking as I do to the distinctive *chi-CA-go* call of California quail. If you're lucky, you'll also see a dozen or more little tennis balls following the parents willy-nilly from one shrub to the next, with a large, older male on a fence post or other perch watching for danger. Late in summer, the young and their parents join coveys of thirty to seventy.

Look for: Plump gray-and-brown birds scurrying along the ground, with topknots flapping.

Found: In neighborhoods across Bend, Redmond, and Alfalfa.

Top: *Males have a black throat with a white ring around it. (Photo by Kim Elton)*

Bottom: *Females have shorter topknots and less facial marking. (Photo by Chuck Gates)*

BIRDS OF A FEATHER

Use the Merlin Bird ID app to learn these common and beautiful birdsongs that will make your hikes more fun and entertaining:

- Barred Owl: *who cooks for you?*
- Black-headed Grosbeak: a long, sweet, flute-like song
- Canyon Wren: an unmistakable descending whistle
- California Quail: *chi-CA-go, chi-CA-go*
- Hermit Thrush: *oh, holy holy, ah, purity purity eeh, sweetly sweetly*
- Olive-sided Flycatcher: *quick, three beers!*
- Red-breasted Nuthatch: *yank, yank, yank*
- Western Meadowlark: piercing whistles followed by gurgled warbles

Top: *Males inflate those yellow air sacs, emitting a loud popping sound to attract the ladies. (Photo by Kevin Smith)*

Middle: *Their low, fast flights in poor light lead many to fly into barbed-wire fences. (Photo by Kevin Smith)*

Bottom: *A male strutting his stuff at dawn. (Photo by Alan St. John)*

Greater Sage-Grouse
(Centrocercus urophasianus)

Seen: Year-round

Just about every article I've read about sage-grouse compares them to chickens—chicken-sized, look like chickens, chicken-like. No offense to domesticated chickens, but sage-grouse are wild animals that can fly up to sixty miles per hour and have been gracing our wild areas for forty million years. Unlike your average Cornish cross, sage-grouse are also an indicator of environmental health, reflecting the condition of about 350 other species, from pronghorn to sage sparrows.

A better comparison might be to say that sage-grouse are like footballs: Females are about that size, and these days the whole species is bandied about like a political football. That's because they rely on large swaths of the sagebrush steppe for food, cover, and nesting—and that territory is being gobbled up and destroyed by urbanization, energy development, grazing, climate change, takeover by non-native vegetation, and other threats.

Your best bet to see sage-grouse is to join an organized field trip to an area lek (breeding ground) in April or May, when you can watch the male "boomers" conduct their flamboyant mating displays. It's one of the most spectacular, and increasingly rare, bird-watching experiences in Central Oregon.

Look for: Males are mostly gray-brown with a black head and throat. During spring displays, the white ruff on the breast surrounds two bright-yellow air sacs. Females are gray-brown with white markings behind the eyes.

Found: Specific lek sites in the sagebrush steppe are not publicized to protect this sensitive species.

HERONS

Great Blue Heron (*Ardea herodias*)

Seen: Year-round

The Great Blue Heron is the official bird of Portland, with hundreds nesting within five miles of the downtown area. They're also common in Central Oregon (though not that common) and frequently seen or heard clambering into the air near area waterways.

Great blues spend hours and hours standing stock-still at the edges of water or fields as they hunt fish, snakes, rodents, and anything else that fails to notice them. It's an impressive disappearing act given that they are our second-tallest bird, behind Sandhill Cranes.

Look for: They're up to 4 ft. tall, mostly gray-white, and fly with an S-curved neck.

Found: Near water in summer and agricultural fields in winter. Hot spots: Wickiup Reservoir, Sunriver, and Alfalfa.

Great blues stand up to four feet high but weigh less than six pounds. (Photo by Tom Lawler)

DIURNAL RAPTORS

Turkey Vulture (*Cathartes aura*)

Seen: Mid-March to mid-Oct.

Turkey Vultures are very cool birds. They are also a "disgusting bird," as Charles Darwin so delicately put it. They eat cadavers; defecate on their feet to cool them off and kill bacteria; and when disturbed or harassed, they vomit on their attackers, which is thought to reduce their body weight so they can fly off faster.

So, yes, disgusting. But the birds Ursula K. Le Guin called "quiet lords of the warm towers of the air" are also nature's cleanser. When their populations drop, the number of rotting carcasses rises and diseases like rabies proliferate.

One more cool fact about vultures: Have you ever wondered why they eat carcasses in the middle of the road? Seems dumb, right? It's because their feet

These handsome devils have bald heads because carrion would stick to feathers. (Photo by Kim Elton)

are weak and not designed to carry objects, so they have to eat food where they find it. Vultures can't carry nesting material either, so they lay their eggs on the ground or in crevices.

Look for: A large, dark bird with a featherless red head and wings ending in long "fingers." In flight, wings form a "V" and the birds teeter from side to side.

Found: In open country north and east of Bend. Hot spots: Hatfield Lake, Alfalfa, and Hwy. 20 east of Bend.

> "Let us praise the noble turkey vulture: No one envies him; he harms nobody; and he contemplates our little world from a most serene and noble height." —Edward Abbey

Their name comes from the Latin ossifragus ("bone-breaker"). (Photo by Chuck Gates)

Osprey *(Pandion haliaetus)*

Seen: Early April to mid-Oct.

Like many wealthy folks in Bend, Osprey covet large homes with a commanding view of the water. Along the Deschutes River Trail, you'll see their big nests (up to seven feet tall) high up on dead standing trees, or snags. When Osprey return in April from their thousand-mile migrations, you'll also see them at area reservoirs like Crane Prairie, where snags and ranger-erected poles provide ideal perches.

Osprey are also called fish eagles or fish hawks, and indeed it's fish they're after as they patrol above the water. They'll dive up to a foot deep to catch their prey, then fly back to their nests with the fish facing headfirst to minimize wind drag.

Look for: A large bird with a dark strip along the eyes and down the side of the face. White underbellies are distinctive, and wings have a unique crook when in flight.

Found: Hot spots include Hatfield Lake, Crane Prairie Reservoir, and Tumalo Reservoir. Look for nests atop trees and poles at the Old Mill, beside area highways, and along rivers.

Bald Eagle *(Haliaeetus leucocephalus)*

Seen: Year-round

You probably know the oft-told story of our national symbol: Bald Eagles nearly went extinct in the 1970s due to hunting and pesticide poisoning, but a massive recovery effort restored populations to stable levels.

And, yes, as is often mentioned, the emblem of our great nation does steal food (often from Ospreys) and scavenge garbage and carcasses. But, hey, those big bodies and massive wings—their wingspan is up to eight feet—are heavy, and if baldies had to expend energy catching all their prey, they might not survive.

Bald Eagles and their big nests are a fairly common site in Central Oregon. The "bald" heads (actually covered in white feathers) don't emerge until the eagles are about five years old—which gives you a sense of their longevity. In the wild, they have been known to live up to twenty-eight years.

The white head indicates this eagle is at least five years old. (Photo by Buddy Mays)

Look for: A very big bird with a big head. Adults have white heads and tails with dark-brown bodies and wings. Legs and bills are bright yellow.

Found: At high mountain lakes in summer and open farmland and rivers in winter. Hot spots: Crane Prairie Reservoir, Wickiup Reservoir, Alfalfa, and Hwy. 20 east of Bend.

Sharp-shinned Hawk *(Accipiter striatus)*

Seen: March to mid-Oct. (some in winter)

Sharp-shinned Hawks are the smallest hawks in North America, and for good reason: They require speed and agility, not great size, to track down and kill their main prey of small birds. Their long tails and short wings are exactly what they need to maneuver through trees or dart through the air to kill a songbird as it leaves your feeder.

Sharpies look a lot like Cooper's Hawks; it's a sign that you're a good birder if you can tell them apart. Some tips: Sharpies have smaller heads that don't protrude past their wings in flight, and they usually have a square-tipped tail, not rounded like that of a Cooper's Hawk.

Look for: Nearly identical to a Cooper's Hawk, with a dark-gray back and wings, and reddish-orange barring on the breast. Kestrels are smaller, but they're not true hawks.

Found: Wherever there are trees for nesting and small birds to eat. Hot spots: Green Ridge, city feeders in winter, and Calliope Crossing.

Note the small head and squared-off tail. (Photo by Kris Kristovich)

Cooper's Hawk *(Accipiter cooprii)*

Seen: April through Oct. (some all year)

Nature has its own ways of controlling bird populations, and one of them is the remarkably fast and agile Cooper's Hawk. These crow-sized bird ambushers are small enough to tear through cluttered forests in pursuit of their prey, and big enough to take down medium-sized birds like doves, jays, and robins.

Cooper's Hawks kill their prey not by biting but by squeezing them to death with their talons. They've also been known to drown prey. So, no, there probably won't be any children's books written about Cooper's Hawks, but they are phenomenal at what they do.

Male Cooper's Hawks are usually submissive to females. The males build the nest and provide nearly all the food to the female and their young for about three months, until the young fledge.

Look for: A crow-sized bird with rounded wings, long and rounded tail, and long yellow legs. They flap their wings slowly a few times, then glide. Sharp-shinned Hawks are smaller and far more common in Central Oregon.

They have a rounder tail and bigger, blockier heads than Sharp-shinned Hawks. (Photo by Kim Elton)

Found: Mostly in forests but will stay near urban birdfeeders and along songbird migration areas. Hot spots: Green Ridge, Black Butte, and Lava Butte.

Red-tailed Hawk *(Buteo jamaicensis)*

Seen: Year-round

Red-tailed Hawks are the most common raptors in Central Oregon, seemingly mass-produced for our viewing pleasure on every utility pole between Sunriver and Madras. They're also believed to be the most common hawk on the continent, relying not on forests but on agricultural fields and other open areas that offer up squirrels, rats, pigeons, and other small delicacies.

This hawk's *kee-eeeee-arr* scream is the sound most people associate with hawks. You might hear that call during their "sky dance" in spring, when the male performs a series of roller-coaster dives and climbs, before approaching the female from above and briefly touching or grasping her with his talons. Sometimes the pairs then clasp each other's beaks or talons and spiral toward the ground before letting go.

Look for: If you see a raptor, it's probably this one. When they're perched, look for a dark band of feathers across the belly and white shoulder streaks. When they're soaring, look for the dark leading edge of the wings (most adults also have reddish tails).

Top: Note the dark band across the belly. (Photo by Kim Elton)

Bottom: Note the broad wings with dark shoulders. (Photo by Spondylolithesis)

Found: All over open country, especially north and east of Bend. Hot spots: Hatfield Lake, Alfalfa, and Hwy. 20 east of Bend.

FUN FACT

How much do Red-tailed Hawks weigh? Given their length (18–22 in.) and wingspan (45–52 in.), would you guess ten pounds? Five? In fact, even the largest females weigh only about three pounds.

Rough-legged Hawk *(Buteo lagopus)*

Seen: Nov. to early April (uncommon)

Take a drive in winter along Hwy. 20 east of Bend, and you might spot these visitors from the Arctic tundra, which are sometimes perched on utility poles or soaring (or hovering) above fields.

The "rough legs" of the Rough-legged Hawk are thanks to an abundance of white feathers that provide warmth in frigid weather. The only other raptors with similar leg warmers are the Ferruginous Hawk and Golden Eagle.

Look for: A large hawk with long wings. Plumage varies, but it's mostly light in color, with a dark belly and dark wrist patches.

Found: In open country east of Bend. Hot spots: Alfalfa, Hatfield Lake, and Hwy. 20 east of Bend.

The white-feathered legs give this large hawk its name. (Photo by Kevin Smith)

Golden Eagle *(Aquila chrysaetos)*

Seen: Year-round

You think a Bald Eagle is tough? Please. Golden Eagles are America's largest birds of prey, able to dive at speeds up to 150 miles per hour and seize prey with talons that dwarf those of the Bald Eagle. Jackrabbits are their staple food, but these so-called lords of the sagebrush sky have been known to take down young bighorn sheep, pronghorn, coyotes, bobcats, and deer. Because, you know, they can.

Most of the Golden Eagles in North American live in the high desert that includes Central Oregon. At least for now, this is where they can find the isolated nesting sites (often on cliffs) and abundant populations of ground squirrels and black-tailed jackrabbits that their lives depend upon.

Look for: The largest bird around. Mostly dark brown, with golden feathers at the back of the head and neck. In flight, look for a huge, dark bird gliding with broad wings, "fingers" spread at the end of the wings, and a rounded tail.

Found: In desert-like areas with jackrabbits; they often nest in canyons. Hot spots: Powell Butte, Fort Rock, and Alfalfa.

Top: *They're dark brown overall, with a golden nape. (Photo by Gerald Corsi)*

Bottom: *Wingspans can extend more than seven feet. (Photo by Tom Lawler)*

> **"Eagles were given the gift of far sight, so it is their duty to watch over us. . . . What is the duty of humans? . . . It is said that only humans have the capacity for gratitude. This is among our gifts."**
> **—Robin Wall Kimmerer,** *Braiding Sweetgrass*

Top: *Kestrels are one of the real beauties of the raptor world.* (Photo by Jon Nelson)

Bottom: *They have long, square-tipped tails.* (Photo by Tom Lawler)

American Kestrel *(Falco sparverius)*

Seen: Year-round

There are many reasons to appreciate and even cheer for the American Kestrel. First, it's North America's smallest falcon, about the size of a mourning dove. As such, it's preyed upon by a lot of bigger birds like Red-tailed Hawks, Barn Owls, Sharp-shinned and Cooper's Hawks, and even crows. Who doesn't love an underdog?

Kestrels are also one of the most colorful raptors around, and their populations have been declining just about everywhere—two more reasons for your heart to leap whenever you see one hunting for insects or hovering above a field in search of mice, voles, and other small prey.

Look for: Adult males have blue-gray wings and a reddish-orange back. Females have tan wings with black markings. Look for the vertical black stripe on their faces. In flight, look for pale undersides and pointed, swept-back wings.

Found: In open country north and east of Bend. Hot spots: Hatfield Lake, Alfalfa, and Hwy. 20 east of Bend.

DID YOU KNOW?

Kestrels can see ultraviolet light, so they track rodents by following their fluorescent trails of urine. When they catch a surplus of rodents or other prey, they think ahead—storing their kills in bushes and other hiding spots to provide a food source for lean times.

Peregrine Falcon *(Falco peregrinus)*

Seen: May to June and mid-Aug. to mid-Sept.

How can we not stand in awe of the sheer athleticism of the Peregrine Falcon? They're the fastest birds in the world, and the most skilled of all flyers. As they cruise through the sky at about thirty miles per hour, they scan for prey using eyesight that's eight times better than ours and twice as strong as that of the Golden Eagle. (When soaring at 3,500 feet, peregrines can spot a pigeon five miles away.)

Peregrines were among the first birds to reveal the horrors of DDT, which led them to the brink of extinction. DDT was banned in 1972, but even as of 1979 there was just one pair of breeding peregrines in Oregon.

Peregrines are still uncommon in Central Oregon, but thanks to a cooperative effort by government agencies, nonprofits, birders, and others, it's at least possible to see them speeding through the area now and then.

Top: *Peregrines often feed on ducks and shorebirds.*

Bottom: *Note the long, pointy wings and barred underparts. (Photos by John Williams)*

Look for: The dark head and facial feathers resemble a helmet, with a contrasting white neck and breast. Also look for dark barring on the lower breast and a slate-gray back.

Found: Near shallow lakes and shorelines. Hot spots: Hatfield Lake, Tumalo Reservoir, and Green Ridge.

WHY ARE FEMALE RAPTORS BIGGER THAN MALES?

Most female raptors, including Peregrine Falcons, are larger than males. Why is that? Possible explanations include:

- So they can hunt separate prey (for instance, female peregrines pursue waterfowl and other larger birds, while males hunt smaller birds like songbirds).

- Copulation requires the male to rest at least briefly on the female—larger female bodies simplify that task.

- Larger females may be more effective at protecting young in the nest.

Top: *Note the dark armpits contrasting with the otherwise whitish undersides. (Photo by Kevin Smith)*

Bottom: *The mustache is distinctive. (Photo by Tom Lawler)*

Prairie Falcon (*Falco mexicanus*)

Seen: Year-round

While walking in Crack in the Ground, I looked up at a cliff wall and found I was being hunted by a Prairie Falcon. Or, okay, not hunted (they prefer squirrels and medium-sized birds), but certainly watched closely by the large falcon. It wasn't a good feeling—not because I was nervous but because I was trespassing on the falcon's territory.

Like Golden Eagles, Prairie Falcons live and nest in our rocky canyons and cliffs. They're uncommon in Central Oregon, and their sensitivity to our presence is why places like Cline Buttes Recreation Area and Dry River Canyon are closed to humans for several months each year.

Look for: A large falcon with a sandy-brown back and whitish, streaked underside. Its face has a white eyebrow stripe and brown mustache mark. In flight, look for a long tail, pointed wings, rapid wing beats, and dark armpit patches.

Found: In open country east of Bend. Hot spots: Alfalfa, Hatfield Lake, Hwy. 20 east of Bend, and Smith Rock State Park.

SHOREBIRDS

Killdeer (*Charadrius vociferus*)

Seen: All year except winter

Killdeer are quirky little birds—shorebirds that live in our arid climate. They're most famous for their broken-wing display, an act they put on to draw predators away from their nests. But that's not their only theatrical performance.

Giraffe legs, teeny head, long tail. There's no mistaking a Killdeer. (Photo by John Williams)

Killdeer will also rush over to fake nests to lure predators away from the real thing. And if large animals like cows or deer walk toward their nests, they've been known to scream, raise their tail, and charge the beasts. In fact, a writer in the 1800s recalled seeing a Killdeer successfully use that display to part a stampeding herd of bison.

Killdeer are common in Central Oregon, but their overall populations are declining. As their *vociferus* name suggests, those that remain are not shy about letting you know they're around. Chicks start peeping before they hatch, and they seemingly never stop; you can hear their loud, piercing *kill-dee* and *dee-dee-dee* calls day and night near area ponds.

Look for: A medium-sized bird with black breast bands, a red eye ring, and a brown head with white forehead and eyebrow stripe. In flight, look for long white stripes on their wings and a reddish-orange rump.

Found: Near slow-moving rivers and ponds with gravel. Hot spots: Hatfield Lake, any farm pond east of Bend, and Fireman's Pond in Redmond.

DOVES

Mourning Dove *(Zenaida macroura)*

Seen: Year-round

Just because a bird is seemingly everywhere doesn't mean it's not worth noticing. Mourning Doves are common across the continent—you've no doubt heard their sweet, owl-like lament (*coo-ah, coo, coo, coo*) and the unique whistling noise when they take off.

By human standards, these doves are wonderful family birds that are monogamous, share chores, and take turns incubating (males get the day shift). Heck, both parents even produce the crop milk they feed to their young.

Local birders say they're seeing fewer of our native Mourning Doves and more non-native Eurasian Collared-Doves—that's a trend worth watching. Mourning Doves are the most hunted species on the continent and many also die from consuming lead shot on the ground, which is another reason for hunters to use non-lead shot.

Note the dark spots on the wings and side of the head. (Photo by Tom Lawler)

Look for: A dove with a wee head atop a plump body. They're smaller than collared-doves with spots on the side of the brown neck, black spots on brown wings, and a long tail that tapers to a point.

Found: In open countryside, burned forests, and urban areas. Hot spots: Hatfield Lake, urban neighborhoods, and Crooked River National Grassland.

GREAT FINDS

Put these birds on your Central Oregon bucket list. They're relatively easy to find here but tough to spot in most other areas of the state:

- American Dipper
- Barrow's Goldeneye
- Calliope Hummingbird
- Mountain Bluebird
- Northern Pygmy-Owl
- Pinyon Jay
- Pygmy Nuthatch
- White-headed Woodpecker

Top: *A juvenile. (Photo by Susan Berger)*

Bottom: *An adult. (Photo by John Williams)*

OWLS

Great Horned Owl *(Bubo virginianus)*

Seen: Year-round

If you've seen an owl in Central Oregon, it was probably the Great Horned Owl. They're found nearly everywhere east of the Cascades, from forests to open country, and have the quintessential owl look and deep-throated *who-hoo-hoo-oo* call.

Appropriately nicknamed the "feathered tiger," Great Horned Owls are among the world's fiercest birds. Their specially designed talons allow them to take down not only small prey but also larger animals like jackrabbits, herons, and skunks. One researcher even found a deer leg in a Great Horned Owl nest.

On the softer side, these owls are tender caregivers and deeply protective of their mates and young. Local naturalist Jim Anderson wrote of a Great Horned Owl mother covering her owlets to shield them from two hungry ravens. When one raven hopped onto her back and pecked at her head, Jim wrote that the owl's mate swooped in "like an F-16" and slammed into the raven, eventually killing it to save his young.

Look for: A big, thick-bodied owl with two big tufts on the head (they're feathers, not horns or ears). They're a mottled gray-brown color overall with reddish-brown faces.

Found: In just about every habitat. Hot spots: Hatfield Lake, south end of 15th St. in Bend, and Sunriver Nature Center.

Northern Pygmy-Owl *(Glaucidium gnoma)*

Seen: Year-round

You can learn a lot by paying attention to what the birds around you are doing. If your summer hike takes you into an area forest and you hear a noisy commotion, it just might be a mob of jays, warblers, or other birds attacking a small but mighty Northern Pygmy-Owl.

The owls are diurnal, meaning they hunt during the day, and songbirds are among their favorite targets. Although not much bigger than a House Sparrow, a Northern Pygmy-Owl can take down prey up to three times its size, including woodpeckers and domestic chickens.

They're one-third the size of a Great Horned Owl. (Photo by Sue Dougherty)

Look for: A very small owl (6–7 in.) without ear tufts. Usually grayish-brown with striking yellow eyes and dark "eyespots" on the back of the head (to fool predators).

Found: Uncommon but widespread across mid-level forested areas in summer and lower elevations (even juniper woodlands) in winter. Hot spots: Cold Springs Campground, Wickiup Reservoir, the Ochocos, and Forest Service Rd. 11.

Northern Spotted Owl *(Strix occidentalis)*

Seen: Extremely rare

I'm pretty sure this is the only bird in Central Oregon that has graced the cover of *Time* magazine. Since the 1980s, these owls have been the poster-child for the ongoing debate about what to do with the Northwest's remaining old-growth forests.

Spotted owls depend on the dense canopy of old-growth forests as shelter from the cold and to protect their young, which lack flight feathers for their first summer. Count yourself fortunate if you see or hear these owls, and work to preserve our remaining old-growth forests to give the same opportunity to future generations.

Look for: A big owl, mostly brown, with dark eyes and creamy-white mottling on the breast and abdomen.

Found: In old-growth forests.

Where Northern Spotted Owls have spots, Barred Owls generally have vertical streaks. (Photo by Tom Lawler)

Barred Owl *(Strix varia)*

Seen: Rare in all seasons

Barred Owl populations were once limited to the eastern U.S., but their numbers are rising in the Pacific Northwest and south into California. That's bad news for spotted owls because their larger cousins are more aggressive, eat a more varied diet, and nest in more varied habitats (not just old-growth forests).

Barred Owls, which have a distinctive *who cooks for you?* call, are for now a rare find in Central Oregon, but the one spotted in the Old Mill District in 2013 may be a harbinger of things to come.

Look for: A grayish-brown owl with no ear tufts, distinctive horizontal bars across the throat and upper breast, and vertical brown streaks on the lower breast and abdomen.

Found: Mostly in forested areas. No known hot spots in Central Oregon.

Compared to spotted owls, Barred Owls have lighter heads and faces. (Photo by Kris Kristovich)

> "Sometimes owls came near to warn of death. Sometimes they just asked people to be careful. Sometimes they were just owls."
> —Louise Erdrich, *The Night Watchman*

A six-pack of saw-whets. (Photo by Dick Tipton)

Northern Saw-Whet Owl *(Aegolius acadicus)*

Seen: Spring and summer (a few roost in canyons in winter)

We are fortunate to have a relative abundance of Northern Saw-Whet Owls—not that you're likely to see them. These little owls with big heads are highly nocturnal and rarely spotted, although you might get lucky and hear their *too-too-too* call in area forests.

The saw-whet's unusual name apparently comes from early settlers who thought one of the bird's several calls sounded like a saw being sharpened on a whetting stone (not exactly a common sound these days).

Look for: A very small owl with a big, rounded head and catlike face. Facial disc is pale; rest of body is largely brown, with some white spots. Note that they don't hoot—they toot.

Found: Mostly in forests but all over during migration. Hot spots: Any forested area, such as near Tumalo Falls and Virginia Meissner Sno-Park.

HOW TO HELP NATIVE BIRDS

Want to make sure future generations can enjoy the 350 or so bird species in Central Oregon? Local birding expert Chuck Gates has these suggestions:

- Join a local bird club.
- Plant native, bird-friendly plants in your yard or garden.
- Learn to recognize common local birds.
- Find out where local politicians stand on conservation and wildlife issues, and use your vote wisely.
- Contribute time and/or money to local and national birding organizations.
- Be a mentor and role model to young people, introducing them to birds and other aspects of nature.

Common Nighthawk *(Chordeiles minor)*

Seen: Early June to mid-Sept.

Common Nighthawks are entertaining birds with a misleading name (they're becoming less common, can be seen during the day, and aren't hawks). Go kayaking on the Deschutes River or one of the Cascade Lakes on a summer morning or early evening to hear their sharp *peent* call and see them patrolling the skies above in their endless quest for insects.

Nighthawks migrate farther than just about any other bird on the continent, arriving here in June from as far south as Buenos Aires. On a warm evening soon after their arrival, you might get lucky and catch one of their dramatic flight displays. Males will dive fast for the ground, peeling up at the last moment and flexing their wings downward, creating a whooshing sound like a train whistle.

Look for: A medium-sized bird with long, pointed wings. In flight, look for the white bar near the tip of each wing. They fly like swallows, but they're bigger and flap their wings more slowly.

Found: Often spotted eating insects above waterways in early evening or morning. Hot spots: Skyliners Rd. at Forest Rd. 430, the Deschutes River, Hatfield Lake, and Tumalo Reservoir.

Top: *That itty-bitty beak becomes a gaping mouth for catching insects on the fly. (Photo by Kevin Smith)*

Bottom: *Look for the white bar on each wing. (Photo by Tom Lawler)*

DID YOU KNOW?

Nighthawk populations are declining because of habitat loss and pesticide use that kill the insects they depend on. You can watch them flying erratically above waterways as they try to get their fill.

Vaux's Swift *(Chaetura vauxi)*

Seen: Mid-April to late Sept.

One of the best birding shows in Bend takes place every September, when up to thousands of these swifts swirl around and around in the evening sky, before spiraling in a dramatic rush into area chimneys. The chimneys are a stand-in for the dead standing trees, or snags, that were the swifts' traditional nesting places.

Vaux's Swifts are unusual in that they have weak legs and feet so they can't perch on branches. That's why they fly into chimneys and hollow snags, where they can hook their toenails into cracks and hang overnight like upright bats.

They're shaped like boomerangs. (Photo by Kevin Smith)

Look for: The smallest swift in North America is dark gray-brown overall, with long, pointed wings and stiff wing beats.

Found: They roost in Bend chimneys in spring and fall; in summer, they nest in snapped-off trees in area forests. Usually the best place to see them is the Bend Boys & Girls Club, with peak numbers in mid-September.

Top: Male heads have iridescent, reddish-pink feathers. (Photo by Kris Kristovich)

Bottom: Females have a small patch of pink on their throats. (Photo by Chuck Gates)

HUMMINGBIRDS

Anna's Hummingbird (*Calypte anna*)

Seen: All year (fewer in winter)

These are the "big" hummingbirds in our region, a relative term given that they're smaller than a Ping-Pong ball and weigh less than two pennies. They're also the only hummingbird that toughs it out year-round in Central Oregon—or at least a few do. Their nesting begins in late January or February, with females sometimes snowed on while incubating their eggs.

It's often emphasized that hummingbirds are highly territorial, and indeed they are. Wouldn't you be if your daily survival depended on consuming nectar from up to 2,000 flowers? Anna's Hummingbirds will battle for their territories with others, and females have also been known to defend their nests against jays and even hawks.

Look for: A big hummingbird with a green body and light-colored belly. Males have a fuchsia helmet; females have a spot of the same color on their throat. Their heads aren't green like Calliope Hummingbirds and their bodies aren't reddish like Rufous Hummingbirds.

Found: At urban feeders and wildflower areas. Hot spots: Shevlin Park and the Awbrey Hall burn area.

Calliope Hummingbird (*Stellula calliope*)

Seen: Late April to late Sept.

Calliope Hummingbirds, which weigh less than a stick of gum, are the smallest birds in North America. And the incredible thing is that these tiny birds fly several thousand miles twice a year, from Central America to Central Oregon and back again.

The courting display of our relatively mild-mannered Calliope Hummingbird is also remarkable. A male will perform aerial acrobatics to attract a female, then hover in front of her while issuing a high-pitched buzz. If she's game, they'll fly off and spin in aerial circles, sometimes with bills joined.

Look for: A tiny hummingbird with green upperparts. Male throats are streaked red and white. The female has a whitish or cinnamon-buff chest and belly.

Found: At urban feeders and wildflower areas, including high in the mountains. Hot spots: Shevlin Park and Calliope Crossing.

Top: Note the green upperparts. (Photo by Kris Kristovich)

Bottom: Females have whitish undersides. (Photo by Tom Lawler)

Rufous Hummingbird (*Selasphorus rufus*)

Seen: Late April to early Oct.

To recap: Anna's Hummingbirds are the biggest you'll see, and Calliope Hummingbirds the smallest. The former are aggressive; the latter far less so. Now, meet the Rufous Hummingbird: the feistiest on the continent, and also the most common. These noisy birds buzz, chatter, and chip and will aggressively take over other territories and defend their own.

Rufous Hummingbirds migrate even farther than Calliope Hummingbirds, from Mexico to as far north as Alaska. And they know where they're going: They will return to the same exact spot (such as a feeder in your yard) year after year.

Remarkably, once they arrive in spring, males still have the energy to engage in dramatic courtship displays where they soar hundreds of feet into the sky and zoom down toward females, again and again, to prove their health and vigor.

Look for: *Rufous* (meaning reddish-brown) is the key word: Males have an iridescent red throat and bright orange on the back and belly. Females have reddish flanks and often an orange spot on the throat.

Found: At urban feeders and mountain meadows. Hot spots: Along the Deschutes River and at Crane Prairie Reservoir and Big Summit Prairie.

Top: *That deep-orange area around the throat is called a gorget.* (Photo by John Williams)

Bottom: *Females have greenish-gold heads and backs.* (Photo by Kim Elton)

HOW TO HELP HUMMINGBIRDS

- Grow native flowering plants that bloom from early spring through fall.

- Avoid pesticides (hummingbirds depend on insects and spiders for food).

- Provide a water source in your yard.

- Hang nectar feeders (get details online or at Wild Birds Unlimited).

A female caught mid-gulp. (Photo by Rick Derevan)

KINGFISHERS

Belted Kingfisher *(Megaceryle alcyon)*

Seen: Year-round (scarce in harsh winters)

Belted Kingfishers are popular and distinctive birds, always dressed for a night on the town with their flashy blue suits and spiky pompadours. To see a kingfisher for yourself, sit for a spell along the Deschutes River or just about any other area waterway. You might spy one perched on a bare branch above the water or hear their distinctive rattle as they defend their territory and patrol for fish and other prey.

When a kingfisher spots a small fish in the water, it will take your breath away with its sudden dive. If it snags the fish in its bill, it will fly to a perch, and—there's no gentle way to say this—bash the fish to death against the branch, before swallowing it headfirst.

Look for: A big-headed bird with a shaggy crest and long, thick bill. The back and wings are powder blue and the chest is white with a blue band. Females are actually more colorful than males, with an additional reddish-brown band across the lower chest.

Found: Where the fish are. Hot spots: First Street Rapids, Sawyer Park, and Farewell Bend Park.

WOODPECKER WONDERLAND

Central Oregon has one of the highest densities of woodpecker species in the world, thanks to our ancient ponderosa pines, aspen groves, and post-wildfire sites that attract tasty beetles. Thirteen species have been recorded in Central Oregon, ten of which nest here every year.

Lewis's Woodpecker *(Melanerpes lewis)*

Seen: Late April to early Oct.

These are very odd woodpeckers. They don't excavate their own nest holes, preferring to move into those of other woodpeckers. From the back, they look like crows. And they catch insects on the wing, which is more like a swallow than a typical woodpecker.

As snags fall or are salvaged, fewer natural homes are left for Lewis's Woodpeckers. That's one reason their populations have been declining since the 1960s. In Shevlin Park, you can see these birds nesting near the top of snags (standing dead trees) and in volunteer-provided nest boxes.

They have a gray collar and reddish breast and face. (Photo by Tom Lawler)

Look for: A woodpecker with a red face, pink belly, gray nape that looks like a necklace, and dark wings and back. Look for them at the tops of poles or dead trees, or flying slowly in a direct flight pattern (unlike most woodpeckers that undulate).

Found: In burned-over areas with bare snags and open spaces. Hot spots: the site of the Awbrey Hall fire, along China Hat Rd., and at Shevlin Park.

Red-breasted Sapsucker *(Sphyrapicus ruber)*

Seen: April to Nov. (some in winter)

Have you ever seen an orderly series of holes on the side of a tree, rather like a cribbage board? It's likely the work of the Red-breasted Sapsucker, which drills those pea-sized "sap wells" to get at the sugary sap just under the bark.

If the sap wells are seeping, you can bet there are Red-breasted Sapsuckers in the area. There may also be Rufous Hummingbirds nearby, since they smartly follow the sapsuckers around to steal sips from their sap wells.

Look for the red breast and white stripe along the wing. (Photo by Mark Lundgren)

Look for: A medium-sized woodpecker with a red head and breast (others have red on the head, but no others have red on the breast). A white stripe runs up the side of its body.

Found: Forested areas; prefers the soft wood of quaking aspen for easy nest excavation. Hot spots: Glaze Meadow, Cold Springs Campground, and Calliope Crossing.

DID YOU KNOW?

Lewis's Woodpeckers are one of many bird species that benefit from wildfires and the snags they leave behind (as well as the insects they attract). After the 1990 Awbrey Hall fire, the Christmas Bird Count found record numbers of Downy, Hairy, and even Black-backed Woodpeckers.

Downy and Hairy Woodpeckers have a big white patch on their backs. (Photo by John Williams)

Downy Woodpecker *(Picoides pubescens)*

Seen: Year-round

If you spot a mostly black-and-white woodpecker near an urban area, odds are good that it's a Downy Woodpecker. At less than seven inches, they're the smallest woodpeckers on the continent, and one of the more active and fun to watch.

The diminutive size of Downy Woodpeckers allows them to perform gymnastic feats like feeding on tiny branches or cattails. You might also see them scurrying quickly across and down tree trunks in their quest for insects and other food.

Like their look-alike the Hairy Woodpecker, they prefer to nest in dead trees or dead parts of live trees. The wood is softer, and the trees don't produce sticky sap that might otherwise build up in their nests.

Look for: A small woodpecker with a short bill, black-and-white face, and black wings spotted with white. Males have a red patch on the back of the head. In flight, watch for the undulating pattern common to most woodpeckers.

Found: Often near water and in areas with deciduous trees. Hot spots: Calliope Crossing, Indian Ford Campground, Glaze Meadow, and Cold Springs Campground.

They're half-again larger than Downy Woodpeckers, with much longer bills. (Photo by John Williams)

Hairy Woodpecker *(Picoides villosus)*

Seen: Year-round

The Hairy Woodpecker looks a lot like its cousin the Downy Woodpecker. Both have black-and-white heads and black wings with spots of white. Males even share a similar red patch on the back of the head. Look more closely, though, and you'll see that Hairy Woodpeckers are about one-third larger and have much longer bills—the latter is the giveaway, even from a distance.

Another difference is that Hairy Woodpeckers spend more of their time in forested areas where they help ponderosa pines and other conifers by feeding on beetle larvae, ants, moth pupae, and other insects. That's why you'll spot many of them in burned-over forests: They're feeding on insect species like wood-boring beetles that thrive in those areas.

Look for: A medium-sized woodpecker with a long bill (about as long as the head). Heads are black and white; males have a red patch on the back of the head.

Found: In conifer forests. Hot spots: Any burned area near Sisters, Shevlin Park, and southwest Bend.

White-headed Woodpecker *(Picoides albolarvatus)*

Seen: Year-round

There's only one bird in North America that has a white head and a black body, and there's only one woodpecker that relies heavily on ponderosa pine seeds: the beautiful White-headed Woodpecker.

In Sisters, these woodpeckers are frequently seen pecking away at the bark of ponderosa pines. They don't drill deep into the wood like most woodpeckers, preferring instead to probe the cracks and pry off flakes of bark. They also pull seeds out of pinecones and wedge them into crevices in the tree bark, where they hammer away to break the seeds open and get at the tasty interiors.

Note the white wing patch.
(Photo by Mark Lundgren)

Look for: A medium-sized woodpecker with a black body, white head, and flashy white patch on each wing. If there's a red patch on top of the head, it's a male.

Found: In park-like ponderosa pine forests. Hot spots: Cold Springs Campground, near the Best Western in Sisters, and at the city park near downtown Sisters.

Northern Flicker *(Colaptes auratus)*

Seen: Year-round

You've almost certainly seen Northern Flickers, the most common woodpeckers in Central Oregon. But have you really *seen* these woodpeckers, beyond their flashy white rumps as they fly away? Up close, they're beautiful "clown birds" (as a birder friend says)—with a crazed mix of bars and spots all over, a black necklace, and salmon-colored wing undersides.

Whether you've seen flickers or not, you've no doubt heard them in the spring. Woodpeckers don't sing to attract mates; they drum. And many flickers have adapted to urban life by drumming like mad on any metal surface they can find—including metal roofs, gutters, and chimney tops.

Flickers often use a single-note kyeer *call.*
(Photo by John Williams)

Look for: A foot-long bird foraging on the ground for ants and beetles. In flight, look for the white rump patch and roller-coaster flight pattern. We have red-shafted flickers, with red under the tail and underwings; in eastern states, they have yellow-shafted. Sometimes we get hybrids of the two.

Found: Common all over, from cities to dense forests. Hot spots: Shevlin Park, Hatfield Lake, and Bend parks (but really they're everywhere).

FUN FACT

Male and female White-headed Woodpeckers share the job of incubating eggs, communicating with each other by softly drumming back and forth from inside and outside the nest cavity.

The long white stripe makes them look like they're wearing an unbuttoned vest. (Photo by Kim Elton)

FLYCATCHERS

Olive-sided Flycatcher (*Contopus cooperi*)

Seen: Mid-April to mid-Sept.

Olive-sided Flycatchers are world travelers that winter in Panama and South America, then wing their way up to the Northwest by May. That long journey seems to make them thirsty because they belly up to the forest bar all day long, demanding with gusto: *Quick, three beers!* It's one of the most distinctive bird calls you'll hear.

Seeing these small flycatchers is a little tougher, but look for them on exposed branches near the tops of trees. They'll flap around for a bit to catch insects before quickly returning to the branch to order up another few beers.

Look for: Flycatchers in general are tough to tell apart. These are olive-gray overall with a whitish stripe down the middle of the breast and belly. Also look for white on the chin and white patches between their wings and lower back.

Found: In open areas such as clearcuts and burned-over sites. Hot spots: Shevlin Park, site of Awbrey Hall fire, Suttle Lake, and Cold Springs Campground.

VIREOS

Cassin's Vireo (*Vireo cassinii*)

Seen: Mid-April to mid-Sept.

Look for the yellowish flanks and those white-rimmed glasses. (Photo by Mark Lundgren)

Cassin's Vireos are cute little birds that appear to wear white-rimmed spectacles ("Cassin's wear glasses") as they diligently search for insects along branches and twigs.

Cassin's are tough to spot, but you'll hear their persistent singing if they're around. The song consists of short phrases with a pause between, alternating between ending on a high note and a low note. It sounds for all the world like they are holding a Q&A session with themselves.

Look for: A small songbird with a brownish-gray head and white spectacles. Belly is white and flanks yellowish. Each wing has two white bars.

Found: In pine and fir forests. Hot spots: Shevlin Park, Skyliners Rd. at Forest Rd. 430, Cold Springs Campground, and Calliope Crossing.

JAYS AND CROWS

Pinyon Jay *(Gymnorhinus cyanocephalus)*

Seen: Year-round

It won't surprise you to hear that Pinyon Jays have a strong preference for the cones of pinyon pines. We don't have those pines in Central Oregon, but we do have a couple good substitutes in junipers and ponderosa pines. The jays expand their throats to carry dozens of juniper and pine seeds at a time, and they cache thousands of those seeds each year. Incredibly, they also recall where they place ninety-five percent of their caches.

Pinyon Jays are corvids, so their excellent memories are to be expected, as well as the fact that they're highly social and monogamous (even when a demonic researcher separated mated pairs and brought in attractive replacements, the jays would not cheat). Drought, climate change, habitat destruction, and other threats have led to declines in Pinyon Jay populations, so they'll have to be awfully smart, and adaptable, to survive the years ahead.

Look for: A small jay that's entirely dull blue, aside from its whitish chin. They often fly in large flocks.

Found: At borders between juniper woodlands and ponderosa forests. Hot spots: South Bend on 3rd St., Ray's Market in Sisters, Eagle Crest, and McKinney Butte Rd. in Sisters.

Top: *A stocky jay with a blue-gray body. (Photo by Tom Lawler)*

Bottom: *They are social and gregarious birds. (Photo by Chuck Gates)*

FUN FACT

Bumper crops of pinyon cones typically result in bumper crops of Pinyon Jays. In fact, the mere sight of green pinyon cones physically stimulates reproduction—female ovaries start developing and male testicles get bigger and start producing more sperm.

With their spiked crests, it's tough to mistake this jay. (Photo by Sue Dougherty)

Steller's Jay *(Cyanocitta stelleri)*

Seen: Year-round

These handsome jays are "crows in a blue suit"—another smart, social bird in the corvid family. They're the only crested jay in the West, but their good looks are somewhat overshadowed by their loud and raspy calls, propensity for stealing eggs from nests, and bullying antics at backyard feeders, where they swoop in and chase off smaller birds.

Steller's Jays (currently named after the naturalist Georg Steller) can mimic the sounds of many other animals, including cats, dogs, chickens, and squirrels—even the scream of a Red-tailed Hawk.

Look for: A big corvid with a black head and shoulders, transitioning to deep-blue wings, tail, and belly. The big head is topped by a spiky black crest.

Found: Mostly in forested areas but also in other areas, such as rural Bend. Hot spots: Skyliners Rd. at Forest Rd. 430, Shevlin Park, Sawyer Park, and Cold Springs Campground.

The hardy Central Oregon version of a blue jay. (Photo by John Williams)

Western Scrub-Jay *(Aphelocoma californica)*

Seen: Year-round

A lot of things arrived in the 1980s: Cabbage Patch Kids, MTV, Air Jordans, and stirrup pants, to name a few. Oh, and Western Scrub-Jays, which landed in Central Oregon at about the same time as the Deschutes Brewery and have since become ubiquitous.

As the name implies, scrub-jays prefer "scrub" habitat—areas with shrubs and a smattering of trees. They're smart and adaptable creatures that raise a ruckus with their rasping scolds, but what's less known is that they have at least twenty different calls in their repertoire, including a sweet, soft medley exchanged during courtship.

Look for: A jay with deep-blue coloring on the head, neck, wings, and tail, and a blue band across the breast. The back is brownish-gray and underparts are pale gray.

Found: Mostly in urban parks and neighborhoods. Hot spots: Across Bend, Redmond, and Prineville.

Clark's Nutcracker
(Nucifraga columbiana)

Seen: Year-round

Near the top of Tumalo Mountain, my friend and I stood in wonder as a Clark's Nutcracker tore viciously into a pinecone at the end of a whitebark pine branch. In one of nature's wonderfully symbiotic relationships, whitebarks depend on these nutcrackers to do just that: to yank out those seeds with their strong beaks, carry off the seeds and bury them, and forget about a few that will someday become the next whitebark pine.

They have white patches on their wings that show in flight. (Photo by Mark Lundgren)

Clark's Nutcrackers have pouches under their tongue that allow them to hold up to a hundred seeds at a time (making them look like miniature pelicans). From July through early winter, they carry and bury up to 100,000 pine seeds in 5,000 separate mini-caches. During the coldest months of the year, when other food sources are usually covered in snow, those cached seeds provide essential nourishment—especially for a bird that starts nesting as early as January.

Remarkably, the nutcrackers return to find nearly all the seeds they've stashed, even many months later. Which makes me feel rather foolish for forgetting where I set my car keys nearly every day.

Look for: A jay-sized bird mostly a cool gray in color, with black wings. Listen for the loud *kraak* call.

Found: In pine forests and juniper woodlands. Hot spots: Eagle Crest, Black Butte, and the China Hat area.

CACHE ME IF YOU CAN

The more you know about the relationship between Clark's Nutcrackers and whitebark pines, the more interesting it becomes. For instance:

- Nutcrackers eat other types of seeds, but whitebark pine seeds are especially rich and fatty, with more calories per ounce than chocolate.

- The wind can't carry dense, heavy, wing-less whitebark seeds very far. That's why the trees need nutcrackers to disperse the seeds.

- Squirrels cache whitebark seeds too, but in big heaps that don't germinate well. Nutcrackers store a few seeds in each cache, so they're more likely to grow into trees.

Top: *One of the more dapper corvids.*
(Photo by Kris Kristovich)

Bottom: *Keep an eye out for magpies*
flying near Hwy. 20 east of Bend.
(Photo by Kevin Smith)

Black-billed Magpie *(Pica hudsonia)*

Seen: Year-round

If you've spent time in open areas east of Bend, you've probably seen the flash of black and white that's a sure sign of the Black-billed Magpie. As you'd expect of a corvid, magpies are smart, social, and bold (they even snuck into tents to steal food during the Lewis and Clark Expedition).

Magpies are also similar to another species—the coyote—in being demonized by some as vermin, even though they provide a variety of valuable services, such as eating carrion.

Look for: A long-tailed bird a bit larger than a jay. Upperparts are mostly black with a white patch in the outer wing and two white straps on the back. They flap steadily in flight.

Found: Mostly in agricultural areas. Hot spots: Alfalfa, Hwy. 20 east of Bend, Cloverdale, and Hatfield Lake.

Crows are much smaller than ravens, and their tails open differently, like a fan. (Photo by Tom Lawler)

American Crow *(Corvus brachyrhynchos)*

Seen: Year-round

You probably know that crows are smart, but do you know just how smart? Consider, for instance, that they can recognize different human faces, count, solve puzzles, and learn from their dead. They also use tools: One captive crow used a cup to carry water over to a bowl of dry mash. Another can be seen on YouTube using a plastic lid to snowboard down a roof over and over.

Crows are also great communicators. Local naturalist Jim Anderson wrote of a pet crow named Joe that would follow Jim and his brothers to school and tap at the school windows, calling, *"Oh, Jim-my. Oh, Har-ry. Oh, Hor-ace!"* In fact, all crows have the ability to mimic human speech as effectively as parrots, along with the sounds of ducks, dogs, cats, and even machinery.

Among themselves, crows use over twenty distinct calls, including a drawn-out caw that summons reinforcements to mob owls or hawks. Each crow also has a call all its own; if a mate disappears, the remaining crow may mimic that sound in an apparent attempt to call its mate home.

Look for: A large bird (15–20 in.), coal-black in color. In flight, they don't soar or glide; they flap their wings slowly.

Found: Common in most urban areas.

Common Raven (*Corvus corax*)

Seen: Year-round

If there's one bird that may be smarter than the crow, it's the raven. Ravens can solve intricate problems on the first try and will sometimes work together to overcome a new challenge. They will also work together to hunt, or let others do the work for them—research suggests they may attract a predator like a wolf to a dying animal so the wolf will kill the animal and the ravens can feast on the remnants.

In flight, ravens are vastly different from those city-slicker crows. Ravens soar with ease and can perform aerial somersaults and wing-tucked dives. One raven is said to have flown upside down for a half-mile!

In the air and on the ground, ravens display what's tough not to call a sense of humor—teasing each other, humans, and other animals. For instance, ravens (and crows) have been known to nip or pull at the tails of household pets, apparently for the heck of it.

Raven, crow, or hawk? That diamond-shaped tail is a giveaway. (Photo by Tom Lawler)

Look for: A much bigger version of a crow (up to 26 in.). They weigh about 2.5 pounds, which is more than a Red-tailed Hawk. Their main call is a guttural *cr-r-ruck*.

Found: Common across rural areas, especially forested and agricultural areas.

LARKS

Horned Lark (*Eremophila alpestris*)

Seen: Year-round

Horned Larks are one of those adorable little birds that elicit an appreciative "awww" from birders. And why not? They're the only native lark in North America, and their eponymous horns are endearing.

Those "horns" are actually little tufts of feathers that probably help the larks identify each other when they travel in flocks with other bird species. You're most likely to see those flocks on the ground of open fields, where the larks walk and run about in an endless quest for seeds and insects.

Look for: A small songbird with long wings and body. Males have a yellow face with a black mask and mustache, and a black band at the base of the throat. In summer, males have the black horns.

Found: In dry, desert-like areas east of Bend; also at some mountain lakes in fall. Hot spots: Along Hwy. 20 east of Horse Ridge, China Hat Rd., Alfalfa, and Spencer Wells Rd.

Top: A male in a field near Fort Rock. (Photo by Tom Lawler)

Bottom: Fluffed up to greet a cold March dawn near Brothers. (Photo by Alan St. John)

In flight, look for bright-white underparts and short tails. (Photo by John Williams)

SWALLOWS

Tree Swallow *(Tachycineta bicolor)*

Seen: Early March to mid-Sept.

Life is not easy for secondary cavity nesters like Tree Swallows, which depend on woodpeckers and other species to excavate cavities for them. The problem is that European Starlings and House Sparrows want those same cavities, as do native species like bluebirds.

You can help swallows and other secondary cavity nesters by putting up nest boxes. An added benefit? The swallows will gobble up thousands of nearby mosquitoes.

Look for: A small, stocky bird that looks like it's wearing a tuxedo, with a blue-and-black back and snowy-white underparts. They're often in large flocks, and they glide more than other swallows, in a flap-flap-glide flight pattern.

Found: Most common in forested areas with snags that feature abandoned woodpecker cavities. Hot spots: Hatfield Lake, Camp Polk Meadow, and along the Deschutes River in Bend.

Cliff Swallow *(Petrochelidon pyrrhonota)*

Seen: Early April to mid-Sept.

You can spot Cliff Swallows closer to urban areas, but for the best experience, head out to Smith Rock State Park or another cliff-lined area in spring or summer. Then sit back and enjoy the swallows' acrobatic flights as they swoop, zoom, and plunge after insects.

It's also fun to scan cliff walls for these swallows' distinctive, jug-shaped nests. They've been known to form colonies of up to 1,000 nests, and they've also been known to lay eggs in their own nests and then carry the eggs over to another nest (it's not clear why).

Look for: In-flight coloring can be tough to see, but look for a dark throat, white underparts, and a square tail. They also have a pumpkin-colored rump.

Found: In open country where they can find water for drinking and cliffs for nesting. Hot spots: Hatfield Lake, Lower Bridge, First Street Rapids, and Drake Park.

Top: They have square tails—not forked like Barn Swallows. (Photo by John Williams)

Bottom: Can you imagine building that nest one muddy mouthful at a time? (Photo by Chuck Gates)

Barn Swallow *(Hirundo rustica)*

Seen: Early March to late Sept.

Before there were barns, Barn Swallows nested in caves, carrying thousands of spitball-sized mud-and-grass pellets one by one to construct their cup-shaped nests. Now, they build their nests almost exclusively on human-made structures (like under the eaves of your house). That adaptability may be why they're the most abundant and widely distributed swallow species in the world.

Barn Swallows are easy to distinguish from our other swallows because of their deeply forked tails. Why are they forked? Well, legend has it that a Barn Swallow stole fire from the gods to give to humans, which so angered the gods that they threw a fireball that burned away the swallow's central tail feathers.

Look for: A blue-black head, back, wings, and tail, and rufous to tawny underparts. Forehead and chin are cinnamon-orange. And look for that forked tail! Females prefer males with long, symmetrical tails.

Found: In open areas (parks and fields), usually where there's water nearby and structures available for nesting. Hot spots: Open farm country near water, Hatfield Lake, and Tumalo Reservoir.

Top: *Underparts are tawny, not white like that of Cliff and Tree Swallows. (Photo by Tom Lawler)*

Bottom: *Look for the forked tail. (Photo by Chuck Gates)*

CHICKADEES AND BUSHTITS

Mountain Chickadee *(Poecile gambeli)*

Seen: Common year-round

Don't even get me started on chickadees. They're so small and ever-present, with their near-constant *chick-a-dee* and *fee-bee-bee* calls, that they're often dismissed or overlooked. Don't make that mistake! Chickadees are endlessly entertaining and interesting.

Let's start with that *chick-a-dee* call. Ever notice that sometimes it's actually *chick-a-dee-dee-dee*? A study of Black-capped Chickadees found that they tack on a different number of *dees,* depending on the size and type of danger around them—a big but slow goshawk warrants a couple *dees,* while a nimble and highly dangerous pygmy-owl may earn a dozen *dees*.

Another cool thing about chickadees is that they're very friendly—or at least they're one of the more likely birds to land on your foot while you're reading or on your head while you're watching them at a feeder.

Look for: A little bird with a gray back and wings, buff-white underparts, and a black cap with white cheeks and eyebrows.

Found: Wherever there are evergreens. City parks are a great place to look.

They're about five inches tall and weigh less than half an ounce. (Photo by Chuck Gates)

The light eye indicates this is a female fluffball. (Photo by Kim Elton)

Bushtit *(Psaltriparus minimus)*

Seen: Common year-round

Bushtits are the avian equivalent of a box of kittens. The tiny, plump bundles of cute are almost always found out and about with ten to forty pals, chattering *pit, pit* and *tsip, tsip* nonstop from in and under shrubs.

Bushtits' sociability extends to their nesting behavior. Parents work together to build sock-like nests that hang from trees and are rather unusually large for such small birds. Large enough, in fact, to allow all the family members to sleep together during breeding season.

Look for: A chubby little gray bird with a short neck and long tail. Males have dark eyes; females have pale eyes.

Found: In a variety of habitats; often near streams. Hot spots: First Street Rapids, Sawyer Park, North Shore Rd., and Lower Bridge.

SIGNS OF SPRING

Chuck Gates, a fantastic birder who created the Oregon Birding Site Guide, says you know it's spring in Central Oregon when:

- The first migrants (usually Say's Phoebes and Barn Swallows) show up.
- Red-winged Blackbirds and Western Meadowlarks start singing.
- The forest silence is broken by the drumming of woodpeckers.
- Bluebirds start checking out local nest boxes.
- Snowbirds (White-crowned Sparrows and Dark-eyed Juncos) are no longer ever-present under feeders.

Look for the white eyebrow and reddish underparts. (Photo by Steve Byland)

NUTHATCHES AND CREEPERS

Red-breasted Nuthatch (*Sitta canadensis*)

Seen: Common year-round

Once you know the nasal *yank, yank* call of this nuthatch, you'll find it difficult to hike through area forests without hearing it. You're also likely to see Red-breasted Nuthatches winding around and around tree trunks, often facing the ground as they hunt for insects and seeds. They like a wider variety of trees than ponderosa-loving Pygmy Nuthatches and often nest in quaking aspens, which provide the soft wood they need to excavate their cavities.

By the way: It's a common misconception that humans and primates are the only animals that use tools. In fact, a lot of animals do so, including Red-breasted Nuthatches, which use pieces of bark as spatulas to apply sap around entrances to their tree cavities. The sap is believed to prevent insects and other unwanteds from entering.

Look for: A barrel-chested bird with a long bill, short tail, and almost no neck. The white eyebrows, black cap, and reddish breast differentiate them from other nuthatches.

Found: In a variety of forest types. Hot spots: Skyliners Rd. at Forest Rd. 430, Lava Butte, Drake Park, and Deschutes River Woods.

ALERT! ALERT!

Birds vocalize to let others know of danger—and not just others like them. For instance, experiments show that Red-breasted Nuthatches can understand chickadees' calls. They don't simply understand that "danger is coming" but also what kind of predator it is, how far away it is, and precisely how dangerous it's likely to be.

The whitish underparts differentiate pygmies from Red-breasted Nuthatches. (Photo by John Williams)

Pygmy Nuthatch *(Sitta pygmaea)*

Seen: Common year-round

Pygmy Nuthatches are tiny bundles of energy that walk up, down, under, and around ponderosa pine branches and trunks, tittering *tee-dee, tee-dee* all the while. (The distinguished researchers at the Cornell Lab say these nuthatches squeak "like a rubber ducky.") Pygmies and other nuthatches are constantly searching for seeds and nuts, which they jam into tree bark and whack open using their long beaks.

You might wonder how little birds like this survive the winter. Some bird species roost in tree cavities where it's a little warmer. Some huddle closely together. And some go into torpor, their body temperatures plummeting into hypothermia to conserve energy. Pygmy Nuthatches? They do all three, with up to a hundred piling into a single tree cavity to stay warm.

Look for: A wee bird with a brown head, blue-gray back, and buff-white underparts. Red-breasted Nuthatches have a white stripe over the eye and reddish-cinnamon underparts.

Found: Lower-elevation ponderosa pine forests. Hot spots: Shevlin Park, Sawyer Park, Drake Park, and the Best Western in Sisters.

Their long, downturned bill helps them probe for insects in the bark. (Photo by mirceax)

Brown Creeper *(Certhia americana)*

Seen: Year-round

No other bird appreciates conifers quite like the diminutive Brown Creeper, which forages and nests on trees, is camouflaged like a tree trunk, flutters to the ground like a leaf, and even has a song that sounds like *trees, trees, beau-ti-ful trees!*

Their camo makes Brown Creepers tough to see, but listen for that song and their high-pitched calls. Then watch as they scamper up and around the trunks of large conifers, searching for insects with their downwardly curved bills. Once they get near the top of a tree, they'll flit down to the base of the next (or same) tree and do it all over again.

Look for: A tiny songbird with a downturned bill. Their bodies are brown above and white below, and they use their long tails to prop themselves along tree trunks.

Found: Most common in coniferous forests, but also in urban areas and juniper woodlands. Hot spots: Calliope Crossing, Cold Springs Campground, and Trout Creek Swamp.

WRENS

Canyon Wren *(Catherpes mexicanus)*

Seen: April to Nov.

If you haven't hiked in our majestic canyons and been stopped in your tracks by the wonder that is a Canyon Wren's song . . . well, set down this book and get out there; it's a glorious experience.

I think the Canyon Wren's song resembles the opening to the Steve Miller Band's "Jungle Love," but that may betray too much about my musical tastes. Researchers say the descending cascade of notes is reminiscent of the opening and closing of Chopin's "Revolutionary Étude." Either way, it's a joy to hear.

They hold their pretty tails up in a distinctively wren-like way. (Photo by Chuck Gates)

Look for: You're more likely to hear their one-of-a-kind song, but look for a white throat, gray head, rusty-brown underparts and back, bright rufous tail, and long and slightly downturned bill.

Found: In steep canyons and on canyon slopes. Hot spots: First Street Rapids, Farewell Bend Park, Smith Rock State Park, and Lower Bridge.

DIPPERS

American Dipper *(Cinclus mexicanus)*

Seen: Year-round (except in extreme cold spells)

Just when you think you have nature all figured out, along comes a chunky songbird that walks and swims underwater. The American Dipper, or Water Ouzel, is a one-of-a-kind bird that can dive up to twenty feet underwater and swim or simply walk along stream bottoms in search of insects and other prey.

Look for them on rocks and logs in area rivers. (Photo by Tom Lawler)

This was John Muir's favorite bird, and indeed it's an easy bird to fall in love with. A friend and I saw a dipper bobbing beside a stream in the Wallowas (they bob up and down nearly constantly), ignoring us completely as it hunted and preened. We ate our lunch and watched, and near the end of our meal the dipper rewarded us with a private performance, singing a song that was surely made up on the spot, with no repetition that we could detect over the course of several delightful minutes.

Muir must have heard similar performances as he trekked the Sierra Nevadas. "Among all the mountain birds, none has cheered me so much in my lonely wanderings—none so unfailingly," Muir wrote. "For both in winter and summer he sings, sweetly, cheerily, independent alike of sunshine and of love, requiring no other inspiration than the stream on which he dwells."

Look for: A chunky bird, about 8 in. long, with long legs, a slate-gray body, and a short tail. You'll see a protective white membrane cover their eyes when they blink.

Found: In and around rushing streams with clean, cold water. Hot spots: First Street Rapids, Sawyer Park, Deschutes River, and Camp Sherman.

A male showing off his gorgeous colors. (Photo by Kris Kristovich)

THRUSHES

Western Bluebird *(Sialia mexicana)*

Seen: Year-round (few midwinter)

The soft, warbling call of a bluebird is one of the most welcome, beautiful, and increasingly rare signs of spring in Central Oregon. Western Bluebirds are found on both sides of the Cascades, although populations on the west side have dwindled precipitously.

In fact, by some accounts populations of both Western and Mountain Bluebirds have been in trouble since the 1950s. That's why many people put up nest boxes specifically for bluebirds—it helps give them a fighting chance.

Bluebirds face several difficulties, including that they depend on standing dead trees, or snags, which are increasingly hard to come by, as are available nest cavities that must be excavated by others (such as Northern Flickers). Perhaps most damaging is the fact that many available cavities are commandeered by introduced species like European Starlings and House Sparrows.

Look for: Males have a sky-blue back, russet chest and flanks, and a white belly. Females are dusky-gray overall with pale blue on their wings and tail feathers. (The older the bird, the more and brighter the blue and russet colors.)

Found: Fields, pastures, and open woodlands. Hot spots: Neighborhoods on the east side of Bend with junipers, rural areas around Sisters, and Camp Polk Meadow.

These blue beauties can take your breath away. (Photo by John Williams)

Mountain Bluebird *(Sialia currocoides)*

Seen: Year-round (few midwinter)

Mountain Bluebirds are blue jewels that live in the mountains as well as flat, open areas. You're most likely to see them perched on fence posts or atop junipers, or hovering over a field as they hunt for insects, their powder-blue beauty matching that of the high-desert sky.

Bluebirds tend to inspire poetic language, but I'd be remiss if I didn't note that our "bluebirds of happiness" often live nasty, brutish, and short lives. Territorial battles and physical attacks are common, and most bluebirds die in their first year.

The difficulty of their lives may help explain why female Mountain Bluebirds are so focused on nesting and food. A male can sing and show off his cerulean feathers all he wants; a female will choose her mate solely based on the location and quality of the nesting cavity he offers her. Then she'll put him to work: When a female is incubating and brooding, she'll flick the wing farthest from her mate to signal that he should go fetch her a snack.

Look for: Other than larger Pinyon and Steller's Jays, males are the only mostly blue birds in Central Oregon. Females are grayish with pale-blue wings and tail.

Found: Open agricultural areas and burns. Hot spots: Hatfield Lake, Alfalfa, and Hwy. 20 east and west of Bend.

Townsend's Solitaire *(Myadestes townsendi)*

Seen: Year-round

Visit the Badlands Wilderness in winter and you'll almost surely hear a loud and persistent referee's whistle: *tew, tew, tew.* That's the call of the Townsend's Solitaire. If you're lucky, you'll also hear their long, elaborate, and fluty song, which one researcher called "one of the most glorious and beautiful of all bird songs."

Look at the tops of junipers to spy the source of all the noise—long, gray birds insistent on telling the world over and over again that a given territory of junipers is theirs, and theirs alone. It's a tale worth telling (and fighting over) because solitaires survive almost solely on juniper berries through winter, before heading up to high-elevation conifers in springtime.

Look for: A long, slim songbird that's dull gray all over with white rings around the eyes. Also look for a light-colored wing patch and white on the edges of the tail.

Look for the white ring around the eye. (Photo by Mark Lundgren)

Found: High-elevation conifers in summer and juniper woodlands in winter. Hot spots: Badlands Wilderness in winter and areas west of Bend above 3,000 ft. in summer.

Hermit Thrush *(Catharus guttatus)*

Seen: Mid-April to mid-Sept. (very few in winter)

If your yard has trees and shrubs, you might see Hermit Thrushes hopping around on the ground and stirring up insects by picking up leaf litter in their bills or shaking grass with their feet. But the real joy comes at dusk, when they sing their ethereal, flutelike, and somewhat melancholy song, which many birders claim as their favorite of all bird songs.

The secret to thrushes' beautiful songs is that they have a double voice box, or syrinx. The syrinx allows them to create their own harmony, blending notes issued independently from one half of the syrinx with those from the other half.

Look for: A chunky bird that blends well with the forest understory. They're gray to brown overall, with smudged spots on the breast, white eye rings, and a reddish tail that distinguishes them from other thrushes.

Found: Prefer to nest in smaller trees at middle elevations. Hot spots: Suttle Lake, Skyliners Rd. at Forest Rd. 430, High Lakes area, and the Ochocos.

Top: This is a bird that knows how to blend in. (Photo by Chuck Gates)

Bottom: Speckling on the head and back suggests this is an immature Hermit Thrush. (Photo by Mark Lundgren)

There's no mistaking this most common of birds. (Photo by John Williams)

American Robin *(Turdus migratorius)*

Seen: Year-round

American Robins are among the most abundant songbirds on the continent, which makes it easy to observe their interesting behaviors. In fact, you might not be able to avoid those behaviors, such as when they wake you at 3 a.m. by loudly singing *cheerily, cheer-up, cheerio* outside your window. (Yes, Ben Franklin was talking about robins when he wrote his famous line about the early bird getting the worm.)

Robins are so common because we've planted so many lawns and fruiting trees. In the morning, they're hunting for earthworms, cocking their heads to the side so they can see the worms. Later in the day, especially in fall and winter, robins supplement their diet with fermented berries, often getting drunk in the process.

In winter, you aren't as likely to see robins in urban areas. Instead they head out to juniper woodlands and other open places, where they form flocks of up to 5,000 (up to a quarter-million in other regions). When spring rolls around, rising temps and longer days lead robins to break up their huge flocks and return to sing by your window.

Look for: A large songbird, mostly gray-brown, with orange underparts and a dark head (females paler). In flight, look for the white patch on the lower belly and under the tail.

Found: They prefer juniper woodlands in winter and more forested areas in summer, but they're ubiquitous.

TOP SEVEN BIRD SPECIES

According to Partners in Flight, the seven most abundant bird species in North America are:

1. American Robin
2. Dark-eyed Junco
3. Red-winged Blackbird
4. Red-eyed Vireo
5. White-throated Sparrow
6. Yellow-rumped Warbler
7. European Starling

Varied Thrush *(Ixoreus naevius)*

Seen: Mostly early Oct. to mid-Nov.

What a beauty the Varied Thrush is, with its splashes of orange and the sharply contrasting dark band across its breast. Their call is beautiful too—not complex, just a long, sweet, flutelike sound that repeats at different pitches.

Varied Thrushes sometimes overwinter in Central Oregon and are seen in spring, but your best chance to spot them is when they migrate through in late fall.

Look for: A robin-like bird with a plump belly. Look for the bold band across the breast and orange on the breast and head.

Found: In forested areas and urban yards with leaf litter to provide food. Hot spots: Bend and Redmond yards with leaf litter; also at Green Ridge.

Top: *One of the more colorful birds of area forests.* (Photo by Tom Lawler)

Bottom: *Females have a paler breast band.* (Photo by Chuck Gates)

WAXWINGS

Cedar Waxwing *(Bombycilla cedrorum)*

Seen: Transient year-round

There's nothing like a waxwing. Unlike our many territorial birds, Cedar Waxwings are social nomads that fly around in flocks of different sizes all year long, making their high-pitched *zeee* call and eating fruit and little else.

In fact, if you ever wonder where all those chokecherries go in summer, or rosehips in autumn, you can bet some waxwings were behind it. They nest later than most songbirds, waiting until fruits ripen so they can feed themselves and their chicks (chicks can swallow berries whole one day after hatching).

Waxwings are pretty, distinctive-looking birds, with a crest on the head and a bandit-like mask across the eyes. They're also the only bird in North America with a yellow-tipped tail, but it's the waxy red tips on their wings that give them their name—the more red tips, the older the bird and the more preferred it is as a mate.

Look for: A medium-sized songbird with a black mask and chin, brown head and chest, yellow wash across the belly, and yellow tail tip.

Found: In and near ornamental trees with winter fruit. Hot spots: Throughout Bend and Redmond, Hatfield Lake, and Prineville Reservoir State Park.

Top: *Maybe they're discussing who has more red on the wing tips?* (Photo by Sue Dougherty)

Bottom: *Look for the yellow tail tips and the distinctive head shape.* (Photo by John Williams)

Top: *A spectacularly plumed Yellow Warbler. (Photo by John Williams)*

Bottom: *Sweet-sweet-sweet, I'm so sweet is their humble call. (Photo by Kris Kristovich.)*

WARBLERS

Yellow Warbler *(Setophaga petechia)*

Seen: Mid-April to mid-Sept.

Just to confuse us, in Central Oregon we have Yellow-rumped Warblers; Wilson's Warblers, which are mostly yellow; and Yellow Warblers, which are (surprise!) also yellow. Yellow Warblers are one of the most abundant warblers in the world, which is a blessing because they are gorgeous, golden-yellow birds with a too-cute *sweet-sweet-sweet, I'm so sweet* song.

Though they remain quite common, Yellow Warbler populations have declined precipitously in Oregon, according to ODFW. Look and listen for them near willows and other streamside vegetation in spring and summer.

Look for: A small songbird, largely yellow all over (no black cap like Wilson's Warblers). Males have striking red streaks on the breast.

Found: In dense trees and shrubs, especially willows. Hot spots: Willows along the Deschutes River, Tumalo Reservoir, and Camp Polk Meadow.

Top: *In summer, males have yellow on their heads, throats, and flanks.*

Bottom: *And now you know where they got their "butter butt" nickname. (Photos by John Williams)*

Yellow-rumped Warbler *(Setophaga coronata)*

Seen: Early April to late Oct. (some overwinter)

Yellow-rumped Warblers are the warbler you're most likely to see across Oregon—watch for the distinctive flash of yellow as they flutter out from a branch to nab a flying insect, then return quickly to their perch.

Our beloved "butter butts" aren't showy when they stick around for one of our warmer winters, but their spring molt transforms them into colorful characters with yellow on their faces, sides, and rumps.

Look for: In summer, look for a gray bird with a yellow throat, crown, rump, and side patches (females are duller than males). In winter, they're paler brown but still have a yellow rump and some yellow on the sides.

Found: In timbered areas in summer; anywhere in migration. Hot spots: Shevlin Park, Tumalo State Park, First Street Rapids, and Hatfield Lake.

Hermit Warbler *(Setophaga occidentalis)*

Seen: Late April to mid-Sept.

Hermit Warblers aren't really hermits; it's just that they're only found in California, Oregon, and Washington, and they're rarely seen because they spend the bulk of their time up in the canopies of tall evergreen trees. For birders, that makes these hermits worth a special trip or two to find.

East of Sisters is a rare zone of hybridization, where you can spot hybrids of Hermit Warblers and the more common and aggressive Townsend's Warbler. Female Hermit Warblers seem to recognize their competitive superiority and actually prefer mating with the Townsend's instead of their own kind.

This was the toughest bird photo to hunt down—a great find! (Photo by Mark Lundgren)

Look for: A little songbird with a yellow head, gray or olive back, and white underparts.

Found: In the canopies of tall evergreen trees, especially Douglas-firs and true firs. Hot spots: Suttle Lake, Black Butte, and Green Ridge.

Wilson's Warbler *(Cardellina pusilla)*

Seen: Late April to early June; mid-Aug. to mid-Sept.

Local naturalist Damian Fagan accurately compares the *chip, chip, chip* song of the Wilson's Warbler to the sound of an engine struggling to turn over. You're especially likely to hear that sputtering sound during their spring migration, when the warblers forage all day long in deciduous trees and shrubs.

For now, Wilson's are named after the ornithologist Alexander Wilson, but they and other birds named after humans are likely to be renamed, following a decision by the American Ornithological Society. Hello, future Dark-capped Warbler!

Look for: A small, mostly yellow warbler with olive-green on the back. It's our only warbler with a yellow face and dark cap—males have a black eye and cap; females have an olive-colored cap, sometimes with black.

Found: In riparian areas and near ornamental trees and shrubs in urban areas. Hot spots: Tumalo State Park, Tumalo Reservoir, and Lower Bridge.

Top: *Are you sure nature doesn't have a sense of humor? (Photo by Mark Lundgren)*

Bottom: *A female with her yellow underparts and fairly dark cap. (Photo by Kris Kristovich)*

Note the chestnut crown and white throat. (Photo by Chuck Gates)

SPARROWS AND TOWHEES

Green-tailed Towhee *(Pipilo chlorurus)*

Seen: End of April to early Oct.

Head east on Hwy. 20 and maybe at first (before reading this book) you'll think it's a dull region with nothing but sagebrush and juniper. But when you pull off the road and pull out some binoculars, you'll see there are a lot of birds and other wildlife out there—a whole world of activity for those who slow down long enough to notice.

Under a bitterbrush, sagebrush, manzanita, or other shrub, you might come across the colorful Green-tailed Towhee. This smallest of all towhees isn't readily seen because it spends most of its time scratching at the leaf litter under bushes and other cover. Take your time, though, and if you get lucky you'll hear its lovely song or mewing call.

Look for: The olive-yellow wings, back, and tail give it its name, but the eye-catching chestnut crown is usually easier to spot.

Found: In disturbed areas and places with a mix of trees and shrubs. Hot spots: Awbrey Hall burn area, south and west sides of Pine Mountain, Indian Ford Campground, and near Entrada Lodge.

Top: Their eyes are dark red most of the year but bright red during breeding season. (Photo by John Williams)

Bottom: A common and easy bird to spot. (Photo by Chuck Gates)

Spotted Towhee *(Pipilo maculatus)*

Seen: Year-round

If a shrub is making noise and you can't see what's causing it, odds are good it's a Spotted Towhee. They're striking birds when you spot them, but mostly they blend in with the leaf litter as they hop and scratch about for insects.

A wonderful fact about these towhees is that they sing with a purpose. Unlike Song Sparrows and other birds that regale us most or all of the year, male Spotted Towhees sing their hearts out only in the mornings of the early breeding season. As soon as they find a mate, they mostly clam up and focus on other bird business.

Look for: Males have ruby-red eyes and a black hood over the head and upper breast. Females have a slate-brown hood. On both, look for white spots on the wings, a long tail, reddish sides, and white bellies.

Found: In brushy areas. Hot spots: First Street Rapids, Deschutes River, Farewell Bend Park, and Lower Bridge.

Song Sparrow (Melospiza melodia)

Seen: Year-round

With a name like Song Sparrow, you'd better know how to belt out a tune. And indeed these aptly named sparrows sing all year long, both to attract mates and to defend their territory. They have one of the easiest birdsongs to identify, with three short notes followed by some buzzing and then a varied trill. The start of the song sounds like *bees-bees-buzzzzz*.

Researchers have found that young Song Sparrows learn their songs by listening to adults, and females are attracted not simply to the beauty of the song but to how well it reflects the male's ability to learn from his song tutors.

This is likely the most abundant sparrow in Oregon. (Photo by Kris Kristovich)

Look for: They're streaky overall, with brown marks on the breast converging to a central spot. In flight, watch for the pumping action of the tail.

Found: In riparian areas and marshes. Hot spots: First Street Rapids, Deschutes River Trail, and Farewell Bend Park.

White-crowned Sparrow

(Zonotrichia leucophrys)

Seen: Mid-Sept. to mid-April

Winter is the ideal time to go looking for the handsome White-crowned Sparrow, which is (along with the Dark-eyed Junco) one of Central Oregon's so-called snowbirds. Just as many other birds begin their migrations farther south, flocks of White-crowned Sparrows move into Central Oregon from the north, appearing in fields, under shrubs, and at backyard feeders.

Not all White-crowned Sparrows migrate, but those that do typically breed in Alaska and Canada—even above the Arctic Circle—before flying as far south as Southern California for the winter. Their migratory paths can cover over 2,500 miles; researchers tracked one White-crowned Sparrow that flew 300 miles in a single night.

Look for: A large sparrow with a long tail and boldly striped head. It takes two years to acquire adult plumage: Immature birds have reddish head stripes, while adults have bold black-and-white head stripes.

Found: Foraging on the ground in urban areas and nesting in high-elevation clearcuts. Hot spots: Urban birdfeeders and fence rows in winter. Sawyer Park is a good spot in spring.

Top: Look for the bold black-and-white stripes on the head. (Photo by Kevin Smith)

Bottom: They have reddish head stripes for their first two years. (Photo by Tom Lawler)

Top: *Note the white tail feathers sticking out behind the branch.* (Photo by Kris Kristovich)

Bottom: *Females have lighter hoods.* (Photo by Chuck Gates)

Dark-eyed Junco (*Junco hyemalis*)

Seen: Year-round

What do Dark-eyed Juncos have in common with deer and elk? They're all species that spend summer up at our higher elevations, then migrate down to warmer (and less snowy) environs once winter arrives.

These "snowbirds" are among the most common birds on the continent—look for Dark-eyed Juncos on your high-elevation hikes in summer and feeding at or under your feeder in winter.

Look for: Keys include a dark hood, rusty-brown or gray back, pink bill, and whitish underparts. You'll see their white outer tail feathers when they're flushed and hear their high chipping notes as they forage.

Found: At low elevations in winter (rural and open, grassy areas) and high timber in summer. Hot spots: Above 3,000 ft. in summer (Suttle Lake, High Lakes area); in winter, they're in Bend.

Top: *There's a reason these birds grace the covers of so many bird guides.* (Photo by Mark Lundgren)

Bottom: *Females are yellow-green with gray backs.* (Photo by jamesvancourver)

GROSBEAKS AND TANAGERS

Western Tanager (*Piranga ludoviciana*)

Seen: Late April to mid-Sept.

Upon encountering a spectacularly plumed Western Tanager in Central Oregon, you'd be excused for thinking the neotropical bird must be lost—surely it belongs farther south.

In fact, Western Tanagers do winter as far south as Costa Rica. But they also range farther north than any other tanager, nesting in conifers west of Bend and making a welcome appearance in and around our urban areas in spring and early fall.

Look for: Males are yellow with black wings and a flaming orange-red head. Wings are jet-black with two bright bars. Females sport yellow-green feathers on most of their bodies, set off by gray on the back.

Found: Nests in forests west of Bend; widespread during migration. Hot spots: Skyliners Rd. at Forest Rd. 430, High Lakes area, Wickiup Reservoir, and Suttle Lake.

Black-headed Grosbeak
(Pheucticus melanocephalus)

Seen: Late April to mid-Sept.

Black-headed Grosbeaks winter in Central America and in Mexico, where they have an unfortunate predilection for eating Monarch butterflies—millions of Monarch butterflies (they're one of the only birds that can withstand the toxins in the butterflies).

Black-headed Grosbeaks are unusual in another respect: Both females and males like to sing. In fact, a female will sometimes imitate a male's song, possibly to deceive her mate into spending more time at the nest to defend against the mystery man. As for the song itself, it's a sweet, whistled tune said to be like that of a robin . . . if a robin took singing lessons.

Top: *That no-nonsense beak can crack open seeds and hard-bodied insects. (Photo by Mark Lundgren)*

Bottom: *A lighter-colored female with a striped head. (Photo by John Williams)*

Look for: Males have a black head and bright-orange breast, neck, and rump. Females are buff color with pale orange on the belly, a brown back, and a striped head. Evening Grosbeaks have yellow plumage, not orange, and they don't have black or striped heads.

Found: Found along streams in forested areas in summer. They're common visitors to feeders in spring and fall. Hot spots: First Street Rapids, Sawyer Park, Shevlin Park, and Lower Bridge.

BLACKBIRDS

Red-winged Blackbird *(Agelaius phoeniceus)*

Seen: Year-round (few in winter)

Conk-la-ree! Conk-la-ree! When you hear that piercing call in area marshlands, winter is over and one of the continent's most abundant birds has returned.

It's hard to miss the flash of the males' brilliant red epaulets, or shoulder patches—and that's intentional. When the males return in spring, they boldly display those patches as they establish and defend their territories and court the ladies (up to fifteen females each spring).

The funny thing about the males is that after they spend their mornings squawking and attacking other males, they go hunting for food in peaceful afternoon flocks—often with the very same birds they were fighting with earlier. During those afternoon excursions the males hide their red shoulder patches, like matadors stowing their capes.

Top: *Listen for nonstop calls of conk-la-ree!*

Bottom: *Females look completely different than males. (Photos by John Williams)*

Look for: Males are glossy black with red-and-yellow shoulder patches. Females are dark-brownish overall, with streaks all over and a paler throat.

Found: All over, nesting in marshy vegetation like cattails. Hot spots: Hatfield Lake, Deschutes River in Bend, and Fireman's Pond in Redmond.

Males like this one have up to a dozen songs in their repertoires. (Photo by Alison Hardenburgh)

Western Meadowlark *(Sturnella neglecta)*

Seen: Year-round

One of the treats of spending time in open areas east of Bend is the opportunity to hear a Western Meadowlark greet the morning with a melodious song, which starts with a few whistles and ends with a jumbled series of bubbly notes. It's a signature sound of the wide-open West, traveling far and wide over grasses and sagebrush.

The meadowlark's *neglecta* name apparently stems from the fact that early settlers and explorers overlooked the bird. Today, Western Meadowlarks are the state bird of six states, including Oregon. They're not overlooked, but their populations have been declining west of the Cascades.

Look for: A robin-sized bird with a yellow belly and V-shaped black band across the chest. Upperparts are streaked tan and white. Males and females have similar markings.

Found: In open country with grassy areas. Hot spots: East of Bend at Alfalfa, Millican, and Powell Butte Hwy.

FINCHES

House Finch *(Haemorhous mexicanus)*

Seen: Year-round

If you haven't seen a House Finch lately, odds are you haven't been looking. They're an extremely common bird in parks and residential areas, with at least tens of millions of the birds spread across North America.

Since there's such a large sample size, take the time to notice the differences among the birds. The red color in many males comes from the seeds, buds, and fruit they eat—the more pigment in their diet, the redder they become. Females prefer to mate with the reddest male available, possibly because a reddish male is more likely to be a strong forager that can provide for his young.

Look for: Males have a rosy-red (or red-orange, orange, yellow-orange, or yellow) forehead, throat, eyebrow, and rump, with some red in the breast. Females are grayish-brown overall, with a lot of streaks but no red.

Found: Very common in a variety of habitats and at feeders. Hot spots: Juniper woodlands and any yard with a birdfeeder.

Top: This well-nourished male is likely to be popular with the opposite sex. (Photo by Kim Elton)

Bottom: Females are grayish-brown. (Photo by Kris Kristovich)

Red Crossbill *(Loxia curvirostra)*

Seen: Year-round

Put it on your birding bucket list to get close enough to see the crossed upper and lower bills of a Red Crossbill. It's a fascinating sight, and as with so many things in nature, it's also a clever adaptation.

Crossbills use their unique bills to get at the seeds in woody cones. First they bite down and move the lower portion of their bill sideways to spread the scales of the cone. Then they stick in their tongue to pull out the seeds. Amazing!

Crossbills are nomadic, wandering through forested areas in search of cones and breeding up to four times a year, including in winter—whenever they can find enough seed-filled cones.

Look for: Males have deep-red to reddish-yellow or greenish heads and bodies. Females are olive or grayish, with a greenish to greenish-yellow chest and rump. Look for flocks near the tops of area conifers.

Found: In stands of pine, fir, and incense-cedar. Hot spots: Sisters Ranger Station, Best Western Motel in Sisters, Cold Springs Campground, and Mount Bachelor.

Top: *No braces required—that funky bill serves a purpose. (Photo by Kris Kristovich)*

Bottom: *Females are not red at all. (Photo by Tom Lawler)*

Pine Siskin *(Spinus pinus)*

Seen: Year-round

One year your feeder might be mobbed by Pine Siskins, and the next you may see none at all. That's the nature of these nomadic finches, which move wherever they have to in order to find the pine and other seeds they need to survive.

Pine Siskins are tough little birds that can survive even extremely cold temperatures. On subzero nights, they can crank up their metabolic rates far higher than most songbirds. They also put on more winter fat than relatives like the American Goldfinch. And they can store up to ten percent of their body mass in the area of their esophagus known as the crop—enough food to get them through even very cold nights.

Look for: A very small songbird streaked with brown and white, with yellow markings at the base of the tail and on inner flight feathers. They're usually in flocks, so listen for their nonstop, buzzy twittering. In flight, they flap and glide in an undulating pattern.

Found: In coniferous forests. Hot spots: Calliope Crossing, near conifers across Sisters, and Bend city parks.

Top: *A beautifully streaked siskin perched in a pine tree. (Photo by Tom Lawler)*

Bottom: *Note the bright yellow on the folded wing. (Photo by Mark Lundgren)*

Top: *A male American Goldfinch in his summer finery—note the white on the tail. (Photo by John Williams)*

Bottom: *A male Lesser Goldfinch. (Photo by Mark Lundgren)*

Goldfinches *(Spinus* spp.*)*

Seen: Year-round

Lesser Goldfinches are far more common in Central Oregon, but it must be said that American Goldfinches are better looking.

Lessers have a distinctive call, with a high *tee* followed by a lower *yer*. To spot American Goldfinches, watch for the flash of gold and their undulating flight pattern.

Look for: Lessers are the lesser in size; they're not much larger than a hummingbird. Males have a yellow front and black cap. American Goldfinch males are drab in winter but become bright yellow with a black forehead.

Found: In all habitats, but most common near waterways and urban feeders. Hot spots: Deschutes River, Bend neighborhoods, First Street Rapids, and Lower Bridge.

Top: *Males have pale bills and a bold yellow stripe over each eye.*

Bottom: *Females have greenish-yellow bills. (Photos by Tom Lawler)*

Evening Grosbeak *(Coccothraustes vespertinus)*

Seen: Year-round

If Evening Grosbeaks were football players, they'd be linebackers. They're sturdy birds with thick chests and necks, and a massive bill they use to crack open seeds and even cherry pits.

Evening Grosbeaks are also an irruptive, or irregular, winter migrant, so it's tough to predict when and where you'll see them. The best bets are in spring when they perch atop conifers and call as they bounce along in flight (their call has been compared to that of a kid pretending to shoot a laser gun: *tchoo, tchoo*). You also might spot a "gross" of grosbeaks (yes, that's really the term) mobbing your backyard feeder.

Look for: Males are yellow and black with a prominent white patch on their wings, a yellow stripe over their eyes, and pale-ivory bills. Females are mostly gray with black-and-white wings and a greenish-yellow tinge on their necks and sides.

Found: Tough to predict, but often in residential areas outside summer months. Hot spots: Bend city parks, Skyliners Rd. at Forest Rd. 430, Deschutes River Woods, and the High Lakes area.

INVASIVES

European Starling (*Sturnus vulgaris*)
Seen: Year-round

I'm going to go out on a limb here and say there's no such thing as a bad bird species. Birds are just birds, living their bird lives and playing their natural role in the ecosystem. The problem with the European Starling is that it was dragged out of its home ecosystem in Europe and into ours. Doing the dragging was an overly enthusiastic (and literary) Englishman who thought all the birds mentioned by Shakespeare should be in the U.S. Oh, those silly Brits.

Now all of North America is stuck with a bird that kills other birds and their young; kicks bluebirds, chickadees, swallows, and other natives out of their nests; and just generally doesn't play well with others. Incidentally, and ironically, while starlings are now ubiquitous across this continent, in their U.K. homeland their numbers have fallen by up to ninety percent.

It's too bad starlings don't blend in well here because they're wonderful in several ways, including their ability to mimic the sound of everything from barking dogs to croaking frogs. Mozart's beloved pet starling even sang bars of his owner's music.

Look for: A stocky, short-tailed bird. In spring, they're glossy black all over with iridescent layers that glow different colors, depending on the light. By winter, they've added new feathers with white spots that give them their name.

Found: Flocks can be seen all over, but especially in farm country, suburbs, and cities (less so in extensive forest and scrub areas).

Top: *They're invasive and harmful. They're also dazzling.* (Photo by John Williams)

Bottom: *Their summertime plumage is purplish-green with a yellow beak.* (Photo by Chuck Gates)

"MELVIN!"

My friend's grandmother lived with her husband, Melvin, on a beautiful plot of land in the town of Alfalfa. Around noon one day, Grandma Donna walked outside and heard herself call out in a loud, high-pitched voice: "Melvin! Melvin!" She hadn't opened her mouth, but a starling knew it was time to call her husband in for lunch.

Top: *Males have a black throat patch that grows with age.*

Bottom: *Females have buff stripes at each eye. (Photos by Tom Lawler)*

House Sparrow (*Passer domesticus*)

Seen: Year-round

You wouldn't know it from sitting outside at just about any restaurant in Central Oregon, but populations of House Sparrows are actually on the decline. Few people are losing sleep over this because, like the European Starling, House Sparrows are aggressive imports from Europe that evict native birds from their nest holes and have even been known to kill large birds like woodpeckers (and their young) to steal their nest cavities.

Let me try to find a bright side: Because House (aka English) Sparrows are so abundant, you can easily watch them and learn the pleasures of closely observing bird behavior. For instance, you'll notice that they don't walk on the ground; they hop, possibly because it requires less energy than walking. Also look for the black throat patches on the males—the larger the patch, the older the bird is likely to be, and the higher up his position on the sparrow pecking order.

Look for: Flocks of chunky, chirping, rather nondescript birds in urban settings and at backyard feeders. Males have a gray crown and black bib on the throat, and females have a buff eye stripe.

Found: All over urban areas.

Look for the black band around the back of the neck. (Photo by Tom Lawler)

Eurasian Collared-Dove (*Streptopelia decaocto*)

Seen: Year-round

Eurasian Collared-Doves were first observed in Bend in 2006. Within a decade, they had spread across neighborhoods and begun crowding out smaller and less aggressive Mourning Doves.

As for how they got here, the story goes that a pet shop owner in the Bahamas released a flock of about fifty collared-doves in the 1970s, and others were set free on the island of Guadeloupe. From those two places, collared-dove populations spread to Florida by the 1980s, and from there they spread rapidly to the rest of the U.S., including Alaska.

Look for: A light-gray or brown bird, bigger than a Mourning Dove but smaller than a pigeon. Note the black collar around the back of the neck. The tail is not pointed like a Mourning Dove's, but the *coo-coo-cook* call is similar.

Found: Urban feeders and agricultural areas. Hot spots: Bend and Redmond neighborhoods.

Rock Dove (Pigeon)
(Columba livia)

Seen: Year-round

Wild Rock Doves, or pigeons, were domesticated over 5,000 years ago and have served humans in many ways, including by carrying messages for the U.S. Army Signal Corps during the first two world wars. These days you'll see feral populations feeding on garbage, human handouts, and weed seeds.

Derisively called "flying rats" by some, pigeons are occasionally poisoned because people don't like their noise and the smelly mess they leave behind. The problem is that putting poison on roofs or really anywhere can lead to it being eaten not just by pigeons but also by native animals. And even when pigeons eat the poison, unintended targets like Red-tailed Hawks, falcons, and other native birds may also die when they feed on the pigeons.

Their necks often have iridescent green and purple feathers.
(Photo by John Williams)

Look for: Wild pigeons are pale gray overall with two black bars on each wing. Domestic and feral pigeons come in all sorts of colors and patterns.

Found: All over, especially city parks and buildings. Hot spots: Bend Parkway, Smith Rock State Park, and the Crooked River Gorge.

> "I loved that pigeon as a man loves a woman, and she loved me. As long as I had her, there was a purpose to my life."
> —Nikola Tesla

Bobcat. (Photo by Buddy Mays)

Bighorn sheep. (Photo by Greg Burke)

Black bear and cub. (Photo by Alison Hardenburgh)

WILDLIFE

Life is a little wild in Central Oregon. Step outside your door, and you can't help but stumble across deer, coyotes, rabbits and hares, squirrels and chipmunks, yellow-bellied marmots, bats, lizards, and snakes—and that's without trying and without leaving town.

Drive less than an hour outside urban areas, and you can see so much more, from the adorable (pikas) to the impressive (elk) and ancient (pronghorn). Of course, you would've found far more wildlife—more individuals and more species—just a few decades ago. Researchers say wildlife populations have declined by an average of

Western Tiger Swallowtail. (Photo by Dave Rein)

North American river otter. (Photo by Toni Morris)

Pacific treefrog. (Photo by Alan St. John)

Black-tailed jackrabbit.

more than seventy percent since 1970, and we'll lose far more in the years ahead, unless we do more to slow climate change and reduce habitat loss.

The diversity of wildlife in Central Oregon, as well as its decline, is why it feels so critical right now to get to know the animals that still live with and around us. And I do mean get to know them—to learn not only their physical characteristics but also the essence of who they are and why they matter as individuals, valuable contributors to our ecosystems, and symbols of the high desert we all love so much.

AMPHIBIANS

FROGS

American Bullfrog (*Rana catesbeiana*)
Body: 3–8 in.

Although the opening lines of the 1970s song "Joy to the World" may make you think that bullfrogs are friendly, in fact, the American bullfrog is one of the Oregon Department of Fish and Wildlife's twelve most invasive animals and one of the hundred most invasive species in the world—a giant among frogs that doesn't belong here and is the single biggest threat to our native amphibians and small fish. The bullfrog was probably introduced to Central Oregon in the 1920s, when loggers moved to Gilchrist from southern states and brought the tasty buggers along with them.

Bullfrogs don't survive well in areas with long, cold winters, which is one reason we don't have more killer Kermits already. There's trouble ahead, though, as our winters get longer and warmer. To get a feel for the scope of the problem, consider that they can lay 20,000 eggs at a time—even up to 50,000, according to local biologist Jay Bowerman.

To be clear, the bullfrog isn't a "bad animal." There's no such thing. It's just an animal that humans introduced into an environment where it doesn't belong. If you spot a population of bullfrogs (their cow-like bellows are a giveaway), call ODFW. It's legal to kill bullfrogs but also essential that you know what you're doing and don't accidentally harm any of our native animals.

Top: Note the large skin fold right behind the eye. (Photo by Oregon Department of Fish and Wildlife)

Bottom: A blue heron doing us a favor. (Photo by Jim Anderson)

Note: Unless otherwise noted, amphibian photos are courtesy of Alan St. John.

Look for: They're huge! Bullfrogs are much bigger than native frogs, and they have a large tympanum (eardrum) just behind their eyes that creates a distinctive circle.

Found: They're spreading fast across Sunriver and are increasingly common along irrigation canals north and east of Bend, in Crooked River Ranch, and in Prineville.

Oregon spotted frogs require shallow water to survive.

Oregon Spotted Frog *(Rana pretiosa)*

Body: 1.75–4 in.

The Latin *pretiosa* means "precious," and indeed the Oregon spotted frog is a very precious species—the state's most endangered amphibian. After a twenty-three-year wait, the spotted frog finally won listing as a threatened species on the Endangered Species List in mid-2014. A hollow victory indeed.

Deschutes County is one of a few counties in the state that still have spotted frogs, albeit in scattered and isolated wetlands. The frogs once ranged across ten Oregon counties, but urban and agricultural development, livestock grazing, beaver removal, and non-native plants have combined to significantly reduce their available habitat.

Central Oregon's best-known populations are right in the middle of the action at the Old Mill. The frogs were discovered in several spots in the Old Mill in 2012, and two years later landowners and the U.S. Fish and Wildlife Service signed a conservation agreement to protect the frogs' habitat by maintaining water levels, managing vegetation along the riverbanks, controlling predators, and preventing erosion.

The future of the spotted frog is deeply in doubt and depends on restoring wetlands. That means putting beavers back into our ecosystems, yanking out invasive grasses, and removing non-native predators (we're looking at you, bullfrogs).

Look for: Vary in overall color, but have black spots with light centers all over their bodies.

Found: In marshy sites along the Deschutes and Little Deschutes Rivers—try not to bother them!

Treefrogs are the smallest (but definitely not the quietest) frogs in Oregon.

Pacific Treefrog (*Pseudacris regilla*)
Body: 1-2 in.

Oregon doesn't have a state reptile or amphibian, which is a travesty of sorts, since that gave Washington the chance to nab the Pacific treefrog as its own.

The treefrog (or chorus frog) is the froggiest of frogs—the only one that actually makes the *ribbit* sound we associate with frogs. They're the most commonly seen and heard frogs in Oregon, and probably the ones you picture when you think of frogs. They're also a keystone species, meaning their populations have an outsized effect on their environment.

Look for: Treefrogs can be all sorts of colors, but they always have a thick black stripe through their eyes.

Found: Listen for them from late April through June in marshy areas along the Deschutes River Trail, including at Benham Falls and Lava Island.

HOW TO HELP TREEFROGS

Even this most common of frogs is on the decline. If you want to attract more treefrogs to your property, Oregon Department of Fish and Wildlife recommends that you:

- Protect your wetlands, meadows, shorelines, and other natural areas.

- Make sure you have native vegetation along your watery areas.

- Protect paths between their breeding sites and upland areas. You can use logs or brush piles, or even build small tunnels under your roadways.

- Leave some grass unmowed near their sites—and scout for them before you mow.

- Keep stumps, logs, leaf litter, and other debris that provide cover.

- Build a pond! Make sure it offers both sun and shade and is deeper than a foot. Fence large ponds to keep livestock away and protect water quality.

Spadefoots are one of the only toads with vertical pupils.

TOADS

Great Basin Spadefoot *(Spea intermontana)*

Body: 1.5–2.5 in.

Once upon a time, there was a toad that wanted to live in the desert. That would be the fairy-tale opening to the story of the Great Basin spadefoot, the most desert-adapted of our Central Oregon amphibians.

The key is those eponymous feet: The toad uses the sharp-edged nubbins that stick out from the heel of each back foot to burrow rapidly backward into loose soil. Their burrows can be shallow or a few feet deep—even as many as fifteen feet deep—depending on how far the toads need to dig to find cool, humid conditions.

And here's the really incredible part: Great Basin spadefoots can stay in their underground burrows for two years! They basically chill out, completely dormant (not eating or drinking, although they absorb moisture from the soil), until spring or summer rains come along. Then they emerge to eat beetles, ants, and anything else they can find to replenish their fat stores.

If you're lucky, after a rain you might hear the male spadefoots crying *whaa, whaa, whaa* at irrigation ditches, ponds, stream edges—wherever they can find water and mates to help them live happily ever after.

Look for: They're the only toads you're going to see in our dry areas. Look for smooth skin and an hourglass marking on their backs.

Found: You might see them emerging after rains in the sagebrush flats east of Bend where they burrow in the sandy soil.

Western Toad *(Anaxyrus boreas)*

Body: 2-5 in.

How do toads cross the road? Very carefully, we hope. River Road in Sunriver is one of many busy roads western toads have to hop across in a high-stakes version of Frogger.

In spring, adults travel from dry land to ponds, lakes, and wetlands to breed, then head back to forests and meadows. Their young emerge from the water in summer, when the tiny toadlets undertake their first dangerous trek from the water to the dry land where they'll live until spring.

Top: Look for the pale stripe down the back.

Bottom: Kissing the handsome mug of a toad won't give you warts, but it's still best to leave them be.

I wish I could say the story ends there, with the western toad (and their fellow amphibians) living happily ever after. But in fact western toad populations are declining in many areas, and more than one in three of all amphibians is at risk of extinction.

Look for: A pale stripe down their backs and dry, bumpy skin (frogs generally have much smoother skin than toads).

Found: Common at the Cascade Lakes, where hundreds of thousands of tadpoles live along the shorelines. In summer, hike carefully along Todd Lake, Walton Lake, and similar spots where you might spot little toads hopping across the trail.

SALAMANDERS

Long-toed Salamander
(Ambystoma macrodactylum)

Body: 1.5–3.5 in.

Let me be honest here: I wasn't going to cover the long-toed salamander because I just didn't think anyone would notice if I left it out. But, oh, was I wrong. Three people let me know in no uncertain terms that you *cannot* leave out the *only* native salamander you're *ever* going to see in Central Oregon.

Check out those long toes!

So: This smooth, moist character is black, brown, and yellow, with decidedly outsized fourth toes on its hind feet—hence the name. Like other pond-breeding salamanders, they begin life as eggs, become larvae that feed on other small aquatic creatures (occasionally including their brood mates), and then morph magically (or scientifically) into walking adults.

Long-toed salamanders are one of the most widely distributed salamanders on the continent, which tells you that they can live in all sorts of demanding environments. Adults hibernate through our long winters and can live up to ten years, as long they avoid garter snakes, birds, fish, and other predators.

Look for: They're the *only* native salamander in Central Oregon.

Found: In spring, adults can be found under debris or in the shoreline shallows of area rivers, streams, lakes, and ponds.

THREE EASY WAYS TO HELP AMPHIBIANS

- Stop using pesticides and herbicides (they absorb them through their skin).

- Control (by hand, if possible) non-native plants like reed canary grass.

- Find responsible ways to remove non-native predators like the American bullfrog.

INSECTS

BUTTERFLIES

I asked local expert Sue Anderson to help me choose "a couple" butterflies for my book. She was kind enough not to tackle me to the ground and physically pummel some sense into me, but she did let me know that butterflies are too beautiful, abundant, and beloved to get such short shrift. She also graciously provided all the photos in this section of the book. Here, then, is at least a fair sampling of the seven main types of these colorful ambassadors of the insect world.

SKIPPERS

Juba Skipper *(Hesperia juba)*

Size: Small (0.75–1.25 in.)

Skippers are fast flyers that "skip" through the air in a stop-and-go pattern that gives them their name. The Juba Skipper is a fun one with a fat body and really big eyes.

Look for: Triangular in shape and tawny in color, with big silver spots on the undersides of their wings.

Found: All over the region, with peak populations in May and September.

Common Checkered Skipper *(Pyrgus communis)*

Size: Small (0.75–1.25 in.)

The two checkered skippers in Central Oregon (the other is the Two-banded Checkered Skipper) have notably checkered wings and sip nectar from all sorts of annuals, thistles, and more.

Look for: The Common Checkered Skipper's name comes from the distinctive black-and-white checkered pattern on its wings.

Found: From April into fall, you'll find them all over—especially flitting around dry, vacant lots.

SWALLOWTAILS

Western Tiger Swallowtail *(Papilio rutulus)*

Size: Large (2.5–5 in.)

When you picture a butterfly, it's likely a swallowtail that comes to mind. The Western Tiger Swallowtail is well adapted to life in urban areas and is thus our most common swallowtail.

Look for: They're bright yellow, with black, tiger-like stripes on the wings and a single tail.

Found: They're especially abundant along watercourses and have a well-known love for lilacs.

Anise Swallowtail *(Papilio zelicaon)*

Size: Large (2.5–5 in.)

Anise Swallowtails are tigers without the thick stripes. They're beautiful, with a distinctive reddish spot on the hindwing. They're also highly adaptable and can be found in open areas everywhere from deserts to alpine summits.

Look for: Largely black and yellow, with a mostly black abdomen and yellowish to red eyespot on the hindwing.

Found: In many of the same places as the Western Tiger Swallowtail, drinking nectar from many of the same flowers.

WHITES, MARBLES, AND SULPHURS

Western White *(Pontia occidentalis)*

Size: Medium (1.25–2.5 in.)

If you've lived or hiked in Central Oregon for any length of time, you've almost certainly seen whites. The Western White is especially common, but you may see others like the Becker's White (one of the few common to sagebrush) and the Cabbage White (common in vegetable gardens).

Look for: Wings are a white palette dotted by black rectangles, with black edges on the tips.

Found: These are among our most common butterflies, found nearly everywhere from March to October.

Western Sulphur *(Colias occidentalis)*

Size: Medium (1.25–2.5 in.)

This lemon-yellow beauty was discovered near Port Townsend, Washington, in the mid-1850s. Another common one is the Orange Sulphur, also called the "alfalfa butterfly" because it's found in huge numbers in alfalfa fields.

Look for: Males are lemon-yellow with black wing borders; females are a creamier yellow with a black dusting at the base.

Found: Up in the Cascades and near Camp Sherman, with peak populations in midsummer.

MOTH OR BUTTERFLY?

If it's nighttime, you're almost certainly looking at a moth since they're nocturnal. Look closer, and you'll see that moths have pointed or feathered antennae, whereas butterfly antennae have a bulb at the tip.

GOSSAMER WINGS

Purplish Copper *(Lycaena helloides)*

Size: Small (0.75–1.25 in.)

Gossamer wings are smaller butterflies with wings that change color in different lights. Male Purplish Coppers can change from brown to neon purple in the flash of an eye (or sunbeam).

Look for: Like all but one of our seven coppers, the Purplish Copper is mostly orange. It got its name for the purple on its topside that pops out in the right light.

Found: Most common in high-elevation meadows but also in urban areas.

Cedar Hairstreak *(Mitoura grynea)*

Size: Small (0.75–1.25 in.)

Most hairstreaks have hair-like tails that stick out from the back of the hindwings. Of our thirteen hairstreaks, the Cedar Hairstreak is most common, in part because we have the cedars and especially the junipers it depends on.

Look for: Small, reddish-brown butterflies with a white stripe on the underside of their wings.

Found: We're fortunate to have a lot of these butterflies all over Central Oregon—look for them near cedars and junipers.

Greenish Blue *(Plebejus saepiolus)*

Size: Small (0.75–1.25 in.)

Regarding the thirteen blues in Central Oregon, Sue Anderson says, "The sheer beauty of these little shimmering pieces of sky will stop any hikers in their tracks." The Greenish Blue abounds throughout the summer.

Look for: Males get all the glory—while females are mostly brown, males are a pretty blue on top with small black hash marks on their forewings.

Found: They love wet meadows and congregate at puddles and near well-watered clover, especially at higher elevations.

BRUSH-FOOTED

Zerene Fritillary *(Speyeria zerene)*

Size: Medium (1.25–2.5 in.)

Fritillary larvae feed only on wild violets, while adults draw nectar from thistles, mint, and other plants. The Zerene Fritillary is one of ten fritillaries in Central Oregon.

Look for: They're orange with black veins above and shiny silver spots on the undersides of their wings.

Found: In most of the Deschutes Land Trust preserves.

Snowberry Checkerspot *(Euphydryas colon)*

Size: Medium (1.25–2.5 in.)

Snowberry Checkerspots are one of our four gorgeous checkerspot species (Sue Anderson calls them "flying stained-glass windows").

Look for: Colors change from location to location, but ours are mostly dark-black above, with cream-colored spots and red on the margins of the wings.

Found: Prevalent in the Cascades and Ochocos, where they like to feed on dogbane.

Field Crescent *(Phyciodes pulchellus)*

Size: Small (0.75–1.25 in.)

We only have two crescents in Central Oregon: this one and the Mylitta Crescent. They're smaller than checkerspots, with subtler (but still intricate) patterns on their wings.

Look for: Mostly black, with orange and cream "windows" on their wings; the Mylitta Crescent is the opposite (mostly orange with black veins and spots).

Found: Very common butterflies at roadsides and high in the mountains, especially where asters are blooming.

Hoary Comma *(Polygonia gracilis)*

Size: Medium (1.25–2.5 in.)

Also called the Zephyr Anglewing, the Hoary Comma is one of the fastest butterflies in the West. Commas are also called anglewings because of their ragged-edge wings (which make them easy to identify).

Look for: Deep orange with black blotches on top and yellow chevrons on the wing borders. Undersides have a white Nike swoosh on the hindwing.

Found: These are the highest-elevation anglewing, usually found above 3,000 feet along streams, roads, and trails.

Mourning Cloak *(Nymphalis antiopa)*

Size: Large (2.5–5 in.)

The lovely Mourning Cloak is the largest of the three tortoiseshell butterflies in Central Oregon. It feeds on trees and shrubs and is often the only butterfly flying on warm days in early spring.

Look for: When newly emerged, they have a chocolate interior bordered by violet spots, with a golden-yellow fringe. Truly a sight to behold!

Found: Most common in riparian areas; also parks and yards.

West Coast Lady *(Vanessa annabella)*

Size: Medium (1.25–2.5 in.)

You may have heard of Red Admirals, Painted Ladies, Buckeyes, and other "ladies." Of these, the West Coast Lady is our most common, emerging in March and with us through fall.

Look for: The largest colored area on top of the forewing and nearest the wingtip is orange (it's white on the Painted Lady).

Found: All over area gardens, flowerbeds, vacant lots, and meadows.

Lorquin's Admiral *(Limenitis lorquini)*

Size: Large (2.5–5 in.)

We have two beautiful admiral butterflies, the Lorquin's Admiral and the Red Admiral. Lorquin's are especially abundant and can be spotted from February through October.

Look for: Lorquin's have a black interior with a white "necklace" and orange tips on the wings.

Found: All along our riparian areas.

California Tortoiseshell *(Nymphalis californica)*

Size: Medium (1.25–2.5 in.)

You can call the California Tortoiseshell beautiful for its orange-and-black coloring. Just don't call it a Monarch, as many do. It's about half the size of the Monarch, with angular wing edges.

Look for: Mostly orange with black forewing boxes and dots.

Found: Like our real estate prices, California Tortoiseshells go through boom-and-bust cycles. In some years, hikers in the Cascades can encounter thousands coursing along trails.

HOW TO HELP

We don't have a lot of Monarchs coming through Central Oregon, but you can help those that do. Monarchs rely on milkweed to develop, so contact WinterCreek or other local nurseries to buy native milkweed for your garden. Learn more at monarchwatch.org.

SATYRS

Great Basin Wood Nymph *(Cercyonis sthenele)*

Size: Medium (1.25–2.5 in.)

Satyrs are brownish butterflies with a distinctive "whop-whop" flight pattern instead of a flitter. They often have one or more eyespots, which is the case for our three wood nymph species.

Look for: Two-toned underneath with a line on the hindwing that resembles Mount Washington.

Found: Prefer open forest clearings, especially in the Metolius River Basin, but they're also in backyards and sagebrush areas.

Great Arctic *(Oeneis nevadensis)*

Size: Medium (1.25–2.5 in.)

The Great Arctic is our only Arctic species (it's also called the Nevada Arctic, even though it's never been spotted in Nevada). It has a two-year life cycle and is here only in even-numbered years.

Look for: Pale orange above, with a spot on the forewing.

Found: As you'd expect given the name, they're mostly found at higher elevations, in open meadows.

MONARCHS

Monarch *(Danaus plexippus)*

Size: Large (2.5–5 in.)

The most beloved butterfly on the continent is in serious danger, especially the western populations that come through Oregon. With a lifecycle spanning three countries and thousands of miles, Monarchs are a unique and truly wondrous animal that will need a lot of help to survive.

Look for: Monarchs are orange and black with a border of white dots.

Found: Adults prefer meadows, weedy fields, riparian areas, and anywhere milkweed is growing.

WANT MORE?

This is just the tip of the butterfly iceberg. To really get to know our local flyers, sign up for a free guided walk with an expert from the Deschutes Land Trust.

A bee gathering pollen from a sunflower. (Photos of bees by Rich Hatfield)

FOUR EASY STEPS TO HELP OUR NATIVE BEES

1. Find alternatives to herbicides like Roundup and neonicotinoid insecticides. Natural treatments like soapy water or vinegar are simple and non-toxic.

2. Ask nurseries and big-box stores if they pre-treat their plants with neonicotinoids, which make plants toxic to bees and other insects. Don't buy plants from them if they do, and be vocal—ask them to change their policy.

3. Be lazy in parts of your yard. Native bees like overgrown grass, brush piles, and dead wood, and some need bare ground for nesting.

4. Native bees, especially bumblebees, need nectar and pollen from early spring through late fall, so plant native shrubs and wildflowers with different bloom times (see chart on facing page).

NATIVE BEES

I hope I'm not the only one who grew up thinking that honeybees—the kind that live in hives and produce honey—were the only bees around. Honeybees are actually non-native imports from Europe. They're important for pollinating crops, but they're also causing problems for Oregon's more than 700 species of native bees.

In Central Oregon alone, we have 300 or so native bee species, many of which are struggling due to habitat destruction, pesticide use, disease, and climate change. At lease six of our twenty-plus native bumblebee species are at risk of extinction.

Native bees pollinate at least eighty percent of all flowering plants, making them essential to human survival. They come in many sizes, shapes, and colors, and different species build nests in the ground, dead trees, or grasses. Some are generalists and others specialize in pollinating a particular plant.

Top: *Note the difference in color and stripes between the bumblebee at left and the non-native honeybee at right.*

Bottom: *One of the twenty-plus bumblebee species you might see in Central Oregon* (Bombus melanopygus).

While keeping honeybees is a fun hobby with a tasty outcome, we need to focus on helping native bees survive. They're typically the only ones buzzing around in early spring and at higher elevations to pollinate the native plants that make Central Oregon special.

Look for: Honeybees have alternating black and brownish stripes on their abdomens. Native bees vary in appearance, but bumblebees are easy—they're typically big and fuzzy, most commonly with black and yellow stripes.

Found: Native bees can be found from high up in the Cascades down to lower elevations. Look and listen for them on area wildflowers.

APPROXIMATE BLOOM TIMES FOR NATIVE PLANTS THAT SUPPORT BEES

Early	Middle	Late
Balsamroots	Buckwheats	Asters
Bitter Cherry	Douglas Spiraea	Goldenrod
Oregon Grape	Mock-Orange	Gray Rabbitbrush
Serviceberry	Oceanspray	Green Rabbitbrush
Oceanspray	Orange Globemallow	Sunflowers
Western Columbine	Oregon Sunshine	
	Penstemons	

MAMMALS

LARGE MAMMALS

BEARS

American Black Bear (*Ursus americanus*)

Body: 5–6 ft., weight: 125–500 lbs., shoulder height: 3–4 ft.

Since the last grizzly was killed in Oregon in 1931, the black bear has been the state's last bear standing. It no doubt works in their favor that they're solitary animals that tend to stay away from humans, especially as they disappear into their dens for half the year.

Speaking of which, black bear hibernation (technically a state of deep torpor) is fascinating. They hole up in small caves, tree cavities, or other dens where their body temperatures drop significantly, their heart rates decline to as few as eight beats a minute, and they don't eat, urinate, or defecate—for up to seven months.

Female bears may enter hibernation with fertilized eggs, but the eggs don't grow right away. If she doesn't have enough fat stored up, her system will effectively cancel the pregnancy, reabsorbing the eggs before they attach to her uterine wall. If instead her system gives the green light, she'll give birth in January, which gives her cubs as much time as possible to build up the fat stores they'll need to survive the next winter.

Like raccoons, black bears are sometimes attracted to parks and campgrounds where people leave out food. Most often, though, you won't see bears, just "bear trees"—trees they bite, claw, or rub during their summer mating season.

Look for: They're the only bear around, although it's worth noting that they're not always black (they can be brown, cinnamon, bluish-black, etc.).

Found: You're not likely to see them out and about, but they're occasional visitors to forest campgrounds like those at Hosmer Lake, Newberry National Monument, and Lake Billy Chinook, so stow your food appropriately.

Top: A captive and rather content-looking black bear. (Photo by Kevin Smith)

Bottom: A tiny cub on a very large ponderosa pine. (Photo by Oregon Department of Fish and Wildlife)

For those who don't believe in lava bears. (Photo by Jim Anderson)

Lava Bear *(Ursus benditis)*

Body: 2–3 ft.

Lava bears are a myth, a mascot, and a cautionary tale. In the 1920s, a popular reporter and humorist for the *Saturday Evening Post* named Irvin S. Cobb caught wind of a good story: Diminutive bears—weighing thirty-five pounds or less and standing about eighteen inches at the shoulder—had been spotted in lava beds southeast of Bend, near Fort Rock.

Cobb organized the first hunt for what some thought was a new species, and more hunts followed, led most famously by a government trapper named Alfred Andrews. Andrews killed the first small female bear he caught and sold her to the Smithsonian. Then he trapped a male ("Teddy," of course) and made money at exhibitions like one in Portland that drew about 8,000 people.

In 1924, *The Spokesman Review* fueled the lava bear craze in an article about Teddy:

> He has the eyes and head of a coyote, a lip not unlike that of a bear, a nose like a pig . . .
> "Teddy," the meanest, roughest, toughest, and sauciest of bears . . . hates everything
> and everybody who comes within eyeshot. And he has the most active eyes in the
> world. He doesn't growl. He doesn't wait that long before he starts to spring—two
> husky chains prevent the leap.

A funny thing happened in the 1930s, when more little lava bears were caught: They appeared to grow rather rapidly when they had access to, you know, food. It turned out they were almost certainly not a new species, just malnourished black bears that got caught up in an all-too-human tale.

Look for: Small, hungry bears.

Found: NE Sixth St. in Bend.

Bobcats are about twice the size of an average housecat. (Photo by Kevin Smith)

CATS

Bobcat (*Lynx rufus*)

Body: 2–3.5 ft., tail: 5–7 in., shoulder height: 17–21 in.

Like coyotes, bobcats are smart, adaptable animals. They're able to live just about anywhere, from wetlands to deserts, and they eat everything from birds and rodents to the occasional unsuspecting deer. Also like coyotes, bobcats are heavily preyed upon by humans.

Bobcat populations may be dropping due to trapping. (Photo by Jim Anderson)

Although bobcats are by far the most widespread wild cat in the Pacific Northwest, the subspecies east of the Cascades is more highly prized for its pelt, which sells for hundreds of dollars. The desire for fashionable clothing in other countries creates a strong demand. That, on top of habitat loss, could spell trouble for east-side populations.

Bobcat sightings are already rare, in part because the cats are crepuscular, meaning they're most active at dawn and dusk. You're more likely to come across their scat or the scraped ground where they've tried to cover it.

Look for: Bobcats are much bigger than housecats and far more common than lynx, with shorter ear tufts and feet that aren't nearly as big.

Found: In all sorts of habitats, from the Badlands Wilderness to Metolius Preserve. They prefer the cover of rocky outcroppings, ledges, and cliffs, or large brush and log piles in forested areas.

Check out the size of those paws! (Photo by jimkruger)

Canada Lynx (*Lynx canadensis*)

Body: About 3 ft., shoulder height: 18–23 in.

Years ago, Canada lynx lived in the Cascade Mountains, but these days sightings are extremely rare, and while lynx might occasionally pass through high-elevation areas, officials don't know of any that reside in Oregon.

In recent decades, trapping, logging, and human intrusion (via roads, trails, off-road vehicles, and snowmobiles) have decimated lynx populations across the West. They were added to the Endangered Species List as a threatened species in 2000.

Unlike the wide-ranging, adaptable bobcat, lynx are single-minded about their preferred habitat (high, forested areas with deep winter snow cover) and food (snowshoe hares). When there are a lot of snowshoe hares, lynx have large litters. When hare populations drop in their cyclical pattern, lynx sometimes don't breed at all.

Lynx can use those bright eyes to spot mice from 250 feet away. (Photo by John Williams)

Oregon is at the very southern tip of lynx range, so especially with temperatures warming and snowpack less predictable, we aren't likely to see many of these unique cats coming through Central Oregon.

Look for: Huge feet. Lynx leave prints wider than a human hand (more like a cougar print than a bobcat's).

Found: We can hope they'll return to high elevations in the Cascades or the Blue or Wallowa Mountains in northeast Oregon.

Mountain Lion (Cougar)

(Puma concolor)

Body: 3.5–5 ft., tail: 2–3 ft., shoulder height: 26–32 in.

If you want to start a brawl in a bar in Bend, announce that you're a cougar lover. Or a cougar hunter. Or both. We've always had issues with animals at the top of the food chain, including cougars, grizzlies (we killed Oregon's last one in 1931), and wolves (which were driven out by 1947). Some wolves have returned in recent years, but clearly for now the cougar is top dog . . . so to speak.

Cougar basics

A female cougar can come into heat at any time of year. Over about a week, she will mate several hundred times, and six months later will give birth to up to six kittens that each weigh about a pound. Mothers first teach their young to pounce on small prey like grasshoppers, before they graduate to bigger game—and then much bigger game.

Grown cougars subsist on an Atkins-like deer-a-week diet, although they also substitute a lot of smaller animals like skunks, porcupines, and rabbits. Oh, and occasionally the strongest cats can take down an 800-pound elk.

Dominant males have huge territories of up to 300 miles that may overlap with several females. Cougars hunt alone, sneaking up and pouncing on prey with the help of their tremendous leaping ability (they can leap forty feet in a single bound and jump higher than a second-story balcony).

Top: *Not the look you want to see on a cougar's face. (Photo by John Williams)*

Bottom: *They use ridges and other high spots to scout for prey. (Photo by Buddy Mays)*

A cute, and fierce, kitten. (Photo by Dave Rein)

Our lives with cougars

Fortunately for us, cougars do not see us as part of their food chain and generally want nothing to do with us (rather like my housecat, actually). Cougar attacks are terrifying but also exceedingly rare. You're much more likely to die of a lightning strike or in a wildfire. You're also more likely to be killed by mosquitoes (disease), deer (if you hit them with your vehicle), or bees (if you're allergic).

If we can get past our primal fear of them, there's a lot to appreciate about these cats. They're apex predators, and as such their presence has a trickle-down effect on the health of entire ecosystems. Researchers have found that cougars play an essential role in maintaining biodiversity by helping to control populations of deer, elk, and coyotes.

Occasionally a young male cougar will wander through a Central Oregon town, having been booted out of his home territory by a dominant male, often his father. Such encounters are scary for us and probably for the cougars as well. What we should do about them is a hot topic in Central Oregon and part of a continuing process of figuring out how to learn to live with the fiercest predators we have left.

Look for: It's best not to go looking for cougars, but a couple tips are that they're a whole lot bigger than any other cat in this region, and they have a long, black-tipped tail.

Found: Remote rocky, wooded places, generally near mule deer populations. They've been spotted everywhere from Sunriver to Pilot Butte to Smith Rock State Park.

Top: *Sierra Nevada red foxes can be a range of colors. This one was spotted just south of Bend.*

Bottom: *Gray foxes are more common west of the Cascades. Note the black tip on its tail.*
(Photo by Kevin Smith)

FOXES, COYOTES, AND WOLVES

Sierra Nevada Red Fox
(*Vulpes vulpes necator*)

Body: 2–3 ft., tail: 1–1.5 ft., shoulder height: 15 in.

Central Oregon is home to several kinds of foxes. We have tree-climbing gray foxes, although they're more common west of the Cascades. We have the introduced eastern red fox, with the lush red coat you probably imagine when you think of red foxes. And we probably have other foxes that are the result of interbreeding.

Our most compelling fox is surely the Sierra Nevada red fox, a mountain-dwelling subspecies that until about 2012 wasn't known to exist in Central Oregon. They've since been spotted on Mount Bachelor and at Hoodoo Ski Area, among other places, which is not to say they're common. In the Sierra Nevada after which they're named, they're listed under the Endangered Species Act. In Central Oregon, researchers continue to study populations and hope to see them increase.

If you're lucky enough to see any fox, avoid the temptation to feed or interact with them. If they learn to approach humans for food, they'll be more likely to be hit by cars and less likely to live the wild lives they deserve.

Look for: Foxes are smaller than coyotes, with narrower faces and bushier tails. Sierra Nevada red foxes can be black and silver, red, or a mix of colors.

Found: At high elevations in the Cascades.

A coyote in mid-pounce. (Photo by Alison Hardenburgh)

Coyote *(Canis latrans)*

Body: 2.5–3.5 ft., tail: 1–1.5 ft., shoulder height: 23–26 in.

Coyotes are incredibly smart, playful, and loyal animals that often mate for life. They're not the strongest animal around, but they have exceptional endurance and are the fastest of all our dogs, foxes, and wolves. They also have a phenomenal sense of smell and sometimes team up with their partners or in packs to kill rodents, as well as grasshoppers, birds, fawns, and just about every other edible item on the planet.

Those facts aren't what you're most likely to hear about coyotes, though. The animal the Navajo call "God's dog" is now the most maligned and persecuted animal in Oregon—shot, trapped, poisoned, and hunted from planes. The reason seems to be an old and mistaken belief that coyotes are "varmints" that indiscriminately kill a lot of livestock. In reality, repeated studies show that most coyotes live largely on rodents and carrion, with only the occasional individual causing repeated trouble for ranchers.

Many Indigenous stories describe the coyote as Trickster, a cunning, wise creature that teaches lessons in sometimes harsh or funny ways. That description seems particularly apt these days, as the Trickster first expanded its range and population when we removed wolves and now responds to our guns, traps, and poisons by reproducing more often and having larger litters.

As local naturalist Jim Anderson wrote, "When you poke a sharp stick into coyote culture, they fight back." One would hope we'd learn our lesson and try to find a smarter way to live with coyotes.

Top: *Coyotes help keep rodent populations under control. (Photo by John Williams)*

Bottom: *Coyotes howl, bark, and yip. (Photo by John Williams)*

Look for: Color and size can vary, but look for erect ears, a pointy snout, and a bushy tail with no curve to it.

Found: All over Central Oregon, even in the heart of Bend. They prefer grasslands, meadows, sagebrush-covered flats, and other open areas.

Two wolves howling. (Photo by Andyworks)

Gray Wolf *(Canis lupus)*

Body: 3.5–5 ft., tail: 14–20 in., shoulder height: 26–38 in.

In 2011, a two-year-old wolf called OR-7 made a historic, 1,200-mile journey from northeast Oregon to Northern California. Along the way, he earned several "firsts": first known wolf in California in nearly ninety years, first known wolf west of the Cascades since the mid-1940s, and first known wolf in Central Oregon in about seventy years, although wolves have passed through for years.

"Gray" wolves actually range in color from pure white to solid black. (Photo by Kevin Smith)

Today, wolves have returned to Central Oregon, and across the state we have over 170 confirmed wolves. That represents dramatic growth, given that there were fewer than two dozen wolves in Oregon when Journey (as he was later named) made his famous trek.

That's the recent history of wolves in Oregon. Historically, gray wolves lived across most of the lower 48 until the early 1900s. They were nearly wiped out in subsequent decades, until a recovery effort began in the 1980s. By 2009, wolves had finally returned to northeast Oregon, where their populations remain the highest in the state.

As with every other apex predator, there's a great deal of controversy about how to deal with wolves in Oregon. Many people hope that populations will keep growing and their range will continue to expand across the state. Others fear that higher wolf populations will lead to more livestock being killed and more conflicts with people.

OR-7, or Journey, in Jackson County in May 2014. (Photo by Oregon Department of Fish and Wildlife)

Journey is believed to have died in 2020 at age eleven, after fathering at least seven pups and creating the Rogue Pack east of Medford. Whether you view his adventures as heroic or tragic, inspiring or unsettling, you can be sure that the question of how we should manage wolves in Oregon, and Central Oregon, will continue to play out for decades to come.

Look for: They're way bigger and taller than coyotes, and they carry their tails straight back when they run.

Found: They've been spotted across Central Oregon, including in the Metolius River area and between Bend and Sisters.

OUR FAST (AND NOT-SO-FAST) MAMMALS

Exact speeds are impossible to pin down, but this list gives you an idea of how the fastest mammals measure up. It depends on distance and whether it's an average individual or the fastest ever. I gave humans an advantage by listing Usain Bolt's top speed over 100 meters and not my own (which likely compares unfavorably with the river otter).

- Pronghorn (65 mph)
- Cougar (45 mph)
- Coyote (40 mph)
- Elk (40 mph)
- Jackrabbit (40 mph)
- Gray wolf (35 mph)

- Mule deer (35 mph)
- Bighorn sheep (30 mph)
- Black bear (30 mph)
- Human (23 mph)
- River otter (15 mph)

HOOFED MAMMALS

Bighorn Sheep *(Ovis canadensis)*

Body: 4.5-6 ft., weight: 120-340 lbs., shoulder height: 30-45 in.

Bighorn sheep are the only animals that can rival mountain goats in alpine agility—and that's while hauling around those famous horns, which can weigh over thirty pounds. Despite their heavy heads, bighorns are so surefooted they can race across boulder fields with nary a misstep.

Bighorns once thrived in Oregon, both in steep, rocky terrain and in arid regions east of the Cascades. Overhunting, diseases from domestic sheep, and human encroachment led to their demise in Oregon, but in 1954, an effort began to reintroduce them.

We now have fewer than 4,000 bighorn sheep across the state, including 800 Rocky Mountain bighorn sheep in northeast Oregon. The rest are California desert bighorn sheep that prefer to live in drier parts of the state. They're the bighorns you're most likely to see in and around Central Oregon, if you're lucky.

Look for: The large, curled horns are a dead giveaway.

Found: California desert bighorns are along the lower John Day River, in the lower Deschutes River Canyon near Maupin, and in the Hart Mountain National Antelope Refuge.

Top: The "big horns" of rams like this one weigh more than all the other bones in their bodies combined. (Photo by Greg Burke)

Bottom: A herd of bighorns on the move. (Photo by Alison Hardenburgh)

FUN FACT

The largest herd of California bighorn sheep in North America isn't in California—it's in the Owyhee Canyonlands in southeast Oregon.

A 2014 photo in Dry River Canyon, before the billy moved on to Newberry National Monument. (Photo by Greg Burke)

Mountain Goat *(Oreamnos americanus)*

Body: 4–5 ft., weight: 100–350 lbs.

In 2014, hikers in the Dry River Canyon east of Bend were treated to a rare sight in Central Oregon: a big ol' billy with a shaggy white coat hanging out on the steep cliffs bordering the canyon. It also happened a few years earlier, in 2010, with each mountain goat taking in the beautiful canyon views for a spell before moving on to Newberry National Monument.

Mountain goats aren't actually goats (they're in the same family as buffalo and cattle), and they aren't at all common in our area, although they are native to the Cascades. Overhunting wiped out Oregon populations by the 1850s, but they've been slowly reintroduced in recent years, with the nearest band up on Mount Jefferson.

Mountain goat adaptations for living on steep, rocky cliffs up to 13,000 feet include a thick wool undercoat topped by six-inch guard hairs to fight off wintry weather. They also have the animal equivalent of great rock-climbing shoes, with hard-edged hooves surrounding rubbery, concave footpads that act like suction cups.

Most remarkable of all: These five-foot-long relatives of the cow are so agile it's said they can fit all four of their hooves on a ledge smaller than this book—and even turn around on that tiny precipice to head the other way.

Look for: The black, stiletto-like horns and thick, white coat are tough to miss.

Found: The largest nearby population is on Mount Jefferson, where they're sometimes spotted from the Canyon Creek Meadows Trail.

A young mountain goat in the Elkhorn Mountains in northeast Oregon. (Photo by Oregon Department of Fish and Wildlife)

Does typically give birth to one or two fawns each spring. (Photo by Kevin Smith)

Mule Deer *(Odocoileus hemionus)*

Size: 4.5–6 ft., weight: 68–470 lbs., shoulder height: 3–3.5 ft.

Deer are everywhere, both in our imagined and real lives. As children, we cry over *Bambi* and *The Yearling*. As adults in Central Oregon, we cry over the flowers and shrubs and trees that deer gnaw and rub and pee on in our backyards.

They may frustrate us, but in a world that's becoming less and less wild, deer stand tall as the biggest, wildest creature many of us will ever encounter. They're the most common large mammal left in the wild, in part because for decades we've reduced the numbers of predators like wolves that would naturally control their populations.

The antlers often branch into multiple forks. (Photo by Greg Burke)

Every Central Oregon community now has a resident (non-migrating) population of mule deer. Common as they may be in neighborhoods, mule deer populations across Central Oregon are far below ODFW's targets due to issues including poaching, vehicle strikes, and climate change.

Like elk and other wildlife, deer are also losing critical habitat as we expand our communities, roads, and trails into their winter grazing areas. In fact, pretty much all of Bend was once their valuable winter habitat. It's no wonder deer act as though our backyards are theirs—up until recently, they were.

Look for: Whitish rump patch, black-tipped tail, and huge ears.

Found: Resident deer populations live year-round in area towns. Thousands more browse to the top of the Cascades in summer and migrate down to lower elevations in winter.

Wildlife corridors

The Cascade Lakes Highway and Hwys. 20 and 97 run right through mule deer habitat and migratory areas, which means thousands of deer (and other animals) have to cross these and other highways each year—a skill their Ice Age ancestors didn't prepare them for.

The results are not good for humans, their vehicles, or wild animals. In 2020, nearly 6,000 vehicles in Oregon hit wild animals—and those are only the reported cases. Each collision had an average insurance cost of over $4,000. Deer were hit most often, but owls, eagles, cougars, and bighorn sheep were among the other victims.

Here's the good news: Today there are almost no vehicle–animal collisions along that four-mile span of Hwy. 97. The reason? The Oregon Department of Transportation built the state's first two wildlife corridors along that stretch, with eight-foot-high fencing guiding animals to one of two vehicle-free underpasses.

It's not just deer—and humans—that benefit from wildlife corridors. Cameras along the two underpasses have caught images of many other animals finding safe passage, including black bears, bobcats, bushy-tailed woodrats, coyotes, Douglas squirrels, elk, feral cats, golden-mantled ground squirrels, mountain cottontails, northern flying squirrels, short-tailed weasels, snowshoe hares, and striped skunks.

Top: *Yellow-bellied marmots don't migrate, but they do stroll through underpasses.*

Bottom: *By taking the low road near Sunriver, these deer are less likely to be involved in vehicle crashes. (Photos by Leslie Bliss-Ketchum)*

HOW TO HELP AREA DEER

- Drive especially slowly and carefully during migration periods, when deer cross highways and other roads.
- Don't feed or approach deer, and don't let dogs chase them.
- In winter, dispose of construction tape, woven wire, cone-shaped tomato cages, hammocks, and other materials that deer get tangled in and die from every year.

A family of pronghorn at Hart Mountain National Antelope Refuge. (Photo by Greg Burke)

Pronghorn *(Antilocapra americana)*

Body: 4–5 ft., weight: 70–140 lbs., shoulder height: 32–41 in.

Sure, we have a sunny climate, good trails, and nice people in Central Oregon. But to me one of the biggest draws is that this land is still wild enough to support an ancient animal like the pronghorn. I will never get over the fact that less than an hour from Bend is a twenty-million-year-old species that may be most closely related to giraffes.

You can tell this is a male by the black patch on the jawline and the long horns—with the distinctive prongs. (Photo by Greg Burke)

Lone survivors

That's right—giraffes. Pronghorn aren't antelope and they don't have any close relatives left because all the others in their family went the way of the dinosaur. Pronghorn survived, but just barely. There were forty million or so in the 1800s, making them as common as bison, but hunting nearly wiped them out by the early 1900s.

Like many other animals, pronghorn were saved by hunting restrictions and creation of protected habitat, particularly at Oregon's Hart Mountain National Antelope Refuge and Nevada's Sheldon National Wildlife Refuge. Those locations are ideal for pronghorn because they feature wide-open spaces filled with the sagebrush, rabbitbrush, bitterbrush, snowberry, bunchgrasses, wildflowers, and other plants the animals love to eat.

What to look for

When you spot pronghorn, they won't seem terribly different from other browsers like deer, so it helps to be aware of a few adaptations that make them special. For one thing, know that by the time you see pronghorn, you've almost certainly already been seen. Their eyesight is eight times better than ours, and they can spot details and movement at three miles. Their eyes also bulge out a bit, giving them a 320-degree field of view.

Pronghorn bucks fight for does, just like elk. (Photo by Alison Hardenburgh)

Maybe the best-known (and coolest) thing about pronghorns is that they're North America's fastest land animal—and second fastest in the world behind the African cheetah. They can cruise along for several miles at up to forty-five miles per hour, and unlike my Subaru, they can also surge quickly to at least sixty-five miles per hour.

Those jaw-dropping speeds are a vestige of the pronghorn's early days outrunning now-extinct animals like jaguars, long-legged hyenas, and the North American cheetah (yes, we used to have cheetahs). Born in May or June, pronghorn fawns can also run like the wind—easily smoking humans within about a week of birth. Even so, many fawns are lost each year to coyotes, bobcats, Golden Eagles, and other predators.

Their unique horns are bone covered with a sheath they shed each year. (Photo by Kim Elton)

To help the remaining pronghorn in Central Oregon continue their twenty-million-year journey, please keep a polite distance. Like most other wildlife, they can ill afford to burn their energy running away from us, however slow we may be by comparison.

Look for: You'll likely see their big, white rump patches first. Then look for the horns and two white bands on their throats.

Found: Mostly treeless, arid areas. The closest herds to Bend are east near Brothers, where they can be seen from Hwy. 20, especially early in the morning, when they get their water from dew-covered grass. They're also in the Crooked River National Grasslands.

Top: *Hunters would recognize this bull as a 6x7, or 6x8, if you count the tiny antler point. (Photo by Kevin Smith)*

Bottom: *A pair of elk in a ponderosa pine forest. (Photo by Oregon Department of Fish and Wildlife)*

Rocky Mountain Elk
(Cervus elaphus)

Body: 6.5–8 ft., weight: 400-1200 lbs., shoulder height: 4-5 ft.

My favorite story about elk comes from the Grand Canyon, where they installed water stations for hikers. Thirsty elk taught themselves to turn on the water by lifting the spring-loaded levers with their noses—and then decided they owned the watering stations.

To keep the elk from aggressively defending "their" watering stations, wildlife biologists tried shooting them with paintballs and water guns. A biologist at the canyon noted one problem: "Sometimes when you shoot them with water guns, they open their mouths."

We don't normally associate such ingenuity with grazers like elk. What gets more attention is their fancy headgear (their antlers can grow to five feet, span nearly four feet, and weigh up to forty pounds). But there is more to elk, including that they can run a good forty miles per hour and jump over eight feet in the air—and even swim across rivers as wide as the Columbia.

Elk are known for their fall bugling, when males let out a breathtaking bellow to attract females and scare off other males. Fights sometimes ensue, as the bulls duke it out to form breeding harems. That leaves the bulls exhausted and hungry at the start of winter, when they head down from the mountains to find forage and, they hope, peace and quiet on their winter rangeland near area towns.

Look for: Roosevelt elk are found west of the Cascades and Rocky Mountain elk to the east; here in the middle, we have Rocky Mountain elk and hybrids. Elk are a lot bigger than deer, with larger antlers on the males, and their rump patches are yellowish or brownish, not mostly white like deer.

Found: Similar habitats to that of mule deer, although they prefer grass to shrubs. They try to stay far from people, but we make that difficult by building neighborhoods and golf courses in their former winter range. If you see elk near towns (often in April and November), please try not to disturb them.

MAMMAL URINALYSIS

It turns out that to know wild animals, it helps to know about their pee and what they do with it. It may not be a sexy topic (unless you're a jackrabbit or porcupine), but it's an interesting one, and sometimes awfully funny.

- **Black bear:** How can black bears hibernate up to seven months without peeing? Their bodies recycle the waste and turn it into new proteins. That helps the bears avoid muscle atrophy, and it means they don't need potty breaks during their hibernations.

- **Black-tailed jackrabbits:** Part of the elaborate mating ritual for jackrabbits involves jumping over each other, again and again—often with the jumper showering the one below with urine, a behavior called enurination.

- **Elk:** Elk dig shallow pits and line them with urine and feces to wallow in. Bulls even use their antlers to toss urine-soaked sod onto their backs. It's thought that the smell tells other bulls if the elk is metabolizing fat (a sign of health) or is metabolizing fresh food or muscle. The healthier the bull, the less likely he is to be challenged (and the more attractive he is to females).

- **Mule deer:** Deer deliberately pee on a little tuft of hair partway up their rear legs. Why? It's like a calling card. They rub their legs together and spread their unique scent to advertise their health, breeding status, and dominance rank.

- **Porcupines:** Let's say you're a guy who wants to mate with a female. How do you let her know you're interested? If you're a porcupine, you rear up on your hind legs and spray the lucky lady with urine, soaking her from head to toe. She might scream at you, punch you, try to bite you, or run away. But if she doesn't do any of those things (and many do), you're in business. Just hurry: Female porcupines have a once-a-year, twelve-hour window of fertility.

- **Ord's kangaroo rats:** These rats don't drink water, and not surprisingly, they produce the most concentrated urine of all mammals—surpassing even camels. They pee only a few drops a day.

MEDIUM MAMMALS

BEAVERS, MUSKRATS, AND PORCUPINES

American Beaver (Castor canadensis)

Body: 2–3 ft., tail: 11–21 in.

With all due respect to Ducks fans, Oregon got it absolutely right in naming the beaver our state animal. Called "little people" by some Native tribes, beavers are second only to people in their ability to shape their own environment, and they also shaped ours by driving the region's economy and growth throughout the early 1800s.

How smart is our state animal? In one study, when researchers stuck a pipe in a beaver dam, the beavers shaped pencil-like sticks to plug up the ends.
(Photo by Steve Hersey)

Dam it!

If you care about water issues in Central Oregon, you have to care about the beaver. That's because long before beavers were money-makers (and then nation-makers), they were dam-makers.

Beavers cut down willow, aspen, cottonwood, alder, and other trees to slowly dam up waterways. Each dam is unique, but the effect is consistent: They create wetlands. And wetlands are a huge deal—especially in our arid region, where we can't afford to waste what little water we get.

Beaver-created wetlands spread water out and slow it down so plants and animals can squeeze more use of out it. Wetlands sponge up floodwaters, reduce erosion, filter out pollutants, stabilize streambanks, and raise the water table.

And because leaky beaver dams allow natural streamflow, they create what you might think of as water nurseries for all sorts of amphibians, birds, bats, fish, and other animals—many of them endangered.

Unlike human-made dams that often block fish passage and create harmful warm-water conditions, beaver dams like this one aid the environment. (Photo by Kevin Smith)

Rodent gold

Europeans nearly trapped their own beaver to extinction by 1900 because they couldn't get enough beaver fur and castoreum—an anal excretion that's been used to treat everything from headaches to epilepsy, and is still used to provide a leathery note in perfumes.

Imagine Europeans' excitement when tens of millions of "new" beavers were discovered in the New World. The Hudson's Bay Company alone auctioned three million beaver pelts from 1853 to 1877—including over a quarter-million in 1875 alone. Killing beavers for their fur continues to this day in Oregon, albeit in smaller numbers.

Thanks to conservation and management efforts and the end of the beaver hat craze, populations of North America's largest rodent have rebounded to about fifteen million, down from a peak of at least sixty million before trappers and fur traders came along.

Look for: Big, chunky creatures with large, paddle-like tails. They're rarely seen during the day, but look for chewed trees and signs of thin trees being dragged across trails and down to their dens and dams.

Found: Fairly common along area rivers, streams, and other year-round waterways. Look for signs at First Street Rapids, Smith Rock State Park, and area reservoirs, as well as in Sunriver and along the Deschutes River Trail.

Top: *And you wondered how beavers cut down such thick trees. (Photo by Jim Anderson)*

Bottom: *These ingenious creatures use their tails as rudders in the water and for balance on land. (Photo by Dave Rein)*

FUN FACT

In the early 1800s in the Ochoco Mountains, John Day—the early fur trapper, not the town or river named for him—reportedly came across beavers that were five feet long and weighed 200 pounds.

5 ft

Muskrats can swim backward and forward—they even mate underwater! (Photo by Kevin Smith)

Common Muskrat (*Ondatra zibethicus*)

Body: 1–2 ft., tail: 8–11 in.

To you and me, the muskrat might be a poor man's beaver—a smaller version of our state animal that isn't quite so attractive or useful. To many Native American tribes, though, the muskrat is a powerful animal that brings good fortune. Several stories even have the muskrat as the mother of the human race or creating the world by bringing mud up from the depths of the sea.

For the record, the muskrat really isn't an undersized beaver. It's actually more of an oversized vole or field mouse that has adapted to the life aquatic with webbed feet and a flat, rudder-like tail. Like beavers, muskrats are phenomenal swimmers that can stay underwater for at least fifteen minutes at a time.

Muskrats are similar to beavers in other ways too, including that they're skilled builders. They don't construct dams, but their lodges are as complex as those of beavers, with separate sleeping chambers for each family member.

Although they sometimes damage dams, dikes, and embankments, muskrats also do a lot of good. By eating cattails, sedges, and other riparian plants, they open up marshy areas for migrating waterfowl.

Look for: Coats have tawny-to-black guard hairs over a brownish-gray undercoat. They're smaller than beavers and have a black, sparsely haired tail.

Found: In riparian areas at lower elevations, especially in marshy areas with cattails. First Street Rapids, the Old Mill, and wetter areas of Sunriver are good bets.

Muskrats feed mostly on plants, as well as insects, fish, and amphibians. (Photo by Kevin Smith)

A juvenile stab rabbit. (Photo by Ken Canning)

North American Porcupine *(Erethizon dorsatum)*

Body: 2–3 ft., tail 5.5–9 in.

I had a great time writing down adjectives used to describe porcupines. In sum, it's said that they're shy, lumbering, ponderous, slow-of-foot, stout-bodied, methodical, clumsy, and lackadaisical animals that don't move far and can't move fast.

And, really, why rush around? Porcupines have 30,000 needle-sharp quills they can stick in anyone, or anything, that threatens them (hence their scientific name, which means "the animal with an irritating back"). Those hollow spines also make a great flotation device, allowing porcupines to swim, presumably slowly, out to pond lilies and other delicacies.

Maybe in part because of their leisurely pace, it's sometimes suggested that porcupines aren't the sharpest tools in the shed. In fact, researchers are finding them to be quite intelligent, with rich emotional lives communicated through noises that range from a teeth-clicking battle cry to various moans, whines, grunts, coughs, wails, and adorable cooing noises (check out Teddy on YouTube).

Especially in winter, porcupines eat the cambium layer under the bark of pine and other trees, stunting and sometimes killing the trees. In the 1950s, that led folks to put up signs on forest roads around Bend: "Please kill porcupines!" A lot of people did, which did a lot of damage to populations of these gentle and unusual creatures.

Look for: If you see an animal walking around with 30,000 spines sticking out of it and it's not a porcupine, call the authorities.

Found: East of Bend in areas like the Badlands Wilderness. Also in Sunriver and along the Deschutes River Trail.

Iron-rich enamel makes their teeth orange. (Photo by John Williams)

Top: *A jackrabbit darting for cover in Crooked River Ranch.*

Bottom: *Jackrabbits use their enormous ears to hear predators and regulate body heat. They release and absorb heat as needed through their ears. (Photos by Kevin Smith)*

RABBITS AND HARES

Black-tailed Jackrabbit *(Lepus californicus)*

Body: 18–22 in., tail: 2–5 in.

Animals get so much more interesting the better you get to know them. That's certainly true for one of my favorites, the black-tailed jackrabbit.

Eastern Oregon once had an estimated twenty million black-tailed and white-tailed jackrabbits. The latter are rare these days, and the black-tailed is fortunate to be a bit more common. Settlers killed millions of jackrabbits, rounding up thousands at a time and clubbing them to death for sport, meat, and fur. In 1915 alone, over a million jackrabbit scalps were turned in to officials in Harney County for a bounty of five cents each.

Still, black-tailed jackrabbits persist. It helps that they can outsprint just about anything, leaping twenty feet in a single bound and bursting to speeds up to forty miles per hour. Coyotes, bobcats, Golden Eagles, and other top predators still catch them, which isn't all bad—jacks are important buffer species that breed fast and are killed often, which reduces the need for predators to kill other types of wildlife.

> "As the sun was going down, we saw . . . the 'jackass rabbit.' He is well named. He is just like any other rabbit, except that he is from one-third to twice as large, has longer legs in proportion to his size, and has the most preposterous ears that ever were mounted on any creature but a jackass."
> —Mark Twain

I can't leave out one other wonderful part of the jackrabbit story, which is their frenetic courtship ritual. You've heard the phrase "mad as a March hare"? That originally referred to European hares, but it applies to our jacks during their courtship displays, as they sprint, leap, and circle each other before settling in for the inevitable—or almost inevitable (pursued females sometimes strike one for women's lib, punching their suitors in the face when they're not ready to copulate).

When both animals are ready, there's peeing involved and, afterward, this ecstatic celebration from the males, as described decades ago by researcher Del Blackburn:

> After copulation the male jackrabbit was observed on several occasions to jump slightly backwards, fall to the ground, emit a hissing squeal and leap up again renewing the chase with subsequent copulations of up to four times.

Look for: Those ears!

Found: All over fields, valleys, and open areas full of sagebrush and other shrubs. Look for them in the Badlands Wilderness and other areas north and east of Bend.

THE GOOD OL' DAYS

Keep in mind that today's wildlife are specific to our little window of time. A hundred years ago, we had more species and way more individuals. And five to forty-four million years ago? Take a field trip to the John Day Fossil Beds to learn about some of the vastly different species that used to live in our area, including:

- **Entelodonts:** Also called hell pigs, these animals were about the size of a Beetle—the Volkswagen kind. They looked and acted like wild boars.

- *Miohippus:* This three-toed horse was smaller and slower than today's horses, an unfortunate reality with those hell pigs running around.

- *Gentilicamelus sternbergi:* Camels (yes, camels) like this one thrived in our region's open habitats.

- *Ekgmowechashala:* This was our neighborhood primate, a lemur-like animal that weighed about five pounds.

- *Eusmilus cerebralis:* This creature, the size of a bobcat, had teeth like a saber-tooth tiger and could hinge its jaw open almost ninety degrees—bad news for small mammals of the day.

Top: *A transitioning snowshoe hare.*
(Photo by Kim Elton)

Bottom: *Note the larger hind feet. (Photo by*
Oregon Department of Fish and Wildlife)

RABBIT OR HARE?

Rabbits are born blind, naked, and vulnerable. Hares tend to be bigger and enter the world fully furred, open-eyed, and ready to run.

Snowshoe Hare (*Lepus americanus*)

Body: 13–18 in., tail: about 2 in.

Snowshoe hares can't outsmart or outmuscle their many predators, but they do have their famous camouflage in summer (brown) and winter (white). Unfortunately for them, if the days get short and trigger the molt to white but it doesn't actually snow, the hares can look a bit silly—and pay for it with their lives.

Canada lynx are a specialized hunter of snowshoe hares, and the two share the same large feet for walking on top of the snow. They also share the same severe population fluctuations.

Just about every other animal you can think of also hunts snowshoe hares, from weasels to coyotes to owls. Like the mountain cottontail, snowshoe hares respond by raising multiple litters a year, with females sometimes breeding within hours of giving birth.

Look for: Cottontails are smaller and jackrabbits are bigger, with longer ears—and none of them turn white in winter like snowshoe hares. Look for their tracks in the snow (they have huge back feet). In summer, they're a rusty-brown color.

Found: Generally at higher elevations in the Cascades and Ochocos, but also lower down, in forested areas like the Metolius Preserve.

Mountain Cottontail
(*Sylvilagus nuttalli*)

Body: 14–16 in., tail: 1.25–2.5 in.

It's never a good sign when a cottontail appears on a nature program. You just know the next frame is going to show a coyote or bobcat or any number of other predators dining on fresh rabbit.

Indeed, our mountain cottontails are extremely important prey for a host of local species. Because of that, nature in all her wonder gave rabbits the perfect adaptation: the ability to breed like . . . well, you know. Females can become pregnant multiple times a year, and after pregnancies of just one month, they give birth to a handful of kittens (yes, they're called kittens, not bunnies).

In *Watership Down*, Richard Adams gives his own sly spin on rabbits' lot in life. His fictional origin story features a rabbit prince named El-ahrairah whom the great Frith rewards for his bravery:

> *El-ahrairah, your people cannot rule the world, for I will not have it so. All the world will be your enemy, Prince with a Thousand Enemies, and whenever they catch you, they will kill you. But first they must catch you, digger, listener, runner, prince with the swift warning. Be cunning and full of tricks and your people shall never be destroyed.*

Top: *Run like the wind, El-ahrairah!*
(Photo by Kevin Smith)

Bottom: *Note the whitish undercoat.*
(Photo by Justin Wilde)

Look for: They're much smaller than jackrabbits. Introduced and pet rabbits may look similar, but wild cottontails have a fairly distinctive, yellowish-brown and gray coat with whitish underparts.

Found: Prefer areas with a lot of cover, often near rocky outcrops and where trees or brushy areas meet meadows. They also like sagebrush and juniper, so the Badlands Wilderness and other areas north and east of Bend are favored spots.

Which gets your vote for best symbol of the U.S.: the Bald Eagle or the raccoon? (Photo by Kevin Smith)

RACCOONS

Northern Raccoon *(Procyon lotor)*

Body: 24 in., tail: 12 in.

Raccoons are one of those wild animals that have become so common in urban areas that we don't really see them anymore. Or at least we don't see them the way they used to be seen.

Raccoons are excellent climbers—and can come down headfirst. (Photo by John Williams)

In 1963, an essay in *Harper's Magazine* titled "Our Most American Animal" proposed that the raccoon be named our second national symbol, right alongside the Bald Eagle. The writer lauded the raccoon's toughness, adaptability, and self-reliance, raving that "nothing about him is rare, delicate, or specialized. He is as common as dirt and as hardy as weeds."

These days, raccoons are fifteen to twenty times more common than they were decades ago. They take advantage of pet food that's left outside and, most famously, trash that's left unsecured. They're also fierce when they have to be—as local naturalist Jim Anderson wrote, "I've seen a male raccoon teach a German shepherd to climb trees."

But mostly raccoons are just quiet bandits, coming out at night to steal food using those astonishing, humanlike fingers that can untie knots, turn door handles, and remove the lid from just about every garbage can ever made.

Although not recommended for the rest of us, President Calvin Coolidge famously kept a pet raccoon named Rebecca at the White House—which shows how the perception and status of raccoons has changed over the past century.

Look for: There's that famous black "mask" over their eyes, plus unmistakable dark rings around the tail.

Found: Prefer forested areas near water, but they've adapted well to agricultural and urban areas. Look for them all along the Deschutes River and at Camp Sherman.

Fear not! Or not much. Skunks generally prefer not to spray because they have limited "ammo," and it can take a week to reload. (Photo by Tom Friedel)

SKUNKS

Striped Skunk *(Mephitis mephitis)*

Body: 13-18 in., tail: 8-14 in.

While most wild animals try to blend in to their surroundings, skunks do their best to announce exactly where they are. That's because both humans and their wild predators know the unholy stink that will result if they don't keep a safe distance.

The skunk defense system gets all the press, so many people don't realize that they're largely beneficial animals. Skunks feed on garden and agricultural pests, from beetles and crickets to insect larvae like beetle grubs and cutworms. They also eat mice, moles, and rats.

Trouble sometimes arises when skunks—usually the larger and bolder striped skunks—take refuge or form dens under houses, sheds, and porches. If that happens, you can simply wait them out (they may just move on) or seek out live-trapping options.

Look for: Pepé Le Pews have glossy black bodies with two big, bold white stripes down their backs.

Found: All over, from towns and suburbs to streambanks and forested areas—usually within a couple miles of a water source.

FUN FACT

Great Horned Owls are one of the only animals to prey on skunks. Not surprisingly, the owls do not have a well-developed sense of smell. Also not surprisingly, the owls and their nests sometimes smell really, really bad.

Western Spotted Skunk
(Spilogale gracilis)

Body: 9–15 in., tail: 4–8 in.

The western spotted skunk is the more reclusive of our two native skunk species. It's tough to tell with such a shy animal, but at least two local naturalists believe populations are declining in Central Oregon, possibly being driven out by the much larger striped skunk.

Spotted skunks are nocturnal loners that roam around the lava rocks at the foothills of the Cascades, holing up for brief periods before moving on their way. They're strikingly beautiful animals, each with a unique pattern of spots and four or more stripes down their backs.

If a spotted skunk stomps its feet at you, take heed—it's warning you to back up. If you or your pet persists, the skunk will rear up in a five-second Cirque du Soleil handstand and let its tail drop out of the way before spraying a highly accurate dose of its infamous sulfurous fluid.

Spotted skunks are among our most beautiful—and rarely seen—animals. (Photo by Jim Anderson)

Spotted skunks are excellent climbers that sometimes den in attics or haylofts and can scurry up trees to escape threats. Most often, we smell spotted and striped skunks but never see them because unfortunately their defense systems do nothing to stop the threat of onrushing traffic.

Look for: Much smaller than striped skunks, with a lot of spots and more stripes.

Found: In a variety of habitats, including farmlands and rocky areas. Compared to their striped cousins, they're less tolerant of human activity and fonder of forests and woodlands.

In Central Oregon, badgers' preferred cuisine is pocket gophers, not cattle, which pleases farmers. (Photo by John Williams)

WEASELS

American Badger *(Taxidea taxus)*

Body: 17–28 in., tail: 5–6 in.

You can have your bear or cougar; when it comes time to pick my team, I'm going with the badger. Badgers will charge porcupines, cougars, horses, rattlesnakes—badger don't care. What's that? You want to shut badger up in a box? Good luck. He can chew through wood an inch thick and break welded metal bars.

Despite all that fierce potential, badgers are actually pretty mellow creatures. Teddy Roosevelt even kept one named Josiah in the White House, where he (Josiah, not Teddy) reportedly chased a gardener up a tree. Although they can take on larger creatures, badgers mostly eat small animals like squirrels, rats, and mice.

What badgers do best is dig—and, oh, do they dig. They're second only to the grizzly in digging prowess; within seconds, they can use their stubby legs, two-inch claws, and even their strong jaw to dig a burrow ten feet into the ground.

Those front claws are made for digging. (Photo by Gerald Corsi)

Badgers often scoop out a new sleeping hole every few days. Their abandoned burrows are a hazard to horses but extremely valuable as dens and shelters to other animals, from snakes and spiders to coyotes. When badger populations decline, many other animals suffer.

Look for: The white stripe down the middle of their heads is distinctive.

Found: Common wherever ground squirrels are prevalent, including in Sunriver, the Badlands Wilderness and Crooked River National Grasslands, and along Hwy. 20 east of Bend.

American (Pine) Marten
(Martes americana)

Body: 13–19 in., tail: 7–9 in.

American martens are members of the weasel family with fox-like faces and lush, chocolate-brown fur. The latter is one of the marten's problems: Trapping is still legal in Oregon, and heavy trapping from frontier days forward (reaching a high of 272,000 pelts in 1820) is one reason they're now listed as a sensitive species in Oregon.

Another issue for the marten is logging. They prefer mature and old-growth forests with abundant down trees and snags where they can hunt prey such as voles, shrews, mice, and squirrels. They're thus often viewed as an indicator species—where they're doing well, forests and other species tend to be doing well too.

You're not likely to see a marten, but it'll be memorable if you do. They're fast, graceful animals that are as playful as river otters and can navigate trees as well as tree squirrels. They're also curious creatures that sometimes tolerate people—Brian Doyle's book *Martin, Marten* provides a fictional example.

Look for: Big ears on triangular faces, with a much bushier tail than the American mink.

Found: In mature and old-growth forests across the upper Cascades (on Mount Bachelor, near Todd Lake, etc.).

Top: *Marten populations appear to be doing well in the Deschutes National Forest (this one was in Yellowstone). (Photo by Tim Gage)*

Bottom: *Marten tracks near Todd Lake. (Photo by James Jaggard)*

Mink aren't the most agile of weasels, until they're in the water. (Photo by Kevin Smith)

American Mink *(Mustela vison)*

Body: 12–19 in., tail: 5–9 in.

While their fellow weasels are better runners and climbers, American mink have cornered the market on streams and rivers. They're considered semiaquatic and can dive to depths of ten feet to snag a fish.

The word *mink* comes from the Swedish *menk*, a charming word that means "the stinking animal from Finland." They're the foulest-smelling weasel, with anal glands that release a musk said to be as bad as—or possibly worse than—that of a skunk (please report back if you find out which it is).

Like martens, mink have the bad luck of having beautiful, thick coats. They're still trapped in Oregon, and there are numerous mink farms in the state that continue to raise the animals for their fur.

Look for: A smaller version of an otter, usually with white spots on the chin and chest. Legs are shorter and tail less bushy than martens.

Found: Prefer forested areas near water—including along the Deschutes and Crooked Rivers and around many irrigation reservoirs.

Their underbelly is orangish. (Photo by GRAWLFF)

Long-tailed Weasel *(Mustela frenata)*

Body: 10–13 in., tail: 5–11 in.

Think of long-tailed weasels and other weasels as the hummingbirds of the mammal world. Like hummers, they're quick, flitty creatures that expend a lot of energy and are hungry all the time.

Naturalist Jim Anderson spotted this weasel near a lava flow at Newberry National Monument, where Jim was looking for pikas, and probably the weasel was too (for different reasons). (Photo by Jim Anderson)

In the weasels' case, that's partly because they have really long, slender bodies and thin fur, making it tough to stay warm. Long-tailed weasels are heavier than short-tailed weasels and have to work their brushy tails off to hunt and kill enough food—about forty percent of their body weight each day

To meet their bodies' needs, weasels have evolved to be fast, ferocious hunters. Night and day, they sprint through burrows, scale trees, swim, and squirm through rock piles in a never-ending search for small rodents like mice, voles, shrews, and squirrels, as well as other animals up to several times their size. For anyone bothered by an abundance of rodents, weasels are a friend indeed.

Ferocious as they are as hunters, it's worth noting that weasels are smart, curious, and even affectionate creatures. The long-tailed weasel is also especially beautiful, with a rich cinnamon-brown coat in summer that turns almost entirely white in winter, so they can blend in as they scour our snow-covered slopes for their next meal.

Look for: A long body and neck, a small head, silky-brown fur with an orangish underbelly, and of course a very long and cat-like tail.

Found: Near water along rivers and streams, or in open habitat near livestock ponds and irrigation canals. They're in Sunriver and all around Newberry National Monument.

They're smaller than their long-tailed cousins.

Short-tailed Weasel *(Mustela erminea)*

Body: 7–12 in., tail: 1.5–3.5 in.

Short-tailed weasels are the smallest true carnivore in the Pacific Northwest, and possibly the most abundant land carnivore. But that's not to say you're likely to see them. They scurry around our forests, above and below snowline, and blend in well to their surroundings with their brown summer and white winter coats.

Short-tailed weasels hunt rodents primarily, just like the long-tailed, and they are hunted by many of the same predators, including owls, small hawks, and foxes. They also share the same ferocity and astonishing strength. In fact, one short-tailed is said to have sprinted 300 yards without pause—while carrying a rodent nearly as large as itself.

Europeans call the short-tailed weasel a "stoat" when it's wearing its summer coat and an "ermine" when it molts to its winter white coat. Whatever you call them, they are impressive animals, with bodies so thin and lithe that the entrance to their dens (under rock piles or stumps) can be as small as one inch in diameter.

A short-tailed weasel showing off its colorful underbelly.

Look for: Along with having a shorter tail, short-tailed weasels are smaller overall and have a white or lemon-yellow belly that distinguishes them from the long-tailed.

Found: Prefer open spaces, from meadows to open woodlands. You might get lucky and see one at Lava Lands Visitor Center or while you're riding a chairlift at Mount Bachelor.

With thick fur and huge paws, they're built for high elevations. (Photo by Gerald Corsi)

Wolverine *(Gulo gulo)*

Body: 26–37 in., tail: 7–10 in.

Wolverines are on the move. After not being seen in Oregon for more than a decade, they've been spotted in Clackamas County, along the Columbia River in Portland, and even at the Oregon Coast. Odds are those animals are climate refugees, traveling through as they search for suitable high-elevation homes.

What are they?

Wolverines are the toughest twenty to thirty-five pounds of mammal you'll find in North America. They're the biggest land-dwelling weasel, but they carry the forest cred of a bear—in fact, they look like small bears and have been known to chase bears (and cougars) off their kills.

Contrary to that tough-guy image, wolverine kits are tiny and vulnerable. At birth, wolverines are less than five inches long and weigh about five ounces. They're born in and depend on high-elevation snow dens through May, which makes them especially vulnerable to climate change. Their lives are also made challenging by their need for vast territories of 200 miles or more.

Current population

We don't know how many wolverines are left in North America. Some experts estimate there are a few hundred in the Lower 48, but when I asked wolverine researcher Rebecca Watters, she said there are only up to fifty wolverines in the North American breeding population. "Beyond that," she said, "who knows?"

A future with climate change?

Climate change has already driven thousands of animal species worldwide northward and upward in elevation. Some, like the wolverine, can't climb much higher. In 2023, the U.S. Fish and Wildlife Service listed wolverines as threatened under the federal Endangered Species Act (they've had threatened status in Oregon since 1975).

A captive wolverine in Washington. (Photo by Clint Long and Dale Pederson)

Federal and state protections alone won't save the animals. "What a listing really represents," Watters said, "is a societal commitment to at least having a conversation about what to do about wildlife in the era of climate change."

Because of wolverines' expansive territories, Watters worries that single-state recovery plans will not be sufficient. She says regional solutions are needed, with people across the West coming together to figure out how to support wolverines and other wildlife—before climate change drives them not only out of Oregon but also all the way to extinction.

Look for: Mainly brown fur, with a pale stripe running down each side of the body.

Found: There's hope that wolverines will return to the Wallowa Mountains and may someday be found high in the Cascades, possibly near the Three Sisters or Mount Jefferson.

> **"They've got this attitude where they will walk up to a grizzly that has a carcass they want and say, 'THAT'S MINE.' They start issuing this wolverine growl that sounds like a Harley-Davidson mating with a chainsaw, and its real velociraptor-quality stuff."**
> **—Douglas H. Chadwick, wildlife biologist**

On land, river otters are about as fast as humans. (Photo by Dave Rein)

North American River Otter *(Lontra canadensis)*

Body: 2–3.5 ft., tail: 12–20 in.

Do river otters really play? Are they having something we'd call "fun" when they sled down snowy hills, bodysurf in river rapids, turn somersaults with family members, or balance floating sticks on their noses? Or when they repeatedly drop pebbles in the water and dive down to retrieve them?

Maybe they're just staying in shape, or taking the fastest way down the slope, or practicing hunting maneuvers. But probably they're having a grand ol' time.

Along with being perhaps the most playful, otters are one of the best swimmers of all land-based mammals, able to stay underwater for five-minute stretches. River otters swim on their bellies, not their backs, which is one way to tell them apart from sea otters (sea otters are also much larger—up to six feet long).

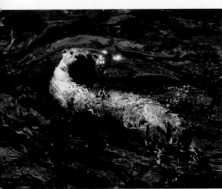

They're most at home in water, where they can easily outpace humans. (Photo by Toni Morris)

The funny thing is that otter pups are often afraid of the water. Their mothers have been known to drag their reluctant offspring into the water by their scruffs, where at first they struggle to keep from drowning.

Look for: Otters are a lot bigger than minks or muskrats. Also look for the long, thick, tapered tail.

Found: Along the Deschutes River Trail, Crooked River, Lake Billy Chinook, and Prineville Reservoir. Look for droppings, such as fine bits of fish bones and scales in a latrine area.

EASY WAYS TO HELP WILDLIFE

Central Oregon has several wildlife rehabilitation facilities that patch up wild animals that have struck windows, have been hit by cars, or are suffering from other injuries or illnesses. Wildlife rehabber Jeannette Bonomo came up with this list of tips to reduce injuries to wildlife:

1. **Slow down.** Drive slowly around town, especially near waterways and in winter when deer are crossing our highways.

2. **Keep your cats indoors.** Outdoor cats live shorter lives, and they shorten the lives of songbirds, squirrels, rabbits, and other native wildlife.

3. **Use humane methods to trap and release** skunks, woodrats, rabbits, and other animals that are bugging you or damaging your property. Please call a wildlife rehab facility for help or advice about humane wildlife eviction methods.

4. **Keep birds from hitting your windows by putting up Window Alert decals.** They're sold at Wild Birds Unlimited.

5. **If you hunt or shoot small game, use non-lead bullets.** Otherwise, hawks, eagles, and other predators eat the dead animals and often suffer lead poisoning. Local bullet-maker Nosler (nosler.com) offers ballistic tip lead-free bullets.

6. **Put up nest boxes for cavity-nesting birds** such as flickers, bluebirds, and swallows.

7. **Don't feed wild animals!** Yes, that means no breadcrumbs and no scraps when picnicking at Drake Park. Tossing that apple core out the car window isn't okay either—small animals will eat it, which will draw raptors to the roadway, where they are often hit by passing cars.

8. **Report suspicious or illegal activity**—including shooting birds, hunting out of season, or any animal abuse—to U.S. Fish and Wildlife, the state police, or other authorities.

9. **Get a reward** if you see evidence of someone poaching deer, elk, cougar, or game birds. Just call 1-800-452-7888.

10. **Call for help if you find a wild animal in distress.** Think Wild's hotline is 541-241-8680. Native Bird Care in Sisters is at 541-728-8208.

SMALL MAMMALS

BATS

Spotted Bat (*Euderma maculatum*)
Body: 4–4.5 in.

Despite the fact that spotted bats are rare and notoriously shy, you can find them fairly easily—by listening for the sounds of them navigating above you. The spotted bat's echolocation calls (which sound like clicks) are at a lower frequency than that of most bats, which means their calls can travel much farther. In fact, spotted bats can use their calls to identify the precise location of a moth and chase it down from a hundred yards away!

"No, really, I'm all ears."
(Photo by Bureau of Land Management)

You won't see spotted bats west of the Cascades because they're true desert dwellers. But head to Smith Rock State Park in August and wait till after dusk. If you're lucky, you may hear the clicks of dozens of these bats overhead, as they hunt for insects and come back to roost in their "bat hotels"—the crevices of the big cliffs.

Look for: Large, pinkish ears; a jet-black body; and two white spots on the shoulder and another on the rump. Old-timers used to call spotted bats the "death's head bat" or the "jackass bat" due to the pattern of white spots on their backs.

Found: Listen for them after dark at Smith Rock State Park, or try the pullout on Hwy. 20 across from Dry River Canyon.

BAT FACTS

- At least one in five (some say one in four) mammals is a bat.
- Central Oregon has hundreds of caves and fourteen species of bats.
- Bats can eat 600 insects an hour—and they routinely consume over half their body weight in insects every night.

Their light-brown bodies contrast with their very long black ears. (Photo by Adam Messer)

Western Long-eared Myotis *(Myotis evotis)*

Body: 3.5–4 in.

After spending a day out birding, why not settle in for an evening bat show? Sit outside a cave mouth on a summer evening, and most of the bats swooping and swirling above you will likely be this long-eared bat, which is drawn to our forests, lava tubes, and ice caves.

The western long-eared myotis is one of fourteen bat species east of the Cascades—far more diversity than you'll find on the west side. These particular bats are known to prefer beetles and moths, and they have long life spans that can reach twenty years or more.

Unfortunately, this and all our bat species face unprecedented threats. Wind turbines kill hundreds of thousands of bats each year. And the dreaded white-nose syndrome that has killed millions of bats across much of the eastern U.S. and Canada could devastate Oregon bat populations.

So, with those issues in mind, please take extreme care. Sit outside and enjoy the show of the long-eared myotis and other bats. Just don't go inside their caves and lava tubes unless you're guided by a professional biologist. Disturbing bat caves during the breeding season or winter hibernation can lead them to burn through their limited energy supplies and starve, or prematurely abandon their pups.

Look for: If you saw these bats up close, you'd discover that they do indeed have very long ears, as well as long, luxurious fur.

Found: All over Central Oregon, including in our forests, lava tubes, and ice caves.

Seeing them side-by-side gives you a good sense of the size and color difference between least chipmunks (left and bottom) and the golden-mantled ground squirrel. (Photo by Kevin Smith)

CHIPMUNKS

Least Chipmunk *(Tamias minimus)*

Body: 3–4 in., tail: 3–4.25 in.

There's no telling if the least chipmunk is offended by its common name, but to be clear, "least" refers to its body size and not its importance. Like other chipmunks, this one spends most of its time on the ground, scurrying around to collect enough food to last through the long winter months.

Look for: They hold their tails erect when they run, which is handy for identification. They're also grayer and paler than the yellow-pine chipmunk and, yes, slightly smaller.

Found: Prefer open areas with sagebrush (look for them sitting atop shrubs), but are on the edges of our forests too.

Listen for their high-pitched "chips" in pine forests. (Photo by Kevin Smith)

Yellow-Pine Chipmunk

(Tamias amoenus)

Body: 4–5 in., tail: 3.25–4.25 in.

An Iroquois legend tells of a trouble-making chipmunk that poked fun at a bear for not being strong enough to stop the sun from rising. The bear got mad and raked several claw marks down the chipmunk—a permanent reminder borne by all chipmunks not to make fun of other animals.

Yellow-pines, like other chipmunks, have those "claw marks," including four light stripes down the back and two light stripes through the eyes.

Look for: Very similar to the least chipmunk but slightly bigger and more brightly colored.

Found: Common throughout open forests, especially ponderosa pine forests. Look for them in Shevlin Park, on the trails near Lava Lands Visitor Center, and throughout Sisters and Sunriver.

CHIPMUNK OR SQUIRREL?

The simple way to tell: Look for light-colored stripes on the head and particularly through the eyes. If there are stripes through the eyes, it's a chipmunk. If not, it's a squirrel.

GROUND SQUIRRELS

Belding's Ground Squirrel

(Urocitellus beldingi)

Body: 7–8.5 in., tail: 2–3 in.

Belding's ground squirrels are dormant almost three-fourths of the year, one of the longest periods of any animal in North America. When they emerge in March, they feed like mad on weeds, seeds, leaves, stems, flowers—all sorts of vegetation, as well as insects (and sometimes each other).

Farmers have long considered them public enemy #1, but in California some farmers may be changing their tune. That's because as the state struggles with crippling drought, their burrows are helping aerate high-elevation fields and meadows—which makes the soils better at filtering and holding on to precious water.

They're also called sage rats and pocket pins. (Photo by J. H. Williams)

Look for: Medium in size and mostly gray, with a broad, reddish-brown strip down the back and cinnamon-pink color on the underside of the tail.

Found: Numerous colonies in grain fields, pastures, golf courses, and other open areas, especially north and east of Bend.

California Ground Squirrel

(Otospermophilus beecheyi)

Body: 9–11 in.; tail: 6–9 in.

California ground squirrels are common across western states, probably in part because they're not terribly picky. They like all sorts of habitats, from pastures to forests and rocky slopes, and although they're called ground squirrels, they often climb trees.

Look for: Large ground squirrels with a dark patch on the upper back and white speckles on their mostly gray fur.

They live in colonies, each squirrel with its own entrance to the communal burrow system. (Photo by Claire Weiser)

Found: They like to climb fence posts and stumps in a wide range of habitats—pastures, grain fields, rocky ridges, and open forested slopes.

FUN FACT

Where rattlesnakes are common predators, California ground squirrels chew discarded snakeskin and then lick their fur and that of their young, presumably to mask their scent.

TREE SQUIRRELS

Douglas Squirrel (*Tamiasciurus douglasii*)

Body: 7-8 in., tail: 4-6 in.

Famed naturalist John Muir admired the Douglas squirrel so much he devoted a whole book chapter to what he calls "the squirrel of squirrels." Here are a few of Muir's many wonderfully lyrical passages about this common, noisy rodent that most people have never given a second thought:

In just one minute, a Douglas squirrel, or chickaree, can nip off twelve Douglas-fir cones or thirty smaller cones.
(Photo by John Williams)

He is the squirrel of squirrels, flashing from branch to branch of his favorite evergreens crisp and glossy and undiseased as a sunbeam. Give him wings and he would outfly any bird in the woods.

He is, without exception, the wildest animal I ever saw—a fiery, sputtering little bolt of life, luxuriating in quick oxygen and the woods' best juices.

He is the mockingbird of squirrels, pouring forth mixed chatter and song like a perennial fountain; barking like a dog, screaming like a hawk, chirping like a blackbird or a sparrow; while in bluff, audacious noisiness he is a very jay.

Look for: The pumpkin-orange underbelly is a giveaway, especially in summer. Also note their reddish-brown tails. And listen for their sassy calls as you walk by "their" trees.

Found: Look and listen for them at Benham Falls and elsewhere along the Deschutes River Trail—but really, they're everywhere there are pine trees.

Golden-mantled Ground Squirrel (*Spermophilus lateralis*)

Body: 7-9 in., tail: 4-5 in.

You don't have to go looking for golden-mantled ground squirrels—they'll find you and beg for handouts every chance they get. Don't give in! It's never a good idea to feed any wild animal, no matter how hard they work the "poor me" angle.

Hold still, child! This is a great view of the golden-brown noggins that gave these squirrels their common name.
(Photo by Kevin Smith)

Why is it so bad to feed wild animals? Because your food might be bad for them and because it's dangerous for them to become dependent on human handouts. Oh, plus golden-mantled ground squirrels may bring something special to the party: fleas and ticks that transmit Rocky Mountain spotted fever, the bubonic plague, and other super-not-fun diseases sure to ruin your future hiking plans.

Look for: Similar to chipmunks, with two white stripes down their backs, but they're bigger and chunkier, and there's no white stripe through the eye.

Found: Famously all over Crater Lake National Park (even on Wizard Island). They're very common in area forests, on the trails near Lava Lands Visitor Center, and wherever people eat (parks, campgrounds, and hiking pit stops like the top of Black Butte).

Northern Flying Squirrel

(Glaucomys sabrinus)

Body: 6–8 in., tail: 4.25–7 in.

Look up in the sky on a cool summer morning, and you may spot a squirrel soaring high overhead, wings spread wide and a pine cone in its mouth as it dodges eagles and other predators on its long flight home.

Those big, black eyes help them see (and fly) at night. (Photo by Alex Badyaev)

Nah, just kidding. Flying squirrels don't actually fly; they float, or hang-glide, from tree to tree in a spectacular display that (alas) almost nobody ever sees because the squirrels are nocturnal. Long, fur-lined skin folds enable the flights, which can cover hundreds of feet, with the squirrels twisting, turning, and spiraling to avoid obstacles along the way.

The only place I've had the good fortune of seeing a flying squirrel was at a local wildlife rehab facility, where the staff included a flying squirrel named Iggy. Iggy lost both feet to burns in the 2013 Browns Creek fire, but thanks to a kind firefighter, he (possibly she) lived a charmed life as a very spoiled animal ambassador.

Look for: You won't see these squirrels during the day, but if you did, you'd notice the large eyes and the long, loose fold of skin along each side of the body.

Found: In cavities of ponderosa pines, Douglas-fir, grand fir, and lodgepole pine. They like to dine on truffles, and spotted owls like to dine on them.

Western Gray Squirrel *(Sciurus griseus)*

Body: 9–15 in., tail: 10–12 in.

Look up the next time you're walking in the west side of Bend or in other urban areas with a lot of evergreens—there's a highway running right above you. Our gray beauties, western gray squirrels, are up there carrying on a high-wire act as they gather pine and other seeds, scurrying from one tree to another and along phone wires and gutters.

We're fortunate to have so many of these beautiful squirrels in our area. (Photo by Carolyn Waissman)

We're lucky to have western grays here. They've been up-listed from threatened to endangered in Washington, and ODFW says populations are declining across Oregon. They're on the state's sensitive-vulnerable list in the Willamette Valley.

Look for: The biggest tree squirrels you'll see. Their silvery-gray color, white bellies, and fancy plumed tails are tough to miss.

Found: They're where the trees are (Sunriver, Sisters, the west side of Bend, etc.), nesting high in ponderosa pines, Douglas-firs, and other conifers.

> **"This squirrel, this squirrel was always travelling, always searching, it couldn't talk about this, not because it lacked the power of speech but because it had absolutely no time." —Franz Kafka**

Big ears, tiny feet, and much larger than mice.
(Photo by Buddy Mays)

RATS

Bushy-tailed Woodrat (Packrat)
(Neotoma cinerea)

Body: 7–9 in., tail: 5–9 in.

To make your next hike in the Badlands Wilderness infinitely more interesting, keep an eye out for woodrat, or packrat, middens. Middens are piles of sticks and other debris tucked in the cavities of old junipers and the crevices of rocky outcroppings.

What's so interesting about a rat that leaves a pile of stinky junk around? Well, take a closer look without trampling their space, and you might see bones, nails, and other interesting objects in those middens—woodrats especially love shiny treasures, from gold watches to spoons and tinfoil.

Middens can be ten feet high and ten feet wide, built by generation after generation of woodrats. Some middens are over 50,000 years old and are highly valued by scientists who use the preserved fossils and other remains to reconstruct thousands of years of changes in plants, animals, and the climate.

If you get annoyed with woodrats that move onto your property, keep in mind that these are native animals not to be confused with the Norway rat or other harmful imports. If you live-trap and release them in remote areas, they can start collecting old silverware to fortify the next great midden.

Look for: You're more likely to see (and smell) their middens, but bushy-tailed woodrats are dashing rodents with big, black eyes and large ears to go with that bushy tail.

Found: The Badlands Wilderness is prime habitat, but they're all over the region.

> "Once, far back in the high Sierra, they stole my snow-goggles, the lid of my teapot, and my aneroid barometer. . . . [When another started dragging off my ice hatchet], I threw bits of bark at him and made a noise to frighten him, but he stood scolding and chattering back at me, his fine eyes shining with an air of injured innocence."
> —John Muir

Yes, these "kangaroos" have pouches—cheek pouches for carrying food, not joeys. (Photo by Jim Anderson)

Ord's Kangaroo Rat *(Dipodomys ordii)*

Body: 4–5 in., tail: about 6 in.

If there's one thing we know about animals, it's that they need to drink water to survive, right? Wrong. The Ord's kangaroo rat is one of the rare exceptions, an animal that can go its whole life without drinking a single drop of water. Which makes the fact that it's a rodent that hops around like a kangaroo only the second most interesting thing about it.

The rats have developed uber-efficient kidneys that squeeze all the vital fluids they need to survive out of the dry seeds, plants, and insects they dine on. They also plug up their burrows during the day so they can stay cool and minimize sun exposure. And they don't sweat or pant like most animals, which further minimizes water loss.

At night, Ord's rats hop around on their enlarged hind legs, very much like a miniature kangaroo. Instead of a belly pouch, they have fur-lined cheek pouches where they store the seeds they compulsively gather, before hopping home to avoid the many owls, snakes, and other predators that appreciate them for more than their clever adaptations.

Look for: If you see a wee, cinnamon-buff creature standing on its hind legs, it's an Ord's.

Found: You can spot their burrows and trails in the Badlands Wilderness and other juniper woodlands and sandy areas east of Bend.

FUN FACT

Ord's kangaroo rats are one of the few animals with such exceptional hearing that they can detect the nearly silent flight of an owl.

Females raise their offspring jointly within a harem—one male with two or three females. (Photo by Kevin Smith)

OTHER MAMMALS

Yellow-bellied Marmot *(Marmota flaviventris)*

Body: 13–19 in., tail: 5–7.5 in.

A lot of people come to Bend to live the good life, sleeping late, eating tasty food, soaking up the warm sun, playing with friends. Yellow-bellied marmots are no different; they just take the low-key Central Oregon lifestyle to comical extremes—swelling their bellies to outrageous proportions so they can sleep through more than half the year.

They're also called rockchucks or whistle pigs. (Photo by Kim Elton)

On rocky slopes, outcrops, and piles in and near area towns, you can see marmots sunning themselves or playing with others in their colony, wrestling and nibbling ears. Mostly, they spend their waking hours gobbling up wildflowers and whatever other vegetation they can find, until their bellies quite literally drag on the ground. They need every ounce of that added fat to survive hibernations that last seven months or more, depending on elevation and climate.

Somewhere near the dozing marmots you see on rocky slopes will be a sentry. Because as relaxed as their lifestyle may seem, our largest squirrels are eternally vigilant, requiring early warning signs to evade eagles, hawks, badgers, and other predators.

A steady whistle from the sentry may indicate that a predator is in sight, while various shrill and sometimes descending whistles likely convey something akin to "Get that big belly of yours into a burrow now!"

Look for: They're far larger than any other squirrel you'll see, and they do indeed have yellow bellies, as well as yellow-brown backs.

Found: There's a famous population in the Old Mill District. They're also at Smith Rock State Park, River's Edge Golf Course, and many other rocky outcroppings around area towns.

Note the bulging "pockets" and the long, sharp claws for digging. (Photo by Kevin Smith)

Northern Pocket Gopher *(Thomomys talpoides)*

Body: 4 in., tail: 2 in.

Yes, gopher mounds are a nuisance in lawns, gardens, agricultural fields, and even forests, where gophers dine on the roots of plants and trees. But before you go all *Caddyshack* on them, take a closer look. Pocket gophers are interesting animals that in some instances do a great service to the environment.

Pocket gophers are named for the fur-lined cheek pouches where they carry their food. They can even turn their "pockets" inside-out for cleaning—genius! Their tunnels (sometimes hundreds of feet long) are quite the finicky engineering feat, with a lower level for food storage and sleeping, and an upper level for foraging and using as a latrine.

But what good are our pocket gophers, you ask? Well, their tunneling aerates soil, which encourages plant growth and slows water runoff. In fact, research suggests that a single gopher can bring over two tons of soil to the surface each year. All that soil churning mixes subsoil with topsoil, reportedly playing a key role in restoring green life to post-eruption Mount St. Helens. It's also said to help alfalfa grow larger and healthier.

Look for: Squat little animals with thick, almost hairless tails. Colors vary, but their underparts are lighter than their upperparts.

Found: All over open areas and less-dense forest understories. Look for their burrows and trails in the Badlands Wilderness and other sandy, semi-desert areas north and east of Bend.

Kayak around Sparks Lake this summer, and you might be serenaded by pikas' distinctive, high-pitched eenk call.
(Photo by Kevin Smith)

American Pika (*Ochotona princeps*)

Body: 6-8.5 in.

One simple effect of climate change is that animals that live at high elevations will be forced to retreat higher and higher, until there's no place left for them to go. Indeed that's already happening to the wolverine and many others. But the pika—a ridiculously cute furball with no tail and Mickey Mouse ears—is telling a more complicated tale.

Is any animal cuter than a pika? (Photo by Alan St. John)

It's not that climate change isn't affecting pikas; it's just that they appear to be adapting by occupying a wider range of habitats than previously thought. Specifically, OSU-Cascades instructor Matt Shinderman and others have found that pikas are living not only high up in the Cascades but also in lower-elevation lava flows and other craggy landforms at spots like Lava Butte.

Pikas perish quickly in high heat, so it makes sense that they typically live at higher elevations. So how are they surviving life in our hot lava flows? By retreating into the labyrinths under the lava flows where they can stay cool—and take cover in a hurry from weasels, coyotes, raptors, and other predators.

Look for: Pikas are notoriously tough to spot, but if you look on the lava flows and rocky areas where they live, you might find their signs: small white "pee-rocks" stained by urine, perfectly round pellets, and sometimes "hay piles" (the vegetation they gather for winter) stashed within the rocks.

Found: In rocky rubble (talus) at high elevations but also in lava flows along the Lava Butte Trail, at the Lava Cast Forest, and all around Sparks Lake.

Canada lynx.
(Photo by John Williams)

Black bear. (Photo by Dave Rein)

American beaver. (Photo by Dave Rein)

North American river otter.
(Photo by John Williams)

American pika.
(Photo by Damian Fagan)

Squirrel with a horse head.
(Photo by Rick Derevan)

Mule deer in wildlife
corridor. (Photo by Leslie
Bliss-Ketchum)

"Surely, the most important part of an animal is its anima, its vital spirit, on which is based its character and all the peculiarities by which it most concerns us. Yet most scientific books which treat of animals leave this out altogether, and what they describe are as it were phenomena of dead matter."
—Henry David Thoreau

Coyote. (Photo by Kim Elton)

Elk in Sunriver. (Photo by Susan Berger)

ANIMAL TRACKS

Let's be honest: Most wild animals want nothing to do with us. They hide, they dart away, they come out only when we're not there. That's why, if you really want to know who you're sharing the land with, you have to learn at least a few animal tracks.

The finer points are complicated, but the basics are easy. Slow down. Look down. At your feet are stories: a bobcat trotting across a ridge, a jackrabbit racing for its life, a raccoon stopping for a drink beside a stream. Once you start seeing those stories, you'll realize that we're not alone, and our trails are not the only ones worth exploring.

HAVE SOME FUN!

Examine each track and read the descriptions. Then look in the bottom-right corner to see if you've correctly guessed which track belongs to which animal. (Note that the drawings are not done to scale.)

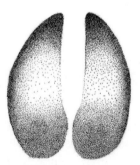

DEER OR ELK?

- Both have hooves roughly shaped like apostrophes.
- Deer tracks are much smaller.
- Elk tracks are rounder and fuller, with rounded tips.

Front print   Front print

COYOTE OR DOG?

- Dog tracks come in all sizes. Coyote tracks are all about 2 in. wide.
- Coyote tracks are more oblong and compact.
- Coyote toes tend to point forward, with less splaying to the sides.

Front print   Front print

COYOTE OR BOBCAT?

- Bobcats usually don't leave claw marks.
- Coyote heel pads have two lobes. Bobcats have three (like an "M").
- Bobcat tracks are broad, almost circular. Coyote tracks are oval.

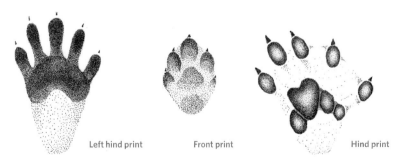

Left hind print   Front print   Hind print

WHAT IN THE WORLD?

- River otters have webbed feet and five sprawling toes with wide nails.
- Raccoon tracks look a lot like human hands.
- Mountain cottontails have oval front tracks with a single lead toe.

Answers: *The deer track is on the left. The dog track is on the left. The bobcat track is on the right. From left to right: raccoon, cottontail, river otter. (Illustrations by Katya Spiecker)*

A pygmy short-horned lizard on Fryrear Butte between Bend and Sisters. (Photos of reptiles by Alan St. John)

REPTILES

LIZARDS

Pygmy Short-horned Lizard (*Phrynosoma douglasii*)

Body: 1–2.5 in.

These plump reptiles are not horned toads, or toads of any kind. They're also not diminutive dinosaurs or dragons, though you'd be excused for thinking so. They are truly unusual little lizards that mostly prefer our semi-arid regions but have also been found in volcanic pumice-sand openings way up near timberline on the eastern slope of the Cascades.

A good-looking mug shot taken near Bend.

Short-horned lizards' adaptations for living in alpine environments are extraordinary. Like the Great Basin spadefoot, they bury themselves underground when weather conditions become inhospitable. In winter, they freeze as solid as an ice cube for months at a time. When the weather warms up in spring, the lizards . . . well, they defrost. And then up they come from their underground refuges to dine on ants and other delicacies.

Though not true of Central Oregon's pygmy variety, a larger kind of short-horned lizard native to regions east of here has a unique defense system. When danger threatens, they swallow a bunch of air, puff up like spiny balloons, and jump up and down while hissing. If that doesn't work (and it would on me), they do what the rest of us can only dream of: They burst a few veins and shoot a thin jet of blood from the corner of each eye to blind their attacker.

Look for: Truly tiny lizards (less than half the size of the desert horned lizards in southeast Oregon), with squat bodies, little spines crowning the head, and two paired rows of dark blotches down their back.

Found: Mostly found in sunny clearings of juniper and pine. Look for them in Cold Springs Campground west of Sisters and in sandy areas (often near anthills) in the Tumalo Natural Area at Bull Flat, the Metolius Preserve, and Fort Rock State Park.

A sagebrush lizard in Fort Rock State Park.

Sagebrush Lizard (*Sceloporus graciosus*)

Body: 3–5.5 in.

Sagebrush lizards and western fence lizards share the same genus (*Sceloporus*) and the same nickname: spiny lizards. In fact, they share just about everything, at least to casual observers.

Both are found most commonly in the arid, sandy regions east of Bend. Both are territorial and show off their blue sides in physically demanding displays. They also share a love for basking in the sun, whether on the ground or on a flat rock or log, and will climb trees to evade predators.

Differences? The sagebrush lizard is smaller and less common than the fence lizard. It looks different too, with a mottled blue chin patch (not solid like the fence lizard's) and often rust-colored armpits. The sagebrush lizard tolerates higher elevations and is the only lizard species in Yellowstone National Park.

Look for: Light strips down the back are a good indicator. The scales on the back of sagebrush lizards aren't as pointy and prickly as the fence lizard's.

Found: In the Badlands Wilderness, Fort Rock State Park, and the Tumalo Natural Area at Bull Flat.

Sagebrush and other area lizards use the tiny claw at the tip of each toe to climb.

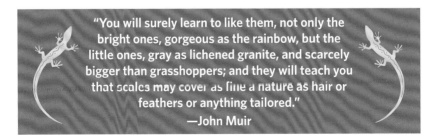

"You will surely learn to like them, not only the bright ones, gorgeous as the rainbow, but the little ones, gray as lichened granite, and scarcely bigger than grasshoppers; and they will teach you that scales may cover as fine a nature as hair or feathers or anything tailored."
—John Muir

A western fence lizard basking on a boulder in Cove Palisades State Park.

The brilliant-blue belly and neck patches on a male fence lizard.

Western Fence Lizard *(Sceloporus occidentalis)*

Body: 3-4 in., tail: 3-5 in.

Western fence lizards are the most common lizard in the Pacific Northwest and can be found just about everywhere in Central Oregon. The only habitats they don't like are shady forests and extremely harsh deserts like the Mojave.

In contrast to so many of our desert-adapted animals, with their variations on gray, brown, dark gray, dark brown, light brown, brownish-gray, gray-brown, and so on, male fence lizards have fantastically blue—blue!— patches on their bellies and throats (the blue is dull or absent in females and juveniles).

Male lizards do pushups to establish dominance and show off their fabulous blue underparts to females. The ladies put in some reps, too, likely to telegraph their strength and interest in mating.

As their name implies, western fence lizards like to bask in the sun on fence posts, as well as on rocks and logs—any open, sunny area will do. Alas, that is not one of the fence lizard's smarter adaptations, as it makes them extremely vulnerable to predators, including hawks, raccoons, and snakes.

Look for: They're bigger than the similar sagebrush lizard and have a dark back with crossbars that often have white flecks.

Found: The Badland Wilderness is a hot spot, but they're all over Central Oregon— the most common lizard you'll come across.

Western Skink (*Eumeces skiltonianus*)

Body: 2.5–4 in., tail: 4–5 in.

The western skink takes the western fence lizard's brash blue belly and raises it one with a blazing-blue tail that it thrashes from side to side, seemingly inviting predators to notice it.

In fact, that's exactly what the skink's doing. When a predator like a kestrel spots the skink, it's likely to focus on that flashy tail. And when the kestrel swoops down and grabs the blue tail, the tail breaks right off, leaving the kestrel with a squirming meal that's a whole lot smaller than expected.

Like many lizards, the western skink will regrow its tail, although future versions will be shorter. The tail also gets paler (less blue) as the skink ages. But don't let all that focus on their back ends fool you: Skinks are not passive little creatures just waiting for predators to bite their tails off. In fact, western skinks are fierce predators themselves, grabbing spiders, beetles, and other prey in their powerful jaws.

Top: *An older adult with a graying tail (it happens to us all).*

Bottom: *A juvenile displaying its electric-blue tail.*

Oh, and that reminds me: Wild lizards are not meant to be pets. And the western skink in particular may let you know its preferences with a strong bite on the hand.

Look for: It's tough to mistake that bluer-than-blue tail, especially on juveniles, but the two white stripes down the body are another giveaway.

Found: Prefer forested, somewhat humid areas, but they've been spotted all the way up to 7,000 ft. Look for them under flat rocks resting on soil and near and under down logs.

SOME OF THE MOST UNUSUAL NAMES FOR THE YOUNGEST WILD ONES

- Bats and beavers: Pups
- Hawks and falcons: Eyases
- Lizards: Hatchlings
- Mountain goats: Kids
- Rabbits: Kittens
- Toads: Tadpoles
- Weasels: Kits

A wandering garter snake in the Sheep Rock Unit of the John Day Fossil Beds National Monument.

SNAKES

Garter Snakes (*Thamnophis* spp.)

Body: 1.5–3.5 ft

For many kids in Oregon, garter snakes are the perfect, safe introduction to snakes. They're harmless, pretty small, and relatively docile. (They do emit quite a stink when picked up, but it's hardly the stuff of horror films.)

Garter snakes are a boon to gardeners because they eat grasshoppers, snails, and other small critters. On the west side of the Cascades, they also gobble up slugs. To encourage garter snakes where you live, add a couple logs or some loosely piled rocks—anything to give them a little cover. And do note that "garter" and "gardener" often get mixed up, but the snakes are "garters."

A valley garter snake in the Deschutes River Canyon near Madras.

There are five garter snake species native to the Pacific Northwest, each with a unique color pattern. The largest ones are females, which can be quite long—nearly four feet! Valley and wandering garter snakes are the most common subspecies in Central Oregon.

Look for: Relatively small snakes with long, bright stripes of various colors.

Found: Watch for them along the Deschutes River Trail, the Crooked River in Smith Rock State Park, the shores of Prineville Reservoir and Lake Billy Chinook, the lakes in Newberry National Monument, and the banks of the Cascade Lakes. Did I mention they're really common?

A rubber boa emerging from a rock crevice late one evening at Fort Rock.

Rubber Boa (*Charina bottae*)

Body: 1.25–2.75 ft.

These small members of the boa constrictor family are timid, gentle, and docile. No, really. They don't move fast and won't bite anyone.

When danger presents itself, rubber boas do what we've all been tempted to do: They roll into a ball, hide their heads, and stick out their stubby tails as decoys (okay, we don't do that last part). Sometimes they even move their tail about, pretending to strike, as they emit a foul-smelling musk (again, human comparisons have their limits).

Mild-mannered rubber boas do have to eat to survive, and that means using their constriction superpowers to kill mice, shrews, and other small animals. They especially like eating infant rodents, and sometimes they use their hard-tipped tail to club the mother while they finish off her infants. But, back to their gentle natures . . .

Would this fool you? This is a rubber boa coiled up and sticking its tail out as a diversionary tactic.

Look for: They resemble racers (another snake in our area), but racers are thinner and much faster. Rubber boas have thicker bodies that really do look like rubber.

Found: In all sorts of habitats, from forests to semi-arid sagebrush areas, usually within a few hundred yards of water (look for them near the Sunriver Nature Center).

Dinnertime: A gopher snake swallowing a rat.

A gopher snake doing its best rattler imitation.

Gopher Snake *(Pituophis catenifer)*

Body: 3–6 ft.

You know that famous poster of a kitty-cat looking in a mirror and seeing a lion looking back? That's kind of what goes on with the common, beautiful, and decidedly non-venomous gopher snake—a snake that will do everything in its power to convince you it's a big, bad rattler.

When confronted with any sort of threat, gopher snakes coil up, flatten their heads, hiss like the dickens, and shake their rattle-free tail, doing a better rattlesnake imitation than many a rattlesnake. Needless to say, that has led to the unfortunate demise of a lot of harmless gopher snakes.

When not engaged in method acting, our Great Basin gopher snakes are helpful members of the Central Oregon ecosystem, hanging out in farmers' fields to help control populations of gophers, mice, voles, and insects.

Look for: Skinnier than rattlesnakes, with slender heads, a "tear" mark through their eyes, and round pupils (unlike the elliptical "cat eyes" of rattlesnakes). Also, their pointed tails lack a rattle, although they may try to convince you otherwise.

Found: Prefer dry brushlands, open juniper and pine woodlands, and the margins of agricultural fields. Look for them east of Bend and on trails near Redmond.

FUN FACT

Gopher snakes frequently live into their teens. The record age is over thirty-three years!

A northern Pacific rattlesnake in the Deschutes River Canyon near Madras.

Western Rattlesnake *(Crotalus oreganus)*

Body: 30–36 in.

The western rattlesnake is the only rattler indigenous to Oregon, and the northern Pacific rattlesnake is Central Oregon's only native subspecies. Now let's get to the common questions:

Will rattlers attack me? No, our rather mild-mannered rattlers will not pursue and attack you. Bites take place when a person reaches onto a ledge or literally stumbles onto a rattler, not realizing it's there. More likely, you'll hear the rattle of the tail, warning you away from where a snake is sunning itself. If you back up, nobody gets hurt.

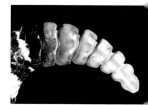

A close-up view of the rattle on the tail-tip of a Northern Pacific rattler.

What do I do if I get bitten? Call 911, and get medical assistance as quickly as possible. To keep the venom from spreading fast, try to stay calm (preventing excessive blood flow) and keep the bitten area below your heart. Bites from the northern Pacific rattler require treatment, but they're rarely fatal.

How common are they? Rattlers appear to be becoming less common in Central Oregon, which reduces encounters with humans but also costs us an ecologically valuable predator of mice, moles, rats, ground squirrels, and other small animals.

How can I avoid them? Avoid the sunny spots where they're commonly found, especially in mornings and evenings on hot days, when they're most likely to be active.

Look for: Broad, triangular heads and large brown blotches down the middle of their back. And of course there's the rattle.

Found: You're most likely to come across them in late spring and summer in dry, rocky areas like Smith Rock State Park, Lake Billy Chinook, Powell Butte, and the Prineville and Ochoco Reservoirs.

The Crooked River flows through Smith Rock State Park, Treasure Hunt 8. (Photo by Ron and Patty Thomas)

TREASURE HUNTS

This book gives you the facts and photos you need to identify over 350 plants and animals native to Central Oregon. But all that book learnin' is just the beginning. The real fun begins when you hit the trail (or river or lake or wastewater treatment facility) and put your know-how to the test.

In this section you'll find treasure hunts for twelve locations within an hour's drive of Bend. Each list features fifty plants and animals divided into highly subjective categories of easy, medium, and hard, depending on how difficult they are to find and identify.

For help locating all the species, be sure to look earlier in the book for details like plant bloom times and the best months to view area birds. Or just get out there and see for yourself what's in season.

I've purposely chosen many well-traveled places, from Pilot Butte to Suttle Lake, because even locations you've visited dozens of times before will offer up new sights and exciting discoveries—once you know what you're looking for.

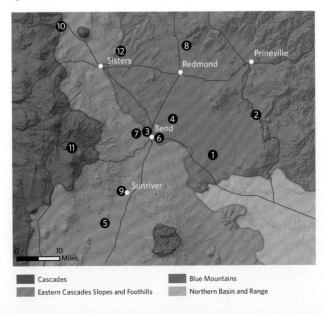

1. BADLANDS WILDERNESS

Think the Badlands Wilderness is a lonely moonscape? Nah, you know better. When the weather's not too hot, this is one of the very best places in Central Oregon to view some of our great survivalists, including ancient junipers (many with packrat nests), buckwheats and bunchgrasses, Canyon Wrens—heck, even some toads and frogs during spring and summer rains.

KEY

☐ Easy ☐ Medium ☐ Hard

TREES

☐ Western Juniper

SHRUBS

☐ Big Sagebrush
☐ Granite Gilia
☐ Gray Rabbitbrush
☐ Green Rabbitbrush

☐ Bitterbrush

☐ Purple Sage

WILDFLOWERS

☐ Cusick's Monkeyflower
☐ Dwarf Monkeyflower
☐ Large-flowered Collomia
☐ Lupines
☐ Oregon Sunshine
☐ Sand Lily
☐ Sulphur-Flower Buckwheat
☐ Threadleaf Phacelia
☐ Western Groundsel

☐ Larkspurs
☐ Western Wallflower
☐ Woolly-Pod Milkvetch

☐ Death Camas
☐ Green-banded Mariposa Lily
☐ Holboell's Rockcress
☐ Parsley Desert Buckwheat
☐ Showy Townsendia
☐ Threadleaf Fleabane

GRASSES

☐ Bottlebrush Squirreltail
☐ Idaho Fescue

☐ Great Basin Wild Rye
☐ Indian Ricegrass
☐ Needle-and-Thread Grass

BIRDS

☐ Common Raven
☐ Mountain Chickadee
☐ Northern Flicker

☐ Canyon Wren
☐ Clark's Nutcracker
☐ Mountain Bluebird
☐ Red-tailed Hawk
☐ Townsend's Solitaire
☐ Turkey Vulture

☐ Cassin's Finch

MAMMALS

☐ Bushy-tailed Woodrat
☐ Least Chipmunk
☐ Ord's Kangaroo Rat

☐ Black-tailed Jackrabbit
☐ Mountain Cottontail

AMPHIBIANS & REPTILES

☐ Sagebrush Lizard
☐ Western Fence Lizard

☐ Western Skink

☐ Great Basin Spadefoot
☐ Pacific Treefrog

Western fence lizard. (Photo by Greg Burke)

2. CHIMNEY ROCK

Want to get a real feel for the dry side? Drive about seventeen miles south of Prineville on Hwy. 27 and hike a mile to the top of Chimney Rock. The views are great, and it's a terrific place to take a closer look at native bunchgrasses and the adaptations (from hairs to light colors to succulent leaves) our hardiest plants use to survive in arid environments. Then hike down to the campground for lunch and a little birdwatching along the Crooked River.

KEY

☐ Easy ☐ Medium ☐ Hard

TREES

☐ Western Juniper

SHRUBS

☐ Big Sagebrush
☐ Bitterbrush

☐ Granite Gilia

☐ Mock-Orange
☐ Purple Sage
☐ Spiny Hopsage
☐ Western Serviceberry

WILDFLOWERS

☐ Cushion Fleabane
☐ Desert Yellow Daisy
☐ Hood's Phlox
☐ Threadleaf Fleabane

☐ Bitterroot
☐ Blue-eyed Mary
☐ Death Camas
☐ Fiddlenecks
☐ Green-banded Mariposa Lily
☐ Lanceleaf Stonecrop
☐ Large-fruited Desert Parsley
☐ Low Pussytoes
☐ Prairie Star
☐ Showy Townsendia
☐ Western Groundsel
☐ Woolly-Pod Milkvetch

☐ Columbia Puccoon
☐ Dwarf Monkeyflower
☐ Gray's Desert Parsley
☐ Lowly Penstemon
☐ Miner's Lettuce
☐ Ragged Robin
☐ Yellow Bell

GRASSES

☐ Bluebunch Wheatgrass
☐ Idaho Fescue
☐ Sandberg Bluegrass

☐ Bottlebrush Squirreltail
☐ Prairie Junegrass
☐ Thurber's Needlegrass

☐ Great Basin Wild Rye
☐ Indian Ricegrass
☐ Needle-and-Thread Grass

BIRDS

☐ American Robin
☐ Cliff Swallow
☐ Common Merganser
☐ Osprey
☐ Rock Dove (Pigeon)

☐ Belted Kingfisher
☐ Golden Eagle
☐ Turkey Vulture

☐ Canyon Wren
☐ Spotted Towhee

Turkey Vulture. (Photo by Dave Rein)

3. FIRST STREET RAPIDS

When I first discovered the First Street Rapids trail near Bend's downtown, I wanted to stop the people speeding by on their way to work. "*This* is your commute? This place with birds singing and beavers building and kingfishers patrolling overhead? You've got to be kidding." But it's no joke. It's Bend at its best.

KEY

☐ Easy ☐ Medium ☐ Hard

TREES

☐ Mountain Alder
☐ Willows

☐ Chokecherry
☐ Elderberry

SHRUBS

☐ Oregon Grape

☐ Douglas Spiraea
☐ Snowberry

☐ Western Clematis

WILDFLOWERS

☐ Fireweed
☐ Larkspurs
☐ Lupines
☐ Silverleaf Phacelia
☐ Western Blue Flax
☐ Western Wallflower

☐ Holboell's Rockcress
☐ Meadow Forget-Me-Not

☐ Columbia Puccoon

WHAT THE HECK IS THAT?

☐ Cattails
☐ Galls
☐ Mistletoe

GRASSES

☐ Idaho Fescue
☐ Bottlebrush Squirreltail

☐ Great Basin Wild Rye

BIRDS

☐ California Quail
☐ Common Merganser

☐ Dark-eyed Junco
☐ Mallard
☐ Mountain Chickadee
☐ Steller's Jay
☐ Western Scrub-Jay
☐ White-crowned Sparrow

☐ American Dipper
☐ American Goldfinch
☐ Belted Kingfisher
☐ Cliff Swallow
☐ Hooded Merganser
☐ Osprey
☐ Pygmy Nuthatch

☐ Anna's Hummingbird
☐ Bushtit
☐ Canyon Wren

MAMMALS

☐ Yellow-bellied Marmot

☐ American Beaver
☐ Muskrat
☐ River Otter

AMPHIBIANS & REPTILES

☐ Sagebrush Lizard
☐ Western Fence Lizard

☐ Pacific Treefrog

☐ Long-toed Salamander
☐ Western Skink

White-crowned Sparrow. (Photo by Chuck Gates)

4. HATFIELD LAKE

Yes, it is a wastewater treatment facility. It's also the best place in Central Oregon to view migrating waterfowl and shorebirds. See how many waterfowl you can pick out on the water and how many songbirds you can spot in the trees. Then check the skies above for raptors soaring and swallows darting after insects. If your goal is to see a lot of different bird species, this place can't be beat.

KEY

☐ Easy ☐ Medium ☐ Hard

BIRDS

☐ American Kestrel
☐ American Robin
☐ American Wigeon
☐ Bald Eagle
☐ Barn Swallow
☐ Black-billed Magpie
☐ Bufflehead
☐ California Quail
☐ Canada Goose
☐ Cinnamon Teal
☐ Cliff Swallow
☐ Common Merganser
☐ Common Raven
☐ Eurasian Collared-Dove
☐ European Starling
☐ Killdeer
☐ Mallard
☐ Mountain Bluebird
☐ Mountain Chickadee
☐ Mourning Dove
☐ Northern Flicker
☐ Red-winged Blackbird
☐ Rock Dove (Pigeon)
☐ Song Sparrow
☐ Tree Swallow
☐ Turkey Vulture
☐ Western Meadowlark

☐ American Goldfinch
☐ Common Nighthawk
☐ Cooper's Hawk
☐ Dark-eyed Junco
☐ Hooded Merganser
☐ House Finch
☐ Pinyon Jay
☐ Red-tailed Hawk
☐ Townsend's Solitaire
☐ Western Bluebird
☐ Yellow-rumped Warbler

☐ Barrow's Goldeneye
☐ Bushtit
☐ Cedar Waxwing
☐ Clark's Nutcracker
☐ Golden Eagle
☐ Hairy Woodpecker
☐ Horned Lark
☐ Peregrine Falcon
☐ Prairie Falcon
☐ Rufous Hummingbird
☐ Wilson's Warbler
☐ Yellow Warbler

American Kestrel. (Photo by Kim Elton)

5. LAPINE STATE PARK

A fraction of the people that visit Pilot Butte State Park visit LaPine State Park, which means you can enjoy a lot more peace and quiet as you explore the lush subalpine pine forest. While there, be sure to visit "Big Red," the largest ponderosa of its kind in the nation, and hike or bike the paths along the Deschutes and Fall Rivers to see some of our more shade- and water-loving plant and animal species.

KEY

☐ Easy ☐ Medium ☐ Hard

TREES

☐ Lodgepole Pine
☐ Ponderosa Pine
☐ Mountain Alder
☐ Willows

SHRUBS

☐ Bitterbrush
☐ Greenleaf Manzanita
☐ Wax Currant
☐ Woods' Rose

☐ Douglas Spiraea
☐ Kinnikinnick
☐ Oregon Grape
☐ Snowberry
☐ Western Serviceberry

WILDFLOWERS

☐ Common Yarrow
☐ False Solomon's Seal
☐ Lupines
☐ Silverleaf Phacelia
☐ Western Blue Flax

☐ Blue-eyed Mary
☐ Pussypaws
☐ Rosy Pussytoes
☐ Wild Strawberry

BIRDS

☐ Canada Goose
☐ Common Raven
☐ Dark-eyed Junco
☐ Mountain Chickadee
☐ Osprey
☐ Red-breasted Nuthatch
☐ Steller's Jay
☐ Tree Swallow
☐ Yellow-rumped Warbler
☐ Yellow Warbler

☐ Common Nighthawk
☐ Hairy Woodpecker
☐ Pine Siskin

☐ Brown Creeper
☐ Cassin's Vireo
☐ Great Horned Owl
☐ Green-tailed Towhee
☐ Hermit Thrush
☐ Northern Pygmy-Owl
☐ Northern Saw-Whet Owl
☐ Olive-sided Flycatcher
☐ Red Crossbill
☐ Vaux's Swift
☐ White-headed Woodpecker

MAMMALS

☐ Douglas Squirrel
☐ Golden-mantled Ground Squirrel
☐ Yellow-Pine Chipmunks

☐ Mule Deer

Golden-mantled ground squirrel. (Photo by Carolyn Waissman)

6. PILOT BUTTE

You've probably been among the million or so people each year who hike or drive to the top of Pilot Butte. But this is not a one-and-done, I've-seen-it-all adventure. The fascinating geology and fabulous views don't change much, but the flora and fauna do. Visit again and again, from late spring through fall, and see how many species (native and noxious) you can spot.

KEY

☐ Easy ☐ Medium ☐ Hard

TREES

☐ Ponderosa Pine
☐ Western Juniper

SHRUBS

☐ Big Sagebrush
☐ Bitterbrush
☐ Gray Rabbitbrush
☐ Green Rabbitbrush
☐ Wax Currant

WILDFLOWERS

☐ Common Yarrow
☐ Large-flowered Collomia
☐ Oregon Sunshine
☐ Sand Lily
☐ Silverleaf Phacelia
☐ Sulphur-Flower Buckwheat
☐ Threadleaf Phacelia
☐ Western Blue Flax

☐ Blazing Star
☐ Blue-eyed Mary
☐ Green-banded Mariposa Lily
☐ Holboell's Rockcress
☐ Low Pussytoes

GRASSES

☐ Bluebunch Wheatgrass
☐ Idaho Fescue
☐ Sandberg Bluegrass

☐ Bottlebrush Squirreltail
☐ Prairie Junegrass

NOXIOUS WEEDS

☐ Cheatgrass
☐ Dalmatian Toadflax
☐ Spotted Knapweed

WHAT THE HECK IS THAT?

☐ Galls
☐ Mistletoe
☐ Mullein
☐ Wolf Lichen

BIRDS

☐ American Robin
☐ Dark-eyed Junco
☐ Eurasian Collared-Dove
☐ European Starling
☐ Mountain Chickadee
☐ Mourning Dove
☐ Northern Flicker
☐ Rock Dove (Pigeon)
☐ Western Bluebird
☐ Western Scrub-Jay

☐ Barn Swallow
☐ Common Nighthawk
☐ Common Raven
☐ House Finch
☐ White-crowned Sparrow
☐ Yellow-rumped Warbler

☐ Cedar Waxwing
☐ Clark's Nutcracker

Sand lily. (Photo by M.A. Willson)

7. SHEVLIN PARK

If you have only one day to see as many species in this book as possible, head to Shevlin Park. The diversity is remarkable, with everything from a mixed-conifer forest to imperiled Lewis's Woodpeckers, plus more beautiful creekside vegetation than you can shake a stick at.

KEY

☐ Easy ☐ Medium ☐ Hard

TREES

☐ Grand Fir
☐ Lodgepole Pine
☐ Mountain Alder
☐ Ponderosa Pine
☐ Quaking Aspen
☐ Western Larch
☐ Willows

☐ Chokecherry
☐ Douglas-Fir
☐ Engelmann Spruce
☐ Red-Osier Dogwood

☐ Bitter Cherry
☐ Elderberry

SHRUBS

☐ Douglas Spiraea
☐ Greenleaf Manzanita
☐ Woods' Rose

☐ Gray Rabbitbrush
☐ Snowberry
☐ Snowbrush

☐ Western Serviceberry

BIRDS

☐ Mountain Chickadee

☐ Brown Creeper
☐ Downy Woodpecker
☐ Lewis's Woodpecker
☐ Northern Flicker
☐ Pygmy Nuthatch

☐ Red-breasted Nuthatch
☐ Tree Swallow
☐ Yellow-rumped Warbler
☐ Yellow Warbler

☐ Cassin's Vireo
☐ Northern Pygmy-Owl
☐ Olive-sided Flycatcher

WILDFLOWERS

☐ False Solomon's Seal
☐ Indian Paintbrush
☐ Lupines
☐ Pearly Everlasting
☐ Red Columbine

☐ Cascades Lily
☐ Cusick's Monkeyflower
☐ Dwarf Monkeyflower
☐ Larkspurs
☐ Oregon Sunshine
☐ Rosy Pussytoes
☐ Sand Lilly
☐ Sulphur-Flower Buckwheat
☐ Threadleaf Phacelia
☐ Western Groundsel

☐ Goldenrod
☐ Jacob's Ladder

Lewis's Woodpecker. (Photo by Kim Elton)

8. SMITH ROCK STATE PARK

Maybe you've heard of this place? Yes, it's one of the state's so-called Seven Wonders. It's also a fantastic site to see and smell our tough-as-nails, arid-climate-loving plant species, and to search the cliffs for bats, falcons, eagle nests, and much more. Or simply walk along the Crooked River and see how many water-loving shrubs, wildflowers, and birds you can spot.

KEY

☐ Easy ☐ Medium ☐ Hard

SHRUBS

☐ Big Sagebrush
☐ Bitterbrush
☐ Red-Osier Dogwood
☐ Wax Currant
☐ Woods' Rose

☐ Golden Currant
☐ Oceanspray
☐ Oregon Grape
☐ Snowberry
☐ Western Clematis
☐ Western Serviceberry

☐ Mock-Orange
☐ Spiny Hopsage

WILDFLOWERS

☐ Arrowleaf Balsamroot
☐ Indian Paintbrush
☐ Lupines
☐ Oregon Sunshine
☐ Sand Lily
☐ Western Blue Flax

☐ Bitterroot
☐ Fiddleneck
☐ Miner's Lettuce
☐ Nineleaf Desert Parsley
☐ Sagebrush Buttercup
☐ Western Wallflower

BIRDS

☐ Black-billed Magpie
☐ Cliff Swallow
☐ Common Merganser
☐ Common Raven
☐ Mallard
☐ Mourning Dove
☐ Osprey
☐ Red-tailed Hawk
☐ Turkey Vulture

☐ Barrow's Goldeneye
☐ Belted Kingfisher
☐ Canyon Wren
☐ Golden Eagle
☐ Great Blue Heron
☐ Prairie Falcon
☐ Peregrine Falcon

AMPHIBIANS & REPTILES

☐ Garter Snakes
☐ Sagebrush Lizard
☐ Western Fence Lizard

☐ Pacific Treefrog
☐ Western Toad

☐ Gopher Snake
☐ Great Basin Spadefoot
☐ Western Rattlesnake
☐ Rubber Boa

Bald Eagle nest at Smith Rock State Park. (Photo by Bobbushphoto)

9. SUNRIVER NATURE CENTER

Bend has a semi-arid climate, but just fifteen miles south and 500 feet higher up, Sunriver offers a cooler, wetter experience where lodgepole pines dominate. Get yourself oriented by visiting the nature center, then go for a morning bird walk or explore the nearby forest and wetlands on the Sam Osgood Nature Trail.

KEY

☐ Easy ☐ Medium ☐ Hard

TREES

☐ Lodgepole Pine
☐ Ponderosa Pine

SHRUBS

☐ Douglas Spiraea
☐ Greenleaf Manzanita
☐ Oregon Grape
☐ Snowberry
☐ Wax Currant

WILDFLOWERS

☐ Indian Paintbrush
☐ Lupines
☐ Sulphur-Flower Buckwheat

☐ Blue-Flag Iris
☐ Goldenrod
☐ Kinnikinnick
☐ Meadow Forget-Me-Not
☐ Oregon Checker Mallow
☐ Red Columbine

MAMMALS

☐ Douglas Squirrel
☐ Golden-mantled Ground Squirrel
☐ Western Gray Squirrel
☐ Yellow-Pine Chipmunk

☐ Beldings Ground Squirrel
☐ Mule Deer
☐ Rocky Mountain Elk

☐ Porcupine

BIRDS

☐ Canada Goose
☐ Common Raven
☐ Eurasian Collared-Dove
☐ House Finch
☐ Mallard
☐ Mountain Chickadee
☐ Northern Flicker
☐ Red-breasted Nuthatch

☐ Barn Swallow
☐ Hairy Woodpecker
☐ Pygmy Nuthatch
☐ Red Crossbill
☐ Red-tailed Hawk
☐ Western Bluebird
☐ Western Tanager
☐ Wilson's Warbler
☐ Yellow-rumped Warbler

☐ Cooper's Hawk
☐ Pine Siskin

AMPHIBIANS & REPTILES

☐ Garter Snakes
☐ Sagebrush Lizard

☐ Pacific Treefrog
☐ Western Skink
☐ Western Toad

☐ Great Basin Spadefoot
☐ Pygmy Short-horned Lizard

Paintbrush and lupine. (Photo by Sue Dougherty)

10. SUTTLE LAKE

The 3.6-mile loop trail around Suttle Lake provides a terrific, easy-to-access example of a mixed-conifer forest and the species that go with it. You'll find a lot of diversity in trees and shrubs, including plants like vine maple that are more typical of the west side of the Cascades. The lake and forest also provide great birdwatching opportunities.

KEY

☐ Easy ☐ Medium ☐ Hard

TREES

- ☐ Douglas-Fir
- ☐ Elderberry
- ☐ Grand Fir
- ☐ Incense-Cedar
- ☐ Subalpine Fir

- ☐ Bitter Cherry

SHRUBS

- ☐ Oregon Grape
- ☐ Snowbrush

- ☐ Pacific Ninebark
- ☐ Red-Osier Dogwood

WILDFLOWERS

- ☐ Common Yarrow
- ☐ False Solomon's Seal
- ☐ Fireweed
- ☐ Western Trillium

- ☐ California Corn Lily
- ☐ Cascades Lily
- ☐ One-sided Wintergreen
- ☐ Orange Honeysuckle
- ☐ Pearly Everlasting
- ☐ Queen's Cup
- ☐ Red Columbine
- ☐ Twinflower
- ☐ Wild Strawberry

- ☐ Heart-leaved Pyrola
- ☐ Pipsissewa

BIRDS

- ☐ American Robin
- ☐ Brown Creeper
- ☐ Bufflehead
- ☐ Canada Goose
- ☐ Common Merganser
- ☐ Dark-eyed Junco
- ☐ Mallard
- ☐ Mountain Chickadee
- ☐ Northern Flicker
- ☐ Red-breasted Nuthatch
- ☐ Yellow-rumped Warbler

- ☐ American Dipper
- ☐ Bald Eagle
- ☐ Barrow's Goldeneye
- ☐ Cassin's Finch
- ☐ Common Nighthawk
- ☐ Hairy Woodpecker
- ☐ Hermit Thrush
- ☐ Hermit Warbler
- ☐ Red Crossbill
- ☐ Western Tanager
- ☐ White-headed Woodpecker

- ☐ Evening Grosbeak
- ☐ Olive-sided Flycatcher
- ☐ Pine Siskin

Bufflehead. (Photo by John Williams)

11. TODD LAKE

Todd Lake is the closest Cascade Lake to Bend and thus is, let's just say, "much-loved." If you go, tread with care. The meadow on the north end is a particularly sensitive environment, with frogs and toads hopping through and delicate wildflowers trying their best to bloom despite repeated trampling by our big boots.

KEY

☐ Easy ☐ Medium ☐ Hard

TREES

☐ Lodgepole Pine
☐ Mountain Hemlock
☐ Subalpine Fir

WILDFLOWERS

☐ Bleeding Heart
☐ Bog Orchid
☐ California Corn Lily
☐ Indian Paintbrush
☐ Jeffrey's Shooting Star
☐ Larkspurs
☐ Pink Mountain Heather
☐ White Marsh-Marigold

☐ Bluebells
☐ Elephant's Head Lousewort
☐ Fiddleneck
☐ Jacob's Ladder
☐ Newberry's Gentian
☐ Pussypaws
☐ Steer's Head

BIRDS

☐ Bald Eagle
☐ Bufflehead
☐ Common Raven
☐ Dark-eyed Junco
☐ Northern Flicker
☐ Osprey
☐ Song Sparrow
☐ Tree Swallow
☐ Yellow-rumped Warbler

☐ Barrow's Goldeneye
☐ Black-headed Grosbeak
☐ Hairy Woodpecker
☐ Olive-sided Flycatcher
☐ Pine Siskin
☐ Red Crossbill
☐ Townsend's Solitaire
☐ Western Tanager
☐ White-headed Woodpecker

☐ Brown Creeper
☐ Cassin's Vireo
☐ Common Merganser
☐ Hermit Thrush
☐ Hermit Warbler
☐ Hooded Merganser
☐ Northern Saw-Whet Owl
☐ Pygmy Nuthatch
☐ Spotted Towhee
☐ Vaux's Swift
☐ Western Bluebird

AMPHIBIANS & REPTILES

☐ Pacific Treefrog
☐ Western Toad

☐ Garter Snakes

Western toad. (Photo by Murphy_Shewchuk)

12. WHYCHUS CANYON PRESERVE

What do you like to explore on your hikes? Canyon country? Verdant valleys? This is one of the rare places in Central Oregon where you can enjoy a bit of everything—all in one 930-acre stretch between Sisters and Redmond. The preserve is owned and maintained by the Deschutes Land Trust, so walk the trails on your own or join the land trust for one of their wonderfully informative (and free) hikes.

KEY

☐ Easy ☐ Medium ☐ Hard

TREES

☐ Mountain Alder
☐ Ponderosa Pine
☐ Western Juniper

☐ Chokecherry
☐ Quaking Aspen

SHRUBS

☐ Big Sagebrush
☐ Red-Osier Dogwood
☐ Wax Currant
☐ Woods' Rose
☐ Snowberry
☐ Mock-Orange

WILDFLOWERS

☐ Arrowleaf Balsamroot
☐ Cow Parsnip
☐ Dwarf Monkeyflower
☐ Gold Stars
☐ Hood's Phlox
☐ Indian Paintbrush
☐ Larkspurs
☐ Prairie Star
☐ Sand Lily
☐ Scarlet Gilia

☐ Bitterroot
☐ Blazing Star
☐ Death Camas
☐ Goldenrod
☐ Green-banded Mariposa Lily
☐ Lanceleaf Stonecrop
☐ Lowly Penstemon
☐ Miner's Lettuce
☐ Oregon Sunshine
☐ Western Wallflower
☐ Yellow Bell

BIRDS

☐ American Robin
☐ Mountain Chickadee
☐ Northern Flicker
☐ Yellow-rumped Warbler

☐ Canyon Wren
☐ Cliff Swallow
☐ Common Nighthawk
☐ Golden Eagle
☐ Hairy Woodpecker
☐ Song Sparrow
☐ Spotted Towhee
☐ Tree Swallow
☐ Western Bluebird
☐ Western Tanager
☐ Yellow-rumped Warbler
☐ Yellow Warbler

☐ Northern Pygmy-Owl
☐ White-headed Woodpecker

Derek Loeb leads a geology hike at the Deschutes Land Trust's Whychus Canyon Preserve. (Photo by John Williams)

LOCAL NONPROFIT ORGANIZATIONS

Do you want to learn more about the local environment? Or get your hands dirty making things better, whether by pulling weeds or twisting arms? These are just a few of the many local nonprofit organizations where you can make friends and make a difference.

Pollinator Pathway Bend

When we paved paradise and put up parking lots across Bend, we destroyed habitat for pollinators. And of course the paving continues. To make sure bees and others can still find enough food, water, and shelter to survive—even in the midst of our fast-growing city—Pollinator Pathway Bend plants thousands of native, pesticide-free plants wherever they can, including in parks, gardens, and roundabouts. Go to pollinatorpathwaybend.org to learn how you can help.

Central Oregon LandWatch

Let's face it: Sometimes the siren call of short-term profits drives people to do irreparable harm to the environment. They log old-growth trees. Pipe pristine waterways. Plop subdivisions on sensitive wildlife habitats. East of the Cascades, LandWatch provides one of the only lines of defense against actions like these. Donate and volunteer to help them continue their fight for a better future. Learn more at centraloregonlandwatch.org.

Deschutes Land Trust

Want to protect the places you care about? Then the Deschutes Land Trust is for you. They work with landowners to conserve and care for lands across Central Oregon. Since 1995, the trust has protected thousands of acres—many of which you can explore on your own, as a volunteer, or on one of their phenomenal trips led by local naturalists. Learn more at deschuteslandtrust.org.

Discover Your Forest

We're surrounded by incredibly rich and diverse national forests and other public lands. The question is, how do we introduce and connect kids and others to these remarkable places? Discover Your Forest provides one answer, with visitor services, a lot of events, and kid-friendly educational opportunities like snowshoeing with rangers on Mount Bachelor. Learn more at discoveryourforest.org.

East Cascades Bird Alliance

So you can't tell a hawk from an eagle? Or you know the basics but yearn to learn more? This lively group is for you. Join them for their weekly birding trips, monthly birders' night, educational events for kids, volunteer work, and more—this is a welcoming, active, fun group of bird lovers. Get involved at ecbirds.org.

The Environmental Center

The aptly named Environmental Center is the center of environmental action in Central Oregon. From the little house on Kansas Avenue (and the learning garden beside it), a small but mighty team produces programs and events about all sorts of sustainability issues, from reducing waste to growing your own food. Get on their newsletter list to learn about local issues and how you can get involved. Find out more at envirocenter.org.

Friends and Neighbors of the Deschutes Canyon Area
Friends and Neighbors (FANs) groups bring people together to learn about, preserve, and restore the land around them. This FANs group focuses on the middle Deschutes River, lower Crooked River, and lower Whychus Creek area. Join them for a field trip or a lecture, and meet some passionate people in the process. Learn more at fansofdeschutes.org.

Great Old Broads for Wilderness
The Great Old Broads got started in 1989 when some gently aged women in Utah banded together in the fight to protect public lands. Fast-forward to today, and there are over 5,000 Broads (and Bros, as men are known) nationwide, including those in our local chapter, the Bitterbrush Broads. Together they tear down fences, sponsor talks, go on trips, advocate for the environment, and have more fun than just about any other group in town. Get involved at greatoldbroads.org.

Native Plant Society of Oregon: High Desert Chapter
In June, make a point to attend the Central Oregon Wildflower Show, organized by our local chapter of the state's Native Plant Society. You can also join NPSO for summer field trips and other activities throughout the year. It's a great way to learn to identify and appreciate some of Oregon's more than 3,600 native plant species. Check it out at npsoregon.org.

Oregon Natural Desert Association
How much of Oregon is rainy, lush, and green? Less than you think. About forty-five percent is actually high desert, and less than one percent of that is permanently protected. That's why ONDA worked so hard to get the Badlands designated as a wilderness area in 2009. And it's why its members and volunteers—you included, I hope—will keep working to protect and restore the state's arid lands. Learn more at onda.org.

Mountain goat. (Photo by Greg Burke)

Sunriver Nature Center & Observatory

We'd need a few pages to explain all that this unique nature center offers, including research, kids' activities, wildlife rehab, a botanical garden, guided walks . . . oh, and the nation's largest public viewing observatory. Since the late 1960s, the nature center has been an invaluable resource for Sunriver and the whole region. Stop by the center with your family, or visit sunrivernaturecenter.org to learn about upcoming activities and events.

Think Wild

Bend-based Think Wild provides medical care to injured and orphaned wildlife across Central Oregon. They're also working hard to reduce the need for rescue by providing education, outreach, and conservation services. Call their wildlife hotline at 541-241-8680 if you find an injured wild animal, and donate or volunteer if you can.

California Quail. (Photo by Alice Doggett)

SELECT BIBLIOGRAPHY

MULTIPLE CHAPTERS

Books

Anderson, Jim. *Tales from a Northwest Naturalist.* Caldwell, ID: Caxton Printers, 1992.

Dietrich, William. *Natural Grace: The Charm, Wonder, & Lessons of Pacific Northwest Animals & Plants.* Seattle: University of Washington Press, 2003.

Ferguson, Denzel, and Nancy Ferguson. *Oregon's Great Basin Country.* Burns, OR: Gail Graphics, 1978.

Furry, Darin. *Beyond Sagebrush: Secrets of Central Oregon's Natural World.* Bend, OR: DF Publications, 2008.

Jackman, E.R., and R.A. Long. *The Oregon Desert.* Caldwell, ID: Caxton Printers, 1964.

Kolbert, Elizabeth. *The Sixth Extinction: An Unnatural History.* New York: Henry Holt and Company, 2015.

Leeson, Tom, and Pat Leeson. *Oregon Wildlife Portfolio.* Helena, MT: Farcountry Press, 2005.

Lichen, Patricia K. *Passionate Slugs and Hollywood Frogs: An Uncommon Field Guide to Northwest Backyards.* Seattle: Sasquatch Books, 2001.

———. *River-Walking Songbirds & Singing Coyotes: An Uncommon Field Guide to Northwest Mountains.* Seattle: Sasquatch Books, 2001.

Mathews, Daniel. *Cascade-Olympic Natural History: A Trailside Reference.* Portland, OR: Raven Editions, 1988.

Mighetto, Lisa, ed. *Muir Among the Animals: The Wildlife Writings of John Muir.* San Francisco: Sierra Club Books, 1986.

Muir, John. *The Mountains of California.* New York: The Century Company, 1894.

Pohs, Keith. *The Wallowa Mountains: A Natural History Guide.* Portland, OR: Northwest Mountain Works, 2000.

Simpson, Ann, and Rob Simpson. *Nature Guide to Yellowstone National Park.* Guilford, CT: Falcon Guides, 2016.

St. John, Alan D. *Oregon's Dry Side: Exploring East of the Cascade Crest.* Portland, OR: Timber Press, 2007.

Taylor, Ronald J. *Sagebrush Country: A Wildflower Sanctuary.* Missoula, MT: Mountain Press, 1992.

Taylor, Ronald J., and George W. Douglas. *Mountain Plants of the Pacific Northwest.* Missoula, MT: Mountain Press, 1995.

Taylor, Ronald J., and Rolf W. Valum. *Wildflowers 2: Sagebrush Country.* New York: Touchstone Press, 1974.

Turner, Mark, and Ellen Kuhlmann. *Trees & Shrubs of the Pacific Northwest.* Portland, OR: Timber Press, 2014.

Twain, Mark. *Roughing It.* Hartford, CT: American Publishing Company, 1872.

Websites

Oregon Dept. of Fish and Wildlife (ODFW): dfw.state.or.us

U.S. Dept. of Agriculture: plants.usda.gov

U.S. Forest Service: fs.usda.gov

World Wildlife Fund's Living Planet Index: www.livingplanetindex.org

Museums & Wildlife Centers

Deschutes Historical Museum

High Desert Museum

Sunriver Nature Center

Tucson Wildlife Center

TREES

Books

Arno, Stephen F., and Ramona P. Hammerly. *Northwest Trees.* Seattle: Mountaineers Books, 1977.

Bass, Rick. "The Larch." *Orion.* 2013.

Cornell, Joseph. *Sharing Nature with Children.* Nevada City, CA: Ananda Publications, 1979.

Halvorson, Ron. "Western Juniper (Juniperus occidentalis)." *Kalmiopsis*, Vol. 20, 2013.

Hatton, Raymond, et al. *Oregon's Sisters Country: A Portrait of Its Lands, Waters, and People.* Bend, OR: Geographical Books, 1996.

Jensen, Ed. *Trees to Know in Oregon.* Corvallis: OSU Press, 1999.

Kerr, Andy. *Oregon Wild: Endangered Forest Wilderness.* 1984.

Kitchen, Stanley G. "Cercocarpus Kunth: Mountain-Mahogany." *Woody Plant Seed Manual.* www.fs.usda.gov/rm/pubs_series/wo/wo_ah727/wo_ah727_381_384.pdf

Lanner, Ronald M., and Christine Stetter. *Trees of the Great Basin: A Natural History.* Reno: University of Nevada Press, 1984.

Miller, Richard F., et al. "Biology, Ecology, and Management of Western Juniper." *Technical Bulletin* 152. OSU Agricultural Experiment Station, June 2005. juniper. oregonstate.edu/sites/default/files/bibliography/documents/phpQ65pOk_tb152.pdf

Murray, Michael. "Our Threatened Timberlines: The Plight of Whitebark Pine Ecosystems." *Kalmiopsis,* Vol. 12, 2005. www.npsoregon.org/kalmiopsis/ kalmiopsis12/timberlines.pdf

Nisbet, Jack. *The Collector: David Douglas and the Natural History of the Northwest.* Seattle: Sasquatch Books, 2009.

Ross, M.R., et al. "Effects of Fuels Reductions on Plant Communities and Soils in a Piñon-Juniper Woodland." *Journal of Arid Environments.* Vol. 79, Apr. 2012. https:// www.sciencedirect.com/science/article/abs/pii/S0140196311003533

Tudge, Colin. *The Tree: A Natural History of What Trees Are, How They Live, and Why They Matter.* New York: Crown Publishers, 2006.

Witty, Jim. *Meet Me in the Badlands: Exploring Central Oregon with Jim Witty.* Bend, OR: Maverick Publications, 2009.

SELECT BIBLIOGRAPHY

Websites

Incense-cedar, Oregon Encyclopedia: www.oregonencyclopedia.org/articles/incense_cedar

Native Plant Society of Oregon, www.npsoregon.org

Oregon Forest Resources Institute, oregonforests.org

SHRUBS, BUNCHGRASSES, NOXIOUS WEEDS, AND WHAT THE HECK IS THAT?

Books

Alexanian, Kev. *"A Weed Warrior's Guide to Crook County."* 2014. co.crook.or.us/Portals/24/WeedWarriorGuide.pdf

Alper, Joe. "Wicked Weed of the West." *Smithsonian Magazine,* Dec. 2004. smithsonianmag.com/science-nature/Wicked_Weed_of_the_West.html

Bowen, Asta. *The Huckleberry Book: All About the West's Most Treasured Berry.* Helena, MT: American Geographic, 1988.

Fillhart, Shannon, and Tobias Policha. "Plant of the Year: Oregon Grape (Berberis aquifolium), Our State Flower." *Kalmiopsis,* Vol. 13, 2006. www.npsoregon.org/kalmiopsis/kalmiopsis13/fillhart.pdf

Garrett, Stuart G. "Plant of the Year: Basin Wildrye (Leymus cinereus)." *Kalmiopsis,* Vol. 9, 2002. www.npsoregon.org/kalmiopsis/kalmiopsis_v09.pdf

Halvorson, Ron. "Plant of the Year: Sandberg Bluegrass (Poa secunda)." *Kalmiopsis,* Vol. 18, 2011. www.npsoregon.org/kalmiopsis/kalmiopsis18/2halvorson.pdf

Jensen, Ed. *Shrubs to Know in Pacific Northwest Forests.* Corvallis: Oregon State University Extension Service, 2013.

Johnson, George. "The Weed That Won the West." *National Geographic,* March 2013. ngm.nationalgeographic.com/2013/12/tumbleweeds/johnson-text

Lawson, Willow. "Study: Lawn Mowing Equals Car Trip." ABC News, 31 May 2001. abcnews.go.com/Technology/story?id=98532&page=1

Mozingo, Hugh N. *Shrubs of the Great Basin: A Natural History.* 1987. Reno: University of Nevada Press, 1987.

Saling, Ann. *Great Northwest Nature Factbook: A Guide to the Region's Remarkable Animals, Plants and Natural Features.* Portland, OR: WestWinds Press, 1999.

Turner, Jason L., et al. *Russian Knapweed and Yellow Star Thistle Poisoning of Horses.* New Mexico State University, 2011. aces.nmsu.edu/pubs/_b/b-710.pdf

WILDFLOWERS

Books

Blackwell, Laird R. *Great Basin Wildflowers: A Guide to Common Wildflowers of the High Deserts of Nevada, Utah, and Oregon.* Guilford, CT: Falcon Guides, 2006.

Buchmann, Stephen L. "Our Vanishing Flowers." *The New York Times* (op-ed), 16 Oct. 2015. www.nytimes.com/2015/10/17/opinion/our-vanishing-flowers.html

Burger, William C. *Flowers: How They Changed the World.* Amherst, NY: Prometheus, 2006.

Fagan, Damian. *Pacific Northwest Wildflowers.* Guildford, CT: Falcon Guides, 2006.

Strickler, Dee. *Wayside Wildflowers of the Pacific Northwest.* Columbia Falls, MT: Flower Press, 1993.

Turner, Mark, and Phyllis Gustafson. *Wildflowers of the Pacific Northwest.* Portland, OR: Timber Press, 2006.

Vance, Nan. "Finding Brown's Peony a Sweet Attraction." *Kalmiopsis,* Vol. 19, 2012. www.npsoregon.org/kalmiopsis/kalmiopsis19/1brownspeony.pdf

Websites

Indian Paintbrush Wildflower, Glacier National Park Travel Guide, www.glacier-national-park-travel-guide.com/indian-paintbrush.html

Oregon Flora Project, oregonflora.org

Turner Photographics' Pacific Northwest Wildflowers, www.pnwflowers.com

BIRDS

Books

Alderfer, Jonathan, and Paul Hess. *Backyard Guide to the Birds of North America.* Washington, DC: National Geographic, 2011.

Brown, Augustus. *Why Pandas Do Handstands and Other Curious Truths About Animals.* New York: Free Press, 2006.

Erickson, Laura, and Marie Read. *Into the Nest: Intimate Views of the Courtine, Parenting, and Family Lives of Familiar Birds.* North Adams, MA: Storey Publishing, 2015.

Sibley, David Allen. *The Sibley Guide to Bird Life and Behavior.* 2009. NYC: Knopf, 2009.

Solomon, Christopher. "When Birds Squawk, Other Species Seem to Listen." The New York Times, 18 May 2015. www.nytimes.com/2015/05/19/science/decoding-the-cacophony-of-birds-warning-calls.html

Strycker, Noah. *The Thing with Feathers: The Surprising Lives of Birds and What They Reveal About Being Human.* New York: Riverhead Books, 2014.

Swanson, Sarah, and Max Smith. *Must-See Birds of the Pacific Northwest.* Portland, OR: Timber Press, 2013.

Tekiela, Stan. *Amazing Hummingbirds: Unique Images and Characteristics.* Cambridge, MN: Adventure Publications, 2010.

Young, Jon. *What the Robin Knows: How Birds Reveal the Secrets of the Natural World.* New York: Mariner Books, 2012.

Mobile App

Merlin Bird ID, Cornell Lab

Websites

Animals, National Geographic: www.nationalgeographic.com/animals

Cornell Lab's All About Birds: www.allaboutbirds.org

National Audubon Society, www.audubon.org

Partners in Flight, partnersinflight.org

AMPHIBIANS, INSECTS, AND REPTILES

Books

Barnard, Jeff. *"Oregon Spotted Frog to Be Protected as Threatened."* Statesman Journal, 29 Aug. 2014. www.statesmanjournal.com/story/tech/science/environment/2014/08/29/oregon-spotted-frog-protected/14813397.

Finn, Charles. *Wild Delicate Seconds: 29 Wildlife Encounters.* Corvallis: Oregon State University Press, 2012.

Glassberg, Jeffrey. *Butterflies Through Binoculars: The West.* Oxford, UK: Oxford University Press, 2001.

Pyle, Robert M. *Butterflies of Cascadia.* Seattle: Seattle Audubon Society, 2002.

Shorack, Ted. *"Spotted Frog Plan Finalized for Old Mill."* The Bend Bulletin, 20 Sept. 2014.

St. John, Alan D. *Reptiles of the Northwest.* Renton, WA: Lone Pine Publishing, 2002.

MAMMALS

Books

Balcombe, Jonathan. *Second Nature: The Inner Lives of Animals.* New York: Palgrave Macmillan, 2010.

Bekoff, Marc. "Animals and Cars: One Million Animals Are Killed on Our Roads Every Day." *Psychology Today,* 21 July 2010. www.psychologytoday.com/us/blog/animal-emotions/201007/animals-and-cars-one-million-animals-are-killed-on-our-roads-every-day

Bittel, Jason. "How Do Porcupines Mate? Very Carefully." *Slate,* 23 Nov. 2012. slate.com/technology/2012/11/porcupine-sex-mating-behaviors-involve-quills-musk-penis-spikes-fights-and-arcs-of-urine.html

Blackburn, Del F. "Courtship Behavior Among White-tailed and Black-tailed Jackrabbits." *Great Basin Naturalist,* Vol. 33, No. 3, 1973.

Cornwall, Warren. "Killer Bat Fungus Jumps to West Coast." *Science,* 1 Apr. 2016. www.science.org/content/article/killer-bat-fungus-jumps-west-coast

Darling, Dylan J. "ODOT Designing Highway 97 Wildlife Overpass." *The Bend Bulletin,* 19 Sept. 2014.

———. *"State Captures, Moves Bighorn Sheep."* The Bend Bulletin, 15 Dec. 2014.

Drabble, Phil. *A Weasel in My Meatsafe.* Leicester, UK: Ulverscroft, 1977.

Eder, Tamara. *Mammals of Washington and Oregon.* Edmonton, AB: Lone Pine Publishing, 2002.

Edson, J.M. "A Visitation of Weasels." *The Murrelet,* Vol. 14, No. 3, Sept. 1933.

"Grand Canyon Plans to Elk-proof Water Stations." *AZcentral,* 1 Oct. 2014.

Graves, Mark. "Oregon Roadkill: Mapping over 42,000 Wild Animal Deaths in 7 Years." *The Oregonian,* 16 Nov. 2014. www.oregonlive.com/commuting/2014/11/oregon_roadkill_mapping_over_4.html

Hartson, Tamara. *Squirrels of the West.* Edmonton, AB: Lone Pine Publishing, 1999.

Ingles, Lloyd G. *Mammals of the Pacific States.* Stanford, CA: Stanford University Press, 1965.

Johnson, Dana. "Porcupines." *Northern Wilds,* 19 Apr. 2015. northernwilds.com/porcupines

King, Carolyn M., and Roger A. Powell. *The Natural History of Weasels and Stoats.* Oxford, UK: Oxford University Press, 2007.

Knoblauch, Jessica A. "Keeping the Wolverine Wild." *Earthjustice*, 10 Feb. 2016. earthjustice.org/blog/2016-february/keeping-the-wolverine-wild

Krautwurst, Terry. "Busy Beavers: Nature's Ecosystem Engineers." *Mother Earth News,* June–July 2010.

Long, Ben. "Pronghorn in Motion." Originally published in *Montana Outdoors,* Nov.–Dec. 2011. fwp.mt.gov/mtoutdoors/HTML/articles/2011/pronghorn.htm#.VwLJMhMrU

Lumpkin, Susan, and John Seidensticker. *Rabbits: The Animal Answer Guide.* Baltimore: Johns Hopkins University Press, 2011.

Maser, Chris. *Mammals of the Pacific Northwest: From the Coast to the High Cascades.* Corvallis: Oregon State University Press, 1998.

Mooallem, Jon. *Wild Ones: A Sometimes Dismaying, Weirdly Reassuring Story About Looking at People Looking at Animals in America.* New York: Penguin, 2013.

Moskowitz, David. *Wildlife of the Pacific Northwest: Tracking and Identifying Mammals, Birds, Reptiles, Amphibians, and Invertebrates.* Portland, OR: Timber Press, 2010.

Muller-Schwarze, Dietland, and Lixing Sun. *The Beaver: Natural History of a Wetlands Engineer.* Ithaca, NY: Comstock Publishing Associates, 2003.

Nugent, Carrie. "Counting Bats in Oregon." *The Oregonian*, 6 Aug. 2008. www.oregonlive.com/news/2008/08/counting_bats_in_oregon.html

Pandell, Karen, et al. *Animal Tracks of the Pacific Northwest.* Seattle: Mountaineers Books, 1981.

Redford, Polly. "Our Most American Animal." *Harper's Magazine.* Oct. 1963.

Rezendes, Paul. *Tracking and the Art of Seeing: How to Read Animal Tracks and Sign,* 2nd Edition. New York: HarperCollins, 1999.

Richard, Terry. "Bighorn Sheep Get New Homes in Oregon After Relocation from Deschutes, John Day Canyons." *The Oregonian*, 6 Dec. 2014. www.oregonlive.com/travel/2014/12/bighorn_sheep_get_new_homes_in.html

Shulins, Nancy. "Hateful Little Cannibal Squirrels Could Help California Drought." *Grist*, 11 Jan. 2015. grist.org/climate-energy/hateful-little-cannibal-squirrels-could-help-california-drought

Weiner, Brittany. "Little Victim of Wickiup Wildfire on the Mend." KTVZ, 31 July 2013.

Weston, Paula. "Kangaroo Rats." Originally published in *Creation*, Vol. 26, No. 3, June 2004. answersingenesis.org/mammals/kangaroo-rats

Wolkomir, Richard, and Joyce Wolkomir. "Prying into the Life of a Prickly Beast." *National Wildlife*, 1 Dec. 1993. www.nwf.org/Magazines/National-Wildlife/1994/Prying-Into-the-Life-of-a-Prickly-Beast

Websites

Beaver Behavior and Biology, Beaver Solutions, www.beaversolutions.com/beaver-facts-education/beaver-behavior-and-biology

National Wildlife Federation, nwf.org/Educational-Resources/Wildlife-Guide/Mammals/Canada-Lynx

Oregon Wild, https://oregonwild.org/resource/the-journey-of-or-7

INDEX

INDEX

ABOUT THE CONTRIBUTING PHOTOGRAPHERS

Jim Anderson was a local writer, naturalist, and photographer. When not chasing bugs and birds or writing nature columns, he and his wife, Sue, spent decades in Oregon's outback surveying Golden Eagle populations.

Sue Anderson is a published nature and portrait photographer who now lives in Eugene.

Alex Badyaev is a professor of evolutionary biology at the University of Arizona. Learn more at tenbestphotos.com.

Susan Berger is a photographer, writer, graphic designer, and former vice president of the High Desert Chapter of the Native Plant Society of Oregon. Learn more at susanbergerphotography.com.

Leslie Bliss-Ketchum has researched wildlife crossings and helped develop two environmental consulting firms, Tall Oaks Environmental Research and Samara Group (where she is principle wildlife ecologist).

Greg Burke is a lover of nature and wilderness who has lived in Bend since 1981. Through his photography he furthers conservation efforts to protect our diminishing wild landscapes. Learn more at pbase.com/gb_photo/root.

Sue Dougherty is a passionate wildlife and nature photographer and veterinarian living, working, and thriving near Bend. Learn more at offleashphotography.net.

Kim Elton—former journalist, commercial fisherman, and politician—now uses a camera to celebrate the flora and fauna of public lands.

Tyson Fisher is a husband, father, and lover of nature and light captured through the lens. Learn more at www.tysonfisher.com.

Tim Gage, Wikimedia Commons, flickr.com/people/16697023@N00.

Dr. Stu Garrett was president of the Native Plant Society of Oregon and has been photographing and enjoying wildflowers in Central Oregon for more than four decades.

Charles Gates is a retired biology teacher, longtime Central Oregon birder, and the author of the Oregon Birding Site Guide website.

Ron Halvorson, BLM botanist (retired), loves that "even though the grass withers and the flowers fade, the word of our God stands forever" (Isaiah 40:8).

Alison Hardenburgh is a wildlife and nature photographer based in Reno, Nevada. You can see more of her work at northerndesert.smugmug.com.

Rich Hatfield is a senior conservation biologist with the Xerces Society (www.xerces.org) and a founder of www.BumbleBeeWatch.org.

Steve Hersey is an amateur nature photographer.

Bruce Jackson is a Sierra Club Grand Prize winner whose large-format fine art photographs are collected worldwide. Learn more at www.brucejackson.com.

James Jaggard is a Central Oregon photographer and adventurer.

Ed Jensen is an award-winning educator and photographer based in Corvallis, Oregon. His popular books include *Trees to Know in Oregon* and *Shrubs to Know in Pacific Northwest Forests.*

Ed Keith worked for Deschutes County, Oregon, where he provided noxious weed management assistance to landowners.

Kris Kristovich is a nature and landscape photographer living in the Sisters area since 1970.

ABOUT THE CONTRIBUTING PHOTOGRAPHERS

Tom Lawler lives in La Pine, Oregon. Learn more at www.avianpics.com.

Clint Long and **Dale Pederson,** The Wolverine Foundation (wolverinefoundation.org).

Ben Legler is a botanist, programmer, and photographer who works for the Herbarium at the Burke Museum, University of Washington.

Mark Lundgren is a photographer based in Oregon.

Rick Martinson founded WinterCreek Restoration and is a recognized national leader in ecology-based landscape design and construction. Learn more at www.wintercreeknative.com.

Adam Messer is the GIS coordinator for Montana Fish, Wildlife & Parks.

Toni Morris and her husband moved in 2010 from the California Sierra to play outdoors in the Central Oregon sun. She has been photographing since 1973 and had a darkroom for years.

Jon Nelson is a biologist and amateur photographer from Central Oregon.

Dr. Richard Old is the author of *1,225 Weeds of North America,* the most comprehensive weed identification reference ever produced. Learn more on that topic, www.Weed-ID.com.

Charmane Powers was a botanist for the U.S. Forest Service in Bend, Oregon.

Mike Putnam is a fine-art landscape photographer based in Bend, Oregon. Learn more at www.mikeputnamphoto.com.

Jane Richardson is a scientist at Duke University who loves making images of scientific, mountain, and wildflower subjects freely available at commons.wikimedia.org/wiki/User:Dcrjsr.

Al Schneider, retired English professor, backcountry guide, and trail designer, is the author of the Colorado Rocky Mountain Wildflowers app and website, swcoloradowildflowers.com.

Clint Shock, professor emeritus of the Oregon State University Malheur Experiment Station, works on crop production problems, watershed protection, and cultivation of relatively undomesticated plants.

Paul Slichter is a nature enthusiast, hiker, and photographer.

Kevin Smith has photographed over 700 bird species, including rare birds and IBBBs (Itty Bitty Brown Birds). Oh, and Lady Bird too, as well as her famous husband.

Alan St. John is a Bend-area nature writer/photographer and author of *Reptiles of the Northwest* and *Oregon's Dry Side: Exploring East of the Cascade Crest.*

Dave Stowe is an environmentalist based in Bend.

Dick Tipton's photos have appeared in several national publications. He is an avid birder, fly fisherman, and woodworker. Dick resides in Sisters, Oregon.

Carolyn Waissman is a local wildlife photographer featured at Artists Gallery Sunriver.

Claire Weiser enjoys horseback riding, kayaking, birding, and photographing beautiful Central Oregon.

John Williams has always enjoyed the outdoors, and photography gives him a way to share what he sees. Learn more at seeingthegift.net.

M.A. Willson was a photographer and wildflower aficionado who lived in Bend for decades.

ABOUT THE AUTHOR

 LeeAnn Kriegh was born and raised on the west side of the Cascades and now calls Central Oregon home. After researching and writing countless (two) nature guides, *Nature of Bend* and *Nature of Portland*, she has become a much slower, more curious, and far happier hiker. She wishes the same for you.

MOUNTAINEERS BOOKS

SKIPSTONE BRAIDED RIVER

recreation · lifestyle · conservation

MOUNTAINEERS BOOKS, including its two imprints, Skipstone and Braided River, is a leading publisher of quality outdoor recreation, sustainability, and conservation titles. As a 501(c)(3) nonprofit, we are committed to supporting the environmental and educational goals of our organization by providing expert information on human-powered adventure, sustainable practices at home and on the trail, and preservation of wilderness.

Our publications are made possible through the generosity of donors, and through sales of 700 titles on outdoor recreation, sustainable lifestyle, and conservation. To donate, purchase books, or learn more, visit us online:

MOUNTAINEERS BOOKS
1001 SW Klickitat Way, Suite 201 • Seattle, WA 98134
800-553-4453 • mbooks@mountaineersbooks.org
www.mountaineersbooks.org

An independent nonprofit publisher since 1960

YOU MAY ALSO LIKE:

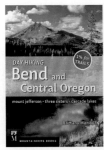